SURVIVING AGGRESSIVE PEOPLE

SURVIVING AGGRESSIVE PEOPLE

Practical Violence Prevention Skills for the Workplace and the Street

Shawn T. Smith

SENTIENT PUBLICATIONS, LLC

First Sentient Publications edition 2003
Copyright © 2003 by Shawn T. Smith

Printed in the United States of America

Cover design by Kim Johansen, Black Dog Design
Book design by Rudy J. Ramos, Rudy Ramos Design Studio

Library of Congress Cataloging-in-Publication Data

Smith, Shawn T., 1967-
    Surviving aggressive people : practical violence prevention skills for the workplace and the street / Shawn T. Smith.— 1st Sentient Publications ed.
        p. cm.
    Includes bibliographical references and index.
    ISBN 1-59181-005-1
        1. Aggressiveness—Prevention. 2. Violence—Prevention. I. Title.
BF575.A3.S55 2003
303.6'9—dc21

2003000084

SENTIENT PUBLICATIONS
A Limited Liability Company
1113 Spruce Street
Boulder, CO 80302
www.sentientpublications.com

For Smitty

Contents

Acknowledgments

EVERLASTING THANKS TO ALL WHO STRUGGLED through the early drafts: Dr. Tony Bandele, Dr. Dave Linke, Dr. Laura Weinman, and Dr. Jon Winterton. Your comments and generosity were more valuable than you know. Arigato, Ron Fearnow. Thank you, Tracy, for your love, support, and eternal optimism. To my agents Janet Rosen and Sheree Bykofsky, and to Sentient, thank you for making this book a reality. To my editor, Sherri Schultz, I'm lucky that we crossed paths. To all the Angels and all the teachers, thank you for educating me. And to Connie Shaw: bless you. Peace and love to y'all.

The Samurai's Sons—
A Parable

ONCE THERE WAS A SAMURAI WHO, in his old age, decided to divide his estate among his three sons. To determine which son deserved the largest inheritance, he tested their skill with the sword. He hung a bag of rice inside a barn door and summoned them one by one. As each son entered, the bag would fall on him. The son with the best response would win the bulk of the estate.

As the first son entered, the bag fell and struck him on the head. Shocked and hurt, he nevertheless managed to react. He drew his sword and cut the bag in half before it hit the ground. *Not bad*, thought the father.

When the second son entered, he sensed the bag even before it struck him, and he sliced it in midair. *Even better*, thought the old man.

When the third son was summoned, he hesitated upon arriving at the barn. Sensing that something was amiss, he didn't enter and never drew his sword. This son won the bulk of the estate.

Introduction

THE POLICE BROUGHT JANICE TO DETOX for the third time in as many weeks. Once again she'd been arrested for public intoxication. As always, her blood alcohol content was through the roof and she was angry, erratic, and hostile.

Janice had developed a lengthy history at this detoxification facility—a history that included hostility and violence toward the staff and other clients. She was particularly malicious toward female staffers, whom she held in special contempt. She would typically accost the first female staffer she came across with a litany of curses and threatening gestures. As often as not, the police who brought her to detox were forced to load her back into the squad car and take her directly to jail, where she could calm herself.

On this particular day, the first female staffer Janice saw was the supervisor on duty, a mild-mannered woman in her late thirties. As soon as she spotted the supervisor, Janice became like a cornered cat, hissing and spitting threats, and ended her tirade with a rather cryptic insult: "You've been nothing but a bitch since you got that dye job!"

She started toward the supervisor with fists clenched and teeth bared. Without missing a beat, the sweet but street-savvy supervisor answered, "You don't know what you're talking about, Janice! I got this dye job before I started working here."

The room erupted in good-natured laughter. Even in her drunken haze, Janice knew she couldn't continue her assault in a cheery atmosphere. She grudgingly smiled, then wandered off to find a snack.

This true story differs only on the surface from the parable of the samurai's third son. In both stories, our heroes responded to the earliest signs of aggression and deftly steered the interaction toward a nonviolent end. Both felt fear and trepidation, but neither succumbed to panic or resorted to force.

If you've never studied violence up close and personal, the skills used by the samurai's son and the detox supervisor may seem a bit esoteric or difficult to develop. In my earliest days of studying verbal de-escalation and violence prevention, these skills seemed almost magical—especially given that they were used during times of stress.

But the truth is, very little in this book will be new to you. It may *seem* new, but it isn't.

The knowledge you need to understand, predict, and prevent violence already resides in you. We just need to unpack it from the dusty, unused boxes in the corners of your mind and to put it in order, as those with whom I studied did for me. Only when we haven't exercised our knowledge of human behavior do attackers seem to strike "out of the blue." The truth is, violence is usually preceded by warning signs.

Consider Janice, for example. She showed several obvious signs of imminent aggression: aggressive body posture, movement toward the supervisor, changed volume and pitch of her voice, clenched fists, and a furrowed brow. When her physical signals are considered next to her history of violence, it's obvious that this is a dangerous individual.

The supervisor understood how dangerous Janice was, and she knew that she needed to respond quickly. She had several options. She could have tried to intimidate Janice into submission, or asked her staff to intervene. She could have threatened Janice with jail time or asked the police to cart her away immediately. She could even have bargained with Janice, offering privileges for good behavior (rarely a good idea). Instead, she chose to use humor—one of the least obvious alternatives. It worked like a charm.

Like most of the people I've studied, this supervisor had been around enough hostile and violent individuals to develop a sort of sixth sense about the subject. She understood why people become violent, and she knew how to respond with speed and finesse.

This book offers a soft approach to violence prevention, similar to the approach taken by the supervisor. The fighting arts include both hard and soft defenses. A hard defense against a punch, for instance, might be an explosive forearm block—standing steadfast and meeting force with force, forearm against forearm, to deflect the attack and hurt the attacker. This type of defense is sometimes necessary—for example, if one is caught by surprise and has no time for a more thoughtful response. But there are drawbacks to such a defense: it doesn't prevent a counterattack, and it's likely to hurt you as much as the attacker.

A soft defense against the same punch might involve ducking quickly aside while parrying the punch—in other words, meeting force with finesse. Getting out of the way puts you in a better position to respond to a second attack, makes escape easier, and doesn't hurt you or the aggressor.

How does this translate into verbal terms? Let's use an example. Imagine yourself as a bartender charged with the task of denying alcohol to an already drunk and obnoxious patron. This person is abusive and clearly seeking to impress the crowd. Any challenge you issue will be met with loud, public confrontation. How do you go about this task without putting yourself and others at risk?

The hard approach might be simply to inform the person, in front of their friends and in no uncertain terms, that they're cut off: a show of force, if you will. There are situations in which such a direct approach is entirely appropriate, and we'll be discussing some of these at length. But here such an approach will likely meet with a drunken temper tantrum as the patron escalates to a higher level of aggression. That's the main reason many bars and nightclubs employ bouncers. It takes skill to reason with a drunkard, so in the interest of efficiency the owners opt for force rather than finesse.

A soft approach, by comparison, might look like this: you take the drunkard aside, affording them the dignity of privacy. You smile, offer a nonalcoholic drink, and say, "Hey partner, the drinks will be a little light from now on. This one's on the house." You've just met force with finesse. While it may not work every time, your chances of a smooth interaction have increased exponentially.

This book primarily teaches *verbal* skills. Some aggressors approach their victims so forcefully, or with such surprise, that words are simply not an option. If ever you find yourself in such a situation—if you ever fear for your life or your safety—your only concern should be to find the quickest escape. Your intuition is your best guide on this matter, and we'll learn more about that subject later in the book.

How did I come to write a book on violence prevention? A combination of events caused me to be fascinated with this subject. As a child, I was a particularly attractive target for bullies and had to devise methods to discourage attacks. Another prime motivator was our family-owned bar, where I spent my nights and weekends. From the sidelines, I watched my father artfully manage armed robbers, angry bikers, domestic disputes, and various arguments over honor and turf. At an early age I began to understand the causes and dynamics of violence, and more importantly, I learned that a quick mind and skillful tongue can usually avert tragedy.

As an adult, I earned degrees in psychology and communication, and I took a special interest in interpersonal conflict. I've also spent seventeen years studying the techniques and philosophies of martial arts, where much of the focus is on de-escalation.

To earn a paycheck over the years, I've worked with hostile drunks, violent teens, and angry customers. I was fortunate enough to spend four years as a patrol leader and trainer with the Denver chapter of the Guardian Angels, an unarmed neighborhood safety patrol founded by New York City citizens in 1973. There I was able to work with world-class, street-savvy experts in the art of verbal de-escalation. These experiences led me to start my own violence prevention training company. The jobs and pastimes I've enjoyed have had one thing in common: they gave me the opportunity to watch and learn from those who know how to prevent violent conflict at its earliest stages. They gave me the skills to write this book.

Now let's talk about how you spend your time, and where violence is most likely to cross your path. The numbers may surprise you. In 1998 (a typical year in America), there were approximately 31.3 million crimes, including 8.1 million crimes of violence. That's one criminal act for every 10 Americans, and one violent crime for every 34. This figure doesn't include homicides, of which there were nearly 17,000.[1]

Eighty-six percent of violent crimes occurred between the hours of 6 a.m. and midnight; 55 percent between 6 a.m. and 6 p.m.[2] Most crimes (90 percent of rapes and nearly 70 percent of assaults) did not involve a weapon, though most robberies did.[3] Only 17 percent of violent crimes occurred at the home of the victim.[4] The rest happened somewhere outside the home.

We could spend several pages on crime statistics, but here's the point: violent crimes aren't confined to dark alleys, and they aren't the bane of "other people." Most importantly, those who commit acts of violence rarely match the stereotype of a gun-totin', crack-smokin' maniac.

The truth is, violent acts occur in large numbers and are most often committed by people we know.[5] They happen while we're going about our daily lives—working, traveling from place to place, shopping, or performing other daily activities. If you work in or around the public, you become that much more accessible to those who would use violence to solve problems. Our jobs can cause us to interact with many more people than we might normally encounter, thereby increasing the risk that a client or colleague might deem us a suitable target. We may be required to represent an organization to a hostile and unpredictable public, follow predictable routines that criminals can use to their advantage, travel far outside our normal stomping grounds, carry valuables, or make decisions that affect other people's lives. Any or all of these aggravating factors, when combined with the inherent risk of leaving the house each day, increase the possibility that we may become the one in thirty-four who is a victim of violence.

My intent is not to frighten; I hope only to paint a realistic picture of the risk that we all face each day. By understanding the risk, we learn how to avoid it, and that's the entire point of this book.

Much has been written about violence, very little of which is useful to the average person in those seconds or minutes before violence erupts. This book will help to remedy that problem. We'll discuss hostility, its warning signs, and preventive measures, using candid language and examples. Here's what you can expect:

- First, we'll cover five simple *ground rules* to follow almost any time you find yourself presented with a potential conflict. These rules will help you understand why some people seem to draw trouble to themselves, while others skate through life untouched by the aggressors of the world.

- Next, we'll examine the *Desperate Aggressor*. This individual feels that they have run out of options and is typically using aggression as a last resort. We'll discuss motivations, early warning signs, and how to respond before the situation spins out of control.

- Finally, we'll discuss the *Expert Aggressor*. This person strikes out in search of social or material gain at the expense of an innocent soul. The Expert Aggressor is a bully and a predator—and can be complex and dangerous to deal with. It's absolutely vital to have early and effective responses at your disposal before you encounter this type of aggressor.[*]

The book uses plenty of examples and scenarios, and looks at the process of violence from its earliest stages. With this knowledge in hand, you gain the ability to think on your feet and quickly find the most appropriate solution—or the quickest escape.

I've written this book for anyone who has a reason or desire to hone their violence prevention skills. It should satisfy one simple purpose: to prevent the statement "I never saw it coming—he just attacked out of the blue."

---

[*] This book is designed primarily to help you respond to potentially violent situations involving strangers and acquaintances. The techniques offered here aren't necessarily the best responses to long-term abusive relationships, be they intimate, professional, or otherwise. If you are in an ongoing abusive relationship, please get yourself and your loved ones to a safe location, then contact your local police or crisis line. Don't wait. Do it now.

PART I
THE GROUND RULES

I KNEW NICK DURING MY LATE TEENS. He was one of the most soft-spoken, kindhearted individuals I've known. He was also a magnet for trouble. People often joked that Nick carried a flashing neon "victim" sign above his head.

Nick attracted bullies the way a sunflower attracts bees. He was even once assaulted by a complete stranger who pulled over in his car, beat Nick into submission, and then drove away. (Nick was battered and bruised, but otherwise okay.)

In my earliest studies of aggression, I focused on the personality traits of people like Nick. What made them such ready targets? Not surprisingly, I found that the typical "volunteer victim" was very kind and trusting and had certain traits that were attractive to people who had a score to settle with the world.

But this line of research quickly reached a dead end. I was gathering a recipe for victimhood, and that wasn't very useful. So I began studying a different kind of personality: the one who repels that which Nick attracted. I began studying the Warrior.

A false and disturbing image of the Warrior predominates in popular culture. Warriors set out to avenge a crime and, in the end, wreak more havoc than an army of bad guys. They're full of anger and vengeance, and while they speak of justice, they often flaunt the law. These "heroes" seem to seek out and create hostility; rarely do they avoid it.

False warriors aren't hard to find. They can be seen in movies, destroying criminals with high-tech explosives; they can be found in children's cartoons, avenging the most recent crime against humanity; they even frequent video games, where they can be seen tearing the spine from a trounced mortal enemy.

True Warriors are much different. It's easy to overlook them, because these relaxed, average-looking people don't match the angry, aggressive stereotype. If you look beneath the calm surface, you'll indeed find passionate and skilled fighters with profound convictions. But what you see in day-to-day interactions are friendly, patient, lighthearted individuals with a sense of humor that puts everyone at ease.

True Warriors don't shy from defending their position, but they do it with dignity and good manners. They walk with their head up and a smile on their face. They command respect but never ask for it. Their modesty masks their strength, and their demeanor isn't sullen or angry. Rather, they're self-confident and calm in the knowledge that, should a threatening situation arise, they have the skills to respond or, at the least, find an escape.

Like so many Warriors before them, they know what's worth fighting for and lose no sleep over trifling problems. With a smile and a kind word they make friends wherever they go, and they never carry the mark of a victim.

Only a fool would attack a true Warrior. Nevertheless, the Warrior's focus is on peace, not war. They're always in pursuit of peace, even when it seems unnecessary.

That brings us to the part of the Warrior personality that most interests us: their methods of dealing with others. We'll examine the types of relationships that Warriors create, and how they establish a persona that makes them an unattractive target for hostility. As the scenarios and case studies in this book will show, the aggressor and the target almost always have an aggression-permissive relationship. Warriors understand how to influence relationships, from the beginning, to discourage hostility.

The initial chapters of this book cover five ground rules that Warriors live by. Think of them as the five commandments of violence prevention:

1. Establish common ground.
2. Don't shame the aggressor.
3. Don't shame yourself.
4. Choose the destination, but be
   flexible in the path.
5. Listen to your intuition.

These rules build the foundation for a mutually respectful relationship that discourages aggression. Of course, mutual respect can wear thin during hostile times, but the true Warrior knows how to steer a relationship through the roughest waters and avoid the most common mistakes.

Reacting versus responding

The story of the samurai's three sons at the beginning of this book illustrates both a *reaction* and a *response*. The first son *reacted* to a threat when he sliced the bag of rice. Reactions are automatic and reflexive, often motivated by pain or anger, and come from the more primitive parts of our brains—circuitry that even lizards possess.[6] (Lizards instinctually strike back when they're threatened.)

The third son, however, *responded* to the situation when he listened to his more evolved gray matter and refused to enter the barn. Responses aren't automatic. They're intelligent; they're based on understanding and training.

During a stressful situation it takes only an instant to do or say something you'll regret for the rest of your life. Responding rather than reacting can literally be a lifesaver.

CHAPTER ONE

Establish Common Ground

People in conflict perceive and react to the threat emanating from the image rather than to a realistic appraisal of the adversary. They mistake the image for the person. The most negative frame contains an image of the adversary as dangerous, malicious, and evil. Whether applied to a hostile spouse or to members of an unfriendly foreign power, the fixed negative representation is backed up by selective memories of past wrongs, real or imaginary, and malevolent attributions.[7]

—AARON T. BECK

FOR CENTURIES MARTIAL ARTISTS HAVE STUDIED *ma-ai*, a concept relating to the physical distance between two combatants. The beginning martial artist usually learns early on how to physically distance himself from an opponent during a sparring contest. An opponent standing more than an arm's or leg's length away poses relatively little threat, because it would take time for them to move in and deliver a blow. An opponent at arm's length calls for caution—they might be able to hit you before you could respond. But the most dangerous position is to be body to body with your opponent. If you can smell the peanut butter sandwich on their breath, watch out.

Manipulating physical distance is vital, but another type of distance is equally important to us: *psychological distance*, or the amount of perceived commonality between an aggressor and the target. It works in the opposite way: while close physical proximity can be dangerous, close psychological proximity (the perception of similarity) can be much safer than a large psychological distance (the perception of dissimilarity).

SCENARIO: The Nervous Taxpayer—Version One

"Next!"*

The woman sitting across from the IRS agent, having not understood his

---

* This book contains numerous case studies and scenarios. Case studies are real incidents that are reproduced here as they happened, with names and places changed to protect privacy. Scenarios,

instructions, looked stunned. After a lengthy question-and-answer session with her, the weary agent had assumed they were finished and had shouted for the next customer. Slowly the woman gathered her papers, rose from her chair, and ambled away, still looking puzzled and frustrated.

Marvin Seidenfeld, next in line, glanced at her with concern as he approached the agent's desk. *This isn't very reassuring,* he thought.

He stood in front of the desk for a moment while the agent scribbled furiously on a series of forms. Uncomfortable and already irritated, Marvin finally decided to take a seat without being invited. He sat down in the hard plastic chair and placed his folder of jumbled papers in a tiny clear patch on the desk.

Marvin was a self-employed duct cleaner. Although intelligent and an expert at his job, he could barely make his way through the maze of paperwork the IRS requires of small businesses. After having several forms returned to him by the IRS as being incorrectly filed, Marvin had been forced to confront the problem directly with a trip to this local IRS office.

After a few moments the agent looked up from his forms only long enough to acknowledge that someone was sitting at his desk. After wearily scanning Marvin's face, he looked back at the forms and, as if speaking to them, asked, "What can I do for you?"

"My name is Marvin Seidenfeld."

The agent looked at Marvin with a blank, tired expression. Perhaps he was too weary to verbalize a response, or perhaps he saw Marvin as just one more complainer who failed to appreciate his greeting.

Marvin paused, hoping for a sign that he should continue. Nothing. Once again he took the initiative. Pulling a letter from his folder, he announced, "I got this letter saying that Form 1120 was filled out wrong and that I owe a bunch of late charges."

"Hmm," the agent grunted as he reached for the letter. Marvin obligingly handed it to him, and the agent quickly scanned it.

"I don't understand what the problem is," Marvin continued. "When I talked to you guys on the phone…"

The agent interrupted: "I see you've claimed yourself as an LLC and not a sole proprietorship."

"I don't understand the difference." Marvin was growing agitated. "Frankly, I don't understand what you people want from me. I paid my taxes."

---

on the other hand, are composite sketches based on one or more real-life incidents. I use them to explore alternate endings to a conflict, while taking great pains to remain true to the events on which they're based.

Making direct eye contact, the agent asked, "Have you read the instructions for Form 1120 and 1120A? It's as clear as possible for people like yourself."

He just insulted me, Marvin thought. He had trouble containing his anger but pressed on. "And where can I find this book?"

"Normally we have them here, but we're out. You have to go online."

"I don't believe this!" Marvin's voice was beginning to break. "The people on the phone told me to come here, and now you're telling me to go online? This is really getting old! Are you going to help me or not?"

"Mr. Seinfeld, I can only recommend that you download the instructions and take your time with the form. If you're still having trouble, come back here or call our 800 number. Thank you. *Next!*"

That last word felt like a punch in the face to Marvin. He jumped to his feet, reached across the desk, and grabbed the agent by the collar, knocking a basket of papers to the floor in the process. "Look at me! My name is *not* Seinfeld! You people sent this letter. Now, are you going to help me or not?"

Psychological Distance

The violence-provoking incident typically consists of several stages: first, there is the classification of the other person as an object or a threat.[8]

—JOHN MONAHAN

Marvin took the low road, and his actions were illegal. By reaching across the desk and grabbing the IRS agent, he committed an assault. No amount of goading by the agent justifies a physical attack.

With that said, the IRS agent was not an innocent bystander; he was an active player. While we can't blame an attack on the victim, we can examine how the agent encouraged Marvin to lash out.

Think about the agent for a moment. Did you find it easy to dislike him? More specifically, did you feel that you had anything in common with him? Would you invite him to your next Super Bowl party or fix him up with your sister? Based on his behavior, probably not. A tiny voice in the back of your head may have even whispered, "Bureaucrat! He deserved it!"

Throughout the scene the agent is cold, uncaring, and even rude. It's obvious how that can encourage anger. But for a moment, disregard his blatant lack of manners. Some of his behaviors were much more subtle and dangerous than his rudeness.

For instance, he never introduced himself. He never shook hands or smiled. He never asked any questions about Marvin, nor did he offer any information about himself.

> **The golden rule of aggression**
>
> We tend *not* to abuse those whom we think are similar to us.

Rudeness is subjective. What one person considers ill-mannered, another might view as efficient. But our agent went beyond rudeness. He created vast psychological distance by making no attempt to establish common ground, or similarity, with Marvin.

Why is this important? No matter what type of attack you're under, narrowing the psychological distance between yourself and your aggressor can discourage violence.

In the early 1950s, researcher Irenaus Eibl-Eibesfeldt wondered what would happen if he placed a rat from one colony in the middle of a different colony.

Rats are social creatures, and they have a great deal of tolerance for the crawling, sniffing, kicking, and scratching of other clan members—as they must, since they tend to live in close quarters.[9] But that tolerance doesn't extend to rats outside their clan. When Eibl-Eibesfeldt removed a rat from Colony A and plunked him down in Colony B, the situation turned into "one of the most horrible and repulsive things which can be observed in animals."[10]

At first, the foreign rat spent several minutes going about his business undisturbed. But the instant a native rat crossed his path, that rat cried to the rest that their perimeter had been breached. The foreign rat was then mobbed by the natives, who bit and scratched and pummeled him, and would have continued until he was torn to bits. (Happily, he was rescued well before being traumatized beyond recovery.)

What gave him away? How did the native rats know he was a stranger, when he looked and behaved just like them?

His scent didn't match, and that one small detail was tantamount to a death warrant.

When Eibl-Eibesfeldt performed a variation of the experiment by imbuing the strange rat with the scent of the different colony, the stranger was this time accepted as one of their own, but then was attacked by his own clan when he returned.

The lesson: Rats, even though they don't have much individuality, are still able to recognize a stranger. And they *don't* like strangers.

Eibl-Eibesfeldt's findings are important to us because they illustrate the danger of being seen as an outsider. The rat is spared if he's perceived as a member of the clan—even if he's not really a member. For rats and humans alike, it's easier to hurt a stranger than one of our own (violence between intimates aside—a very different phenomenon, as noted in the introduction).

This simple truth has been borne out among humans—for example, in the U.S. military. Since the early 1990s, as the United States has engaged in more and more global peacekeeping missions, military psychologists have grown more concerned about the psychological rift that can exist between soldiers and the natives of other nations. If soldiers aren't acclimated to the local customs and belief systems, or if they have no interaction with the locals beyond pointing weapons at them, the soldiers run the risk of developing too much psychological distance. They begin to see the locals as less than human, and the number of violent incidents between soldiers and the locals increases.[11]

One of the most profound demonstrations of the ease with which we can harm strangers comes from hostage situations. You may have seen news footage, particularly from the 1980s, in which hostage takers have placed bags over their prisoners' heads. This isn't to protect the hostages' identity; it's to prevent the hostage takers from getting to know their victims. If they become familiar with the hostages, they might become enamored of them and ultimately be unwilling to do them harm. A wise hostage negotiator will try to cultivate affection between captors and hostages in order to improve the hostages' odds of survival; we can often use a similar strategy when faced with an aggressor.

Whether we're discussing lab rats, soldiers on foreign soil, or hostage takers, the effect seems to be the same: an adversary who perceives you as similar becomes less of an enemy.

The differences we perceive between ourselves and others are usually arbitrary—skin color, accent, clothes, income level, and so on. But this arbitrariness has a positive side. Because these "differences"—which create psychological distance—are imaginary, we can often minimize them, thereby reducing our chances of being attacked.

The IRS agent in our previous scenario may have seemed like a cardboard cutout of a government bureaucrat—the perfect punching bag. But the truth is that he probably has a family, and hobbies, and opinions, and friends and relatives about whom he cares deeply. Had he allowed Marvin to get to know him just a little bit, it would have been much more difficult for Marvin to lash out. Instead he presented himself as a nonhuman, which is generally counterproductive, because dehumanization prevents rapport.

Later in this chapter we'll revisit the situation and see how it could have been handled more effectively.

CLOSING PSYCHOLOGICAL DISTANCE

Ron, an off-duty police officer, was on his weekly trip to the grocery store when he came upon a shoplifting incident gone bad. In the cereal aisle between Cap'n Crunch and Count Chocula, three store security guards were wrestling to control a single shoplifter. He desperately wanted to escape, and the guards were not faring well. Ron felt duty-bound to step in.

As Ron approached, all four parties were gasping for breath, overcome by emotion and aggression, their struggle at a deadlock. Worried that the fight would resume at any second, Ron quickly stepped in and separated the entangled combatants. He then calmly whispered to the shoplifter, "I don't know about you, but I'd like to get out of here and get some fresh air."

The shoplifter grudgingly—but voluntarily—stood up to be handcuffed. Fresh air really wasn't the issue. The message behind the comment was this: "For better or worse, you and I are in this together now. There's no point in continuing to fight against each other. We might as well make the best of the situation."

A similar incident occurred in a senior-care facility. One evening the manager, a registered nurse, was called to the room of an Alzheimer's patient who had become physically violent. The staff members on the scene were unable to restrain the man; he had cornered himself in his room, using a chair as a weapon, and no one was able to get close to him. When the manager arrived, each of the staff members shouted, "I'll go get more help," leaving her alone with the man.

The man glared at the manager with hatred in his eyes.

Alzheimer's is a terrible and undignified disease. It slowly eats away at the mind and separates a person from the world he's always known, until eventually he is unable to communicate even the simplest ideas. The manager, having some idea what the man was going through, gave him a kind look and simply asked, "Are you hungry?"

"Yes!" the man shouted, raising the chair in her direction.

"Me too," she said. "How about if you and I go get a bowl of cereal?"

The man put the chair down and answered, "OK."

The two of them strolled arm in arm to the cafeteria, where they both enjoyed a warm bowl of oatmeal. Rather than adversaries, they had become teammates on a mission to find food. Instead of an enemy, the man now had a comrade in arms.

Both these cases are good examples of bridging psychological distance and establishing common ground between parties who could easily be lifelong enemies (both, strangely enough, involved breakfast cereal). Fortunately, we don't need to let a situation progress this far before putting the other person on our team.

TECHNIQUES

This section presents the first of our many tools for violence prevention: techniques for establishing common ground. These pointers may seem basic, but the failure to take a moment to establish common ground is one of the most common precursors to violence.

- **Use humor when appropriate.** A well placed bit of humor shows that you're comfortable and in control—like a true Warrior. When using humor, of course, you must be careful to avoid accidentally insulting the aggressor by belittling their situation. But if you can tickle an aggressor's funny bone over a shared problem or circumstance, you'll make yourself very difficult to attack.

    One morning while I was working in a local detoxification facility, a highly agitated, severely intoxicated client was berating me, wanting to leave before he was sober. "Surely you can get me out of here!" he shouted.

    I replied with a smile, "Don't call me Shirley." He grinned, and from that moment on was perfectly cooperative.

- **Remember politeness: the preemptive strike.** This needs no explanation. Perhaps if the IRS agent had offered Marvin a seat, introduced himself, and displayed basic manners, Marvin wouldn't have seen him as a target for aggression. Unfortunately, the agent was overworked and underappreciated, and almost everyone around him was agitated, angry, or generally stressed out. That's the easiest time to forget one's manners; it's also the worst time to forget them.

- **Use friendly eye contact.** A bit of friendly eye contact says more than words ever could, especially in stressful situations. In most Western cultures, eye contact says, "I'm listening; I want you to continue." Conversely, a lack of eye contact, as in the agent's case, conveys a lack of interest and can even be perceived as an insult.

- **Use open body language.** The goal in establishing common ground is to break down those imaginary walls. Don't undermine that effort by folding your arms, turning away, frowning, or using any other body language that says, "I'd rather be anywhere than here with you."

- **Discuss shared experiences.** The words "I understand your problem" are often hopelessly ineffective. In fact, they're usually inflammatory. The aggressor almost always responds in this manner: "You don't understand! Nobody understands!" If you've had an experience that is similar to an aggressor's problem, however, you might want to share it. Be brief—an aggressor doesn't want to hear your life story or provide you with a therapy session. But shared experiences can help you team up with the aggressor and start working toward a solution by demonstrating—rather than simply asserting—that you've had genuine experience with his type of problem.

- **State common problems and common goals.** Both the off-duty police officer and the senior-care manager used this strategy. Ron stated that he wanted fresh air. The senior-care manager said that she was hungry too. One way to win a tug-of-war is to pull *with* the other side rather than against them.

- **Apologize if necessary.** It's a natural human tendency to take an accidental affront as a personal insult. An apology simply assures the person that the act was not meant as such. Yet time and time again, pride leads us to deny having stepped on someone's toes, even while we're still standing on their foot.[12] Mom's advice still holds true: If you make a mistake, apologize. Not doing so, even inadvertently, implies that you did it on purpose.

- **Notice general commonalities.** Ron, the police officer, had another trick up his sleeve for closing psychological distance. Occasionally he would work the intake counter at the city jail, where presumably every prisoner coming through the door was hostile from the start. Knowing he was the first person (read "punching bag") they would deal with, Ron made a point of greeting them politely and professionally and, if they weren't too irate, noting some small commonality: "Nice Raiders shirt—are you a fan?" "I have a tattoo like that." "You sound like you're from Texas—whereabouts?" And so on. While it wasn't foolproof, this simple technique was enough to take the edge off many potentially tense encounters.

- **Exchange names.** A famous martial artist once said that only thieves and ingrates come and go without proper greeting. Exchanging names, and using them in conversation, is an old-fashioned, down-home recipe for establishing common ground that is too often forgotten. Don't believe that's true? Tomorrow, take note of how many people you encounter who don't offer their name. Yet doing so would make them much more human—and it's more difficult to berate or assault a stranger if you know their name.

- **Show interest.** This is an excellent technique to use when you don't want (or it isn't appropriate) to share information about yourself, and when you're dealing with an aggressor who might respond to a soft touch—what we call a Desperate Aggressor (see Part Two). Ask a few surface-level questions about the other person, keep your responses generic, and then get down to business. ("Where are you from? New Orleans? I love Mardi Gras. Went there last year. So what can I do for you today?") Use this technique judiciously, though, as a ham-handed execution may be construed as being patronizing or as tap-dancing around the problem.

- **Be mindful of cultural and personality differences.** If your attempts to close distance and establish a connection with your antagonist are going nowhere—if you feel that you're simply not communicating—it may be the result of a cultural or personality difference.

  A psychologist once told me of a marital therapy session he led with a couple from New Jersey. This rather hard-edged pair seemed to bicker constantly, and the psychologist thought therapy would go nowhere until the couple learned to communicate without taking jabs at one another. But when they finally learned to speak to each other in what the psychologist thought was an appropriate manner, all communication seemed to break down. The psychologist then realized that the two came from long lines of bickering couples, and this sparring was simply their mode of communication—in effect, part of their culture. He asked them to return to it, and eventually discovered that their marital problems had nothing to do with the way they communicated. The couple eventually left his practice with their problems solved, happily bickering all the way.

  The point of the story is that two people can pursue precisely the same goal—in this case, successful marital therapy—yet feel completely at odds with one another due to subtle differences in communication styles.

A rule of thumb applies here: If it's not working, don't do it anymore. For instance, one of the points in this list recommends making friendly eye contact. That may be sound advice when dealing with 90 percent of the American population. With certain cultures (and individuals), however, sustained eye contact is perceived as aggressive. Empathy will tell you whether you're on the right track: if your eye contact is met with

Safeguarding sensitive information

Managing psychological distance and establishing common ground doesn't mean compromising your security by giving away information that could be used against you—your last name, for example. And it certainly doesn't mean that you should open yourself to unwanted advances by appearing overly friendly.

When establishing common ground, keep your interaction at a professional level. You don't have to bare your soul when a bit of surface information—or, failing that, good manners—is more than sufficient. Too much self-disclosure can be a dangerous thing.

averted or downcast eyes, you may be inadvertently intimidating the other party. In situations like this, you may want to mirror their behavior: if they avoid eye contact, you're probably well served to do the same. The same notion holds true for humor, showing interest, and all the other distance-closing techniques. It even applies to politeness—some individuals perceive excessive politeness in times of conflict as a sign of deception, and they prefer a more direct approach. When establishing common ground, sometimes you simply have to play it by ear.

Let's revisit our IRS scenario and see how the agent might have fared had he made an early attempt to establish common ground with Marvin.

We'll restart the scenario as Marvin approaches the agent. The chair is still hard, the desk is still cluttered, and the environment is still stressful. But a few well-placed words can overcome all of that, and much more.

SCENARIO: The Nervous Taxpayer—Version Two

"Next!"

The IRS agent, buried in paperwork, scribbled furiously and straightened several forms as Marvin approached his desk. The agent stood up, looked Marvin straight in the eye, and extended his hand.

"Hi, I'm Paul Mendez. And you are?"

> *Taking the initiative and exchanging names—off to a good start.*

"Marvin Seidenfeld."

"Have a seat, Mr. Seidenfeld. What can I do for you?"

> *Extra points for getting the name right this time.*

"Well, you guys sent me this letter saying that Form 1120 was filled out wrong and I owe all kinds of late charges."

> *An accusatory tone—Marvin's not happy.*

"Let me see what we have there," Paul said as he took the papers and glanced over them. "What line of work are you in?"

> *Paul has taken the opportunity to express an interest in Marvin, and it's entirely within the context of work, so Marvin isn't likely to feel patronized.*

"Duct cleaning," Marvin answered.

Paul looked up and met Marvin's eyes with a smile. "No kidding? I have a cousin who does that. Just got his truck paid for."

In an effort to be polite, Marvin half-smiled as Paul looked back at the forms. "Hmm."

> *Paul is sharing some personal information, but staying within the confines of work. He's not overly familiar, nor is he compromising his safety or professionalism. The truck reference demonstrates that he has some familiarity with the challenges of Marvin's business.*

"Well," Paul continued, "it looks like we need to make some changes here."

"That seems to be the situation." Marvin answered with a slight edge. "Do you guys have any idea how complicated these forms are?"

Paul answered with a smile. "Hey, I went to school for four years to learn this stuff. Don't feel bad if you don't get it right the first time. I think we can get this straightened out today if you have a few minutes to work with me."

"Sure," Marvin answered.

> *Marvin's still a bit hostile (note the accusatory comment about the forms). Paul handled this nicely. He could easily have chosen to take this personally. But instead he acknowledged that the forms were indeed complicated, and that they were a shared problem that the two of them could solve together. Now they're teammates, and Marvin will probably think twice before continuing with his negative tone.*

Take the Initiative

Is it easy or pleasant to harm another person? For most of us, no. Is it easy to harm something less than human? For many of us, yes.

Establishing common ground isn't a panacea—none of the ground rules are. But it's difficult to harm someone we regard as similar to ourselves. The more effective you are at bridging the imaginary gaps that exist between yourself and a potential attacker, the less likely you are to become a statistic. Stated simply, the more friends you have in the world, the safer you are.

One last bit of advice on establishing common ground: take the initiative. Offer the first smile, the first words, and the first friendly gesture—and the sooner the better. The best time to close psychological distance is *before* you need to.

CHAPTER TWO

Don't Shame the Aggressor

One should not use rough manners with anyone. . . . It is said, "One is safe when polite, but in danger when ill-mannered."[13]

—TAKEDA NOBUSHIGE

ESTABLISHING COMMON GROUND IS THE LAST thing most of us think of when confronted with an irate person. Closing psychological distance at a time like that runs contrary to our protective instincts. Often what we really want to do is end the interaction as quickly as possible and build a protective wall around ourselves, and most of us do that by running away, which is often the best strategy.

When escape isn't an option, our next instinct seems to be to calm the person down as quickly as possible, by whatever means necessary. We may chant unhelpful phrases such as "Calm down," "Just relax," or "Don't panic" because we don't know what else to do. (Later in this chapter we'll discuss how those phrases can be not only useless but sometimes downright dangerous.)

Dealing with an irate or otherwise threatening person is genuinely frightening. To quote Lieutenant Worf from the *Star Trek: The Next Generation* series, "Only a fool is without fear." But these natural emotions and the desire to avoid conflict, when improperly handled, can lead us to unintentionally shun, challenge, or shame an aggressor. Shaming aggressors implies that they're powerless, and this can be a very dangerous thing to do. Therapist Rollo May put it this way:

> As we make people powerless, we promote their violence rather than its control. Deeds of violence in our society are performed largely by those trying to establish their self-esteem, to defend their self-image, and to demonstrate that they, too, are significant. . . . Violence arises not out of superfluity of power but out of powerlessness. . . . Violence is the expression of impotence.[14]

Pride is arguably one of the most important human emotions. We need to feel that we're at least as important and powerful as everyone else, lest we be ostracized socially or professionally.

In the early stages of human development, when our species' survival skills and mental processes were probably forming, being ostracized meant losing the security of the group, which surely resulted in an unpleasant demise. Pride is the sense that one has power and influence and is deserving of respect as an important contributor to the group, whatever group that may be.

Pride, at its most basic level, is an issue of safety. When it's missing we feel threatened, and that feeling is appropriate. Although being ostracized in the twenty-first century doesn't have the same dire consequences as in the earliest days of humanity, the effects can still be profound: loss of income, failure to find the support of a mate or friends, mental torment from others, physical abuse, and even incarceration.

That's why the opposite of pride—shame—is one of the most important motivators for aggression. To shame people through word or deed is to put them on notice that they are less than you—that they have no power, make no worthy contribution, and are in danger of being left behind.

Shame demands action. Shame demands that honor be restored; that one's reputation be vindicated; that one's worth be reestablished. It can be terribly destructive when applied to an already angry or desperate aggressor. Shame doesn't merely add fuel to the fire; it can turn a smoldering flame into a blazing inferno.

SCENARIO: The Cornered Classmate—Version One

Professor Rosen sat at her desk in her campus office, finishing the semester's business. Classes were over, papers were graded, scores were posted. Only a few more hours' worth of administrative paperwork and she could look forward to two weeks of hard-earned vacation.

She was diligently creating organized piles from the chaos at her desk—student papers here, forms and required paperwork there—when she heard a soft knock. She didn't look up right away; the timidity of the sound told her it was a student at the door, not someone more important. Students had been coming and going all day—some seeking guidance, some arguing over their grades, and some simply wanting to linger and chat.

Little grunts, she thought. *What does this one want? I really don't have time for this.*

Finally, she shouted for the visitor to enter. She vaguely recognized the student who walked through her door, but couldn't place him. She'd had more than three hundred students this semester, most of whom had taken her economics class because it was required of them, not because they wanted to. This one looked absolutely beaten.

She returned to her paperwork for a moment, eventually asking, without looking up, "Yes, what can I do for you?"

There was a long, uncomfortable pause, during which she continued to attend to the papers on her desk. Finally she looked up, as if expecting the student to announce either his name or his problem.

"Brandon," he said quietly. Professor Rosen looked puzzled.

"Brandon Johnson." The professor stared at him. His name still didn't register.

"Economics 204," he continued.

At last, a familiar reference. "Ah yes, Brandon. Have a seat." The professor went back to work for several moments, scribbling her signature and adding more papers to the neat piles. Brandon moved the chair slightly closer to the door, fiddled with his book bag before finding a place for it on the office floor, then sat in uncomfortable silence.

"What can I do for you?" she asked, again without looking up.

Brandon fiddled with his hands. He wished he hadn't set his book bag down. "Well, Professor, um, according to the grades posted outside your office, I got a C in your class."

"Go on," she said, still shuffling her papers.

"The problem is, if I get lower than a B, I lose my scholarship—permanently. That means I have to, um, drop out of college." Brandon's voice was cracking, and he could barely sit still. He felt as if he were going through the humiliation of puberty all over again. The professor offered no response.

"The thing is, I can't let that happen. I mean, it just *can't*."

There was yet another uncomfortable pause as the professor scanned a paper with her eyes and added her signature to the bottom. Finally, she offered some semblance of a response: "And why are you here today?"

"Um, well, I was hoping, ma'am, that there might be an extra-credit assignment, um, or a book I could read, or something." Another uncomfortable pause. "Anything that might raise my grade."

The professor continued her work. *Good Lord*, she thought, *what am I supposed to do with this kid? Am I supposed to hand out grades like candy? If he wanted a higher grade, he should have studied a little harder. Nobody ever gave me anything, and I'm glad. Charity makes you soft.*

Still looking down, she said, "I'm afraid the grades have already been entered into the computer. Besides, that would hardly be fair to the other students."

Brandon took a deep breath and tried to calm himself. *I just told her my entire future is at stake,* he thought, *and she sits there like she couldn't care less. She won't even look at me. I knew this would happen!*

"But Professor, if you check my records you'll see that I'm a solid student, you know? I worked incredibly hard in your class." Another uncomfortable pause. "There must be *something* I can do!" Brandon's voice was becoming high-pitched and strained. He was leaning forward in his chair as if he were ready to sprint at the sound of a starter gun.

Finally the professor looked up. She had listened to whining students all semester and she was tired of them. She usually liked her job and her students, but she needed a break from the incessant complaining.

"Young man, I can understand your problem. But I'd recommend that you calm down and examine the fact that you are responsible for your own grade. There are, after all, consequences to our actions."

Brandon looked stunned. He had always been a good student, and no one had ever spoken to him this way.

"I'm afraid I can't discuss it any further," she continued, "I'm sorry. Now if you'll please excuse me, I'm really quite busy." With that, she turned her full attention to her paperwork.

Brandon sat stunned. He felt as if his entire future had been destroyed in one short conversation. Unable to get up, he muttered to himself, "I can't believe this. . . ."

The professor looked up once again. "I'm sorry, young man, but I do have other matters to attend to."

Astonished, Brandon rose slowly and turned toward the door. His feelings of desperation were quickly turning into anger.

In the bustling hallway, a friend approached. He knew Brandon's plight and had been waiting for him.

"So what happened?" the friend asked anxiously.

By now, Brandon was becoming furious. "It's not taken care of yet, but it will be soon enough."

The friend looked confused. "What does that mean?"

"She just cost me a college degree," Brandon answered. "She thinks she can lecture me about consequences." He let out a disdainful huff. "She's gonna find out about consequences."

Feelin' Little, Feelin' Loud

The most dangerous men on earth are those who are afraid that they are wimps. Wars have been started for less.[15]

—JAMES GILLIGAN

What caused Brandon to make a serious, if vague, threat against the professor? (Brandon's friend would do well to warn the school administration and the professor that she may be in danger, but that's another matter.) Brandon feels that his future is at stake, and that would put anyone on edge. But for most people, that isn't enough to elicit a threat. What the professor failed to see is that Brandon has two concerns, not one: his future and, just as important, his *pride*.

We can't blame the professor for Brandon's reaction; the choice to become violent is always the aggressor's. While the professor didn't directly cause a violent response, however, she did have the opportunity to discourage one—and she failed miserably. She didn't do so on purpose, of course; people rarely do. She simply fell back on a common tactic: she shamed Brandon, humiliated him, "dissed" him.

A training participant once approached me wondering if I could explain why a father, out for a family stroll in the park, had chased her to her car. She had barely escaped being physically assaulted by him. I asked what had happened.

She explained that she had seen a child, who was being pulled in a little red wagon by the father, fall out of the wagon and begin to cry. The wagon was rickety and had tipped. She approached the family to ask if the child was okay. He was, but like any two-year-old receiving attention for his injuries, he was still crying. After a brief conversation, she made the offhand comment "It looks like you need a better wagon."

That's when Dad chased her to her car.

Why was her statement so bitterly offensive to the father? We will never know for sure, but we can take an educated guess.

What we say, and what other people hear, are often two very different things. When the woman commented, quite innocently, that the family needed a new wagon, she had only the best intentions in mind: *It's not your fault that your son is crying, it's the wagon.*

But the father, no doubt feeling responsible for harming his son, may have heard something completely different: *What kind of father are you? You can't provide a decent wagon, let alone pull it correctly! That poor child, stuck being raised by a buffoon like you! Shame on you!* He then joined the ranks of so many who have been pushed into violence by a sense of shame.

Do Your Duty

"Shoot me! Do your duty!" yelled Robert Scott Helfer as he faced a Colorado State Patrol officer in December 1997.

Helfer seemed to feel a profound sense of shame, and thus serves as an extreme example of its effect. A 50-year-old staffer at the Colorado Department of Transportation, Helfer killed one coworker and wounded a second during a disciplinary hearing concerning a disagreement with a third coworker, Donna Archuleta, who was not present at the meeting.

The conflict began earlier that year when Archuleta, under orders from a superior, downgraded Helfer's request for new office furniture. Helfer had been instructed to keep the cost of his requisition below $3,000, and he did. But Archuleta's superior felt that he had requested too much furniture for his relatively small office.

When Archuleta reduced his order to a smaller desk, one chair, and a bookcase (he had asked for a large desk, three chairs, and two bookcases), Helfer confronted her in her office. He trapped her behind her desk, shouting, "So you didn't order what I told you!"

As a result of his belligerence, he received a $200 monthly pay cut and, later, an administrative leave after he failed to improve his behavior. His written response to the pay cut was less than insightful: "The discipline imposed [on me] was not reasonable, given the complainant's conduct. . . . At no time did I use threatening or intimidating body language, or voice, with Donna Archuleta." He hardly felt responsible for his actions.

Months later, when Archuleta expressed concern after her office was placed near Helfer's, he filed a grievance. This was the subject of the tragic meeting that made headlines.

The Little Things

It seemed to be the little things that sent Helfer on a rampage, like being denied a bookcase and chairs, or being instructed not to type e-mails in all capital letters. Superiors told him it was the written equivalent of shouting, but he continued to do so.

And it was a "little thing"—an innocuous statement about a wagon—that caused the father in the park to lose control.

We often read in the newspapers, or hear from friends, that a person "snapped" over a small event or trivial problem: "It wasn't bankruptcy that caused him to jump out of that window. He'd been broke for months. It was the waitress who called him chubby that sent him over the edge."

The problem with the "little things" isn't that they present any serious obstacles in life. It's the shame they contain—the dishonor, the way they chip away at our self-respect. James Gilligan, a psychiatrist who works with the most violent of criminals, has observed:

> In fact, it is well known to anyone who reads the newspapers that people often seem to become seriously violent, even homicidal, over what are patently "trivial" events. Paradoxically, it is the very triviality of those precipitants that makes them overwhelmingly shameful.[16]

Shame and honor, for better or worse, are sometimes more important than life itself. Just consider how many wars, murders, suicides, barroom fights, duels, and hunger strikes have been carried out in the name of honor and self-respect.

And it's that all-important sense of self-respect that can come under accidental assault when someone like Brandon, in this chapter's scenario, feels threatened. Stress and danger can make a person hypersensitive to insults and challenges. When we think we're under attack, we perceive attackers behind every rock and bush.

Two common behaviors, each of which we may engage in with good intentions, can have the effect of instilling in a potential aggressor a dangerous sense of shame:

- accidental insults and challenges
- unintended blaming

Accidental Insults and Challenges

When Professor Rosen said to Brandon, "I'd recommend that you calm down and examine the fact that you are responsible for your own grade," she may as well have said, "You wanna step outside and settle this like a man?" She may not have intended to challenge Brandon, but a challenge is what he heard.

While there may be a large grain of truth in her statement, and while another student might benefit from direct criticism, nothing is to be gained in saying such a thing to a highly agitated individual like Brandon. He simply won't hear the message as intended. Rarely do we accept constructive criticism while in the throes of anger or fear.

What Brandon most likely heard was "This is all your fault. In fact, I enjoyed flunking you. *Nyaah!*"

Them's fightin' words, and it doesn't matter whether or not the professor actually said them. Brandon heard them, and that's all that counts. When a person believes that they're under attack, then for all intents and purposes, they'll behave as if they're genuinely under attack.

How do you avoid accidental challenges? In most cases, paying extra attention to your manners is enough to avoid a slipup. Behaving as you would at a black-tie affair gives you a nonchallenging appearance without the semblance of groveling (which, as will be discussed later, can be as detrimental as making a direct insult).

Unintended Blaming

As a good friend of mine says, you don't have to be a "brain scientist" to know that you shouldn't rub salt in a wound—or, specifically, that you shouldn't say "You asked for it" or "Told ya so" to a highly agitated person stuck in an unfortunate and emotional situation. Yet we often do. Of course, like the accidental insult, blaming is rarely intentional.

Did the woman in the park *intend* to accuse the father of hurting his child? Of course not. But his agitated emotional state created a heightened sensitivity to any perceived assault on his self-respect. When dealing with a frightened or angry person, don't slip into the trap of making suggestions about how the problem could have been avoided, or even asking how the problem came to be.

When in doubt, let them do the talking. When you're ready to speak, focus on solutions; don't dwell on the problem. (Chapter 8, "Listening, Empathizing, and Providing Options (LEO)," will discuss solution-seeking.) You can dissect the situation later, when emotions have simmered down.

It's when we're at a loss for words that we attempt to fill uncomfortable silences. We often feel that saying something—*anything*—is better than saying nothing at all, but in fact that's rarely true. A Warrior knows that silence is preferable to well-intentioned but bumbling effort.

Think back to Brandon's situation, and put yourself in his shoes. Imagine feeling overwhelmed, defensive, and overly sensitive to the professor's words. See if you can guess where she may have inadvertently insulted, challenged, or blamed Brandon.

TECHNIQUES

Here are some guidelines the professor might want to consider next time.

- **Use the aggressor's name and make eye contact.** One of the worst messages you can send to a potential aggressor is that you view them as less than human. Avoiding an aggressor because of a natural aversion to confrontation can be misinterpreted as intentional shunning. Remember also that making nonchallenging eye contact and using their name are powerful signs of respect, in most Western cultures, anyway. Eye contact also helps ensure that you actually listen to them instead of letting your mind wander, which is a natural tendency for many people under stress.

- **Validate their feelings.** Their problem may seem legitimate to you, or it may seem downright silly. But at the moment, their problem is the most important thing in the world to them, and that makes it important to you. Avoid phrases such as "I understand," as they are often inflammatory. Instead, restate the problem in your own words: "Tell me if I understand. You're angry that . . ." You might also use phrases such as "I can see why you'd be angry" and "considering the circumstances, you're handling this really well." Empathy can be a difficult thing to achieve in the heat of the moment. (Chapter 8, "Listening, Empathizing, and Providing Options (LEO)," will discuss empathy in greater depth.)

- **Avoid phrases such as "Calm down."** These are possibly the two most inflammatory words in the English language. What we *mean* is "Things will be okay, we can work this out, please talk to me." What the aggressor *hears* is "Don't be such a baby, this isn't worth having a fit over, shame on you for being so emotional." Unfortunately, it is easy to fall into the trap of saying "Calm down," "Don't panic," "Relax," or "Take it easy," especially when we're trying to fill an uncomfortable silence. Here's a guideline: When you don't know what to say, say nothing. Instead, let the other person talk, ask open-ended questions, and guide the conversation to a discussion of the problem. Generally speaking, the more they talk, the less likely they are to attack.

- **Be mindful of accidental challenges and insults.** Simple good manners are the best prevention against accidental insults. It's often difficult to remember our *pleases* and *thank yous* when we're frightened or angry. Unfortunately, those are the worst times to forget our manners. The scenario training exercises in Appendix C will help you transform good habits into ingrained responses.

- **Watch out for unintended blaming.** It serves no purpose to ask, "How on earth did this happen?" in the heat of the moment. There will be plenty of time later to mull over the causes and explore strategies for conflict prevention in the future. Avoid phrases such as "Maybe you shouldn't have . . ." and "I was afraid this would happen. . . ." It's easy to utter unintentionally callous remarks, so when tensions are running high, the Warrior focuses on the problem at hand.

Shame on You, Shame on Me

Imagine that friends called you in a panic because they had just been in a car accident and the other driver was carted off in an ambulance. You would probably ask what they needed and how you could help. You would not say, "Shame on you"—at least not intentionally. Yet this is precisely what Brandon heard from the professor, whether or not she actually said it.

We return to the scenario as Brandon knocks on his professor's door. As in the first version, the professor is tired and overworked and simply wants to be left alone, but this time she responds differently to Brandon.

SCENARIO: The Cornered Classmate—Version Two

Not again, she thought. *What does this one want? I really don't have time for this.*

She looked up and vaguely recognized the student who stood before her, but couldn't place him. She'd had more than three hundred students this semester, most of whom had taken her economics class because it was required of them, not because they wanted to. This one looked absolutely beaten. "I'm sorry, young man, what was your name?" she asked.

"Brandon," he said quietly. The professor looked puzzled.

"Brandon Johnson." It still didn't register.

"Economics 204."

"Oh, yes," she said, "Brandon. One moment while I mark my place."

The professor scratched her name at the bottom of a page, tidied a few papers, then leaned back in her chair and looked at Brandon.

"Now, Brandon, have a seat and tell me what I can help you with today."

> *She's already ahead of the game. Using Brandon's name and looking him in the eye are a vast improvement from the previous version of this scenario. This time she isn't avoiding Brandon by hiding behind her paperwork.*

Brandon sat down and dropped his book bag at his feet.

"Well, Professor, um, according to the grades posted outside your office, I got a C in your class."

There was a brief but uncomfortable pause before the professor answered. "Go on."

> *Here the professor is actually listening to Brandon— another fine improvement in the interaction.*

Brandon was becoming agitated. "The problem is, if I get lower than a B, I lose my scholarship, um, permanently. That means I have to drop out of school."

"Mmm, I see," Professor Rosen answered. "That is a problem. And what can I help you with today?"

> *She avoided the easily uttered conversation killer "Calm down." Instead, she acknowledged that he had a problem and encouraged him to keep talking.*

"Um, well, I was hoping, ma'am, that there might be an extra-credit assignment, or a book I could read, or something—anything that might raise my grade."

The professor looked concerned. "I see. Well, I'll be forthright with you, Brandon: changing your grade would hardly be fair to the other students. I doubt they'd appreciate being denied a similar opportunity to raise their grade."

"But Dr. Rosen, I'm a solid student. I worked hard in your class." Another uncomfortable pause. "Isn't there *something* I can do?"

The professor thought for a moment, then leaned forward and clasped her hands on her desk. "I'm afraid there isn't a way to raise your grade at this point, Brandon. However, there may be other options. After all, you must be a solid student or you wouldn't be on scholarship, and you certainly wouldn't have passed my class."

> *She has taken his problem seriously—perhaps recognizing that his problem has become her problem. She isn't telling him what he wants to hear, but she is being honest and speaking to him as a human being. This will make it difficult, though not impossible, for Brandon to feel undue shame and resentment.*

She thought for a moment longer while Brandon sat in painful anticipation. "Who provides your scholarship?"

"Stonecutters," Brandon answered anxiously.

"I'll tell you what. Put me in touch with whoever directs the scholarship program there. I'll speak with them on your behalf and see if I can persuade them to support a probationary period rather than expulsion. I can assure them that receiving a C in Econ 204 is no small accomplishment."

> *More honesty—unpleasant, to be sure, but presented appropriately. She is also presenting options that Brandon hadn't considered. Chapter 8, "Listening, Empathizing, and Providing Options (LEO)," will explore this approach in much more detail.*

Brandon was still tense, but eased back in his chair a bit.

"Yes, ma'am. Um, I'll get you the information by the end of the day."

"Now, I have to caution you, Brandon, that I can't guarantee success. But I can see that this is a serious concern for you, and I'll do my best. If this doesn't work, don't give up. There may be other options."

> *She recognizes that Brandon is highly emotional about this and that he isn't in a problem-solving mode. She is taking advantage of a relatively relaxed moment to steer him toward finding solutions. She's also being friendly but professional, a tactic that is always helpful. It's hard to feel shamed (that is, resentful) when you're being treated politely.*

Brandon looked a bit sheepish. "Yeah. Fair enough, ma'am. I'll be in touch. Thank you."

The professor extended her hand. "All right, Brandon. You do that. And best of luck to you."

In the bustling hallway, Brandon's friend saw him emerge from the office. He caught up with Brandon and anxiously asked how it had gone.

"As good as can be expected, I guess," Brandon answered. "It's not fixed yet, but at least she's being decent about it. Come on—I need to call the Stonecutters."

Anger: The Less Unpleasant Emotion

It's much easier to be angry at someone else than to feel guilty about one's own action. Our subconscious minds, if left unchecked by our higher reasoning abilities, can perform mental gymnastics and transform the unpleasant emotion of guilt into the less unpleasant emotion of anger.

It's been shown, for instance, that rapists—men who demonstrate an extreme form of rage toward women—often feel threatened, put down, and shamed by women in general.[17] From that shame arises an intense hatred toward the source.

A person who feels shame, particularly when under the influence of other stressors, will often find a way to transform the source of that shame into the target of aggression. That's where your verbal skills come in. Bolstering an aggressor's self-respect, and assuring them that they are not the object of ridicule or isolation, can literally be a lifesaver.

CHAPTER THREE

Don't Shame Yourself

HAVE YOU EVER NOTICED THAT SOME people seem to be easy targets for aggression, while others seem to naturally command respect? These latter fortunate souls rarely experience trouble, and they seem unlikely to ever be victims of violence. They have a quality perhaps best described as "street savvy." These Warriors simply know how to manage others.

It is possible to develop the type of personality that is unappealing to aggressors, but it isn't done by turning yourself into a "tough guy." In fact, a strutting, tough-guy demeanor can aggravate many situations. The easiest and most direct way of developing an attack-resistant personality is to be clear with yourself and others about your boundaries—especially those that seem insignificant on the surface.

We've examined a few of the ways we can inadvertently shame an aggressor, but compromising our boundaries is one of the quickest ways to shame ourselves, and this is an equally dangerous situation. By shaming ourselves, we're telling the world (including the aggressor) that we're less than human, that we're not worthy of respect or consideration.

Just as we wouldn't intentionally shame an aggressor, most of us wouldn't intentionally shame ourselves, but it can be surprisingly easy to do.

In the following scenario, two people are meeting for the first time. Peter, a client of the law firm at which Gary is a receptionist, is upset over a development in his lawsuit and wishes to speak to his lawyer immediately. As you read, keep in mind that the beginning stages of a relationship set the tone for future interactions. Making your boundaries known early creates an atmosphere of respect. Likewise, any false steps may later return to haunt you.

SCENARIO: The Panicky Client—Version One

Gary was sitting behind his plush reception desk talking to a client on the phone when Peter stormed into the law office, looking frustrated and nervous. Peter waited for a brief moment, hoping that Gary would conclude his phone conversation quickly.

"I'll let Ms. Cooper know that the package is in the mail," Gary said to the party on the other end of the line. "Yes. . . . Is there anything you can fax us in the meantime?"

Unable to contain himself any longer, Peter interrupted. "Excuse me, I need to speak with Sandy Cooper."

Gary covered the phone with his hand and whispered to Peter that he would be finished in a moment, then returned to his phone call.

Peter wouldn't wait. "Excuse me!" he insisted. "I need to talk to Sandy!"

Gary looked annoyed. "I'm sorry, ma'am. May I put you on hold for a moment? Thanks." He turned to face Peter, who was leaning over the counter. "I'm sorry, sir, Ms. Cooper is in a meeting with a client at the moment."

"Well, I'm a client too," Peter countered, "and I have a serious problem with my case. I need to talk to her."

"I'm sorry, sir, she specifically asked not to be disturbed," Gary responded in his most patient tone.

Peter leaned further over the desk. "I said, I *need to see her*! Now get on your intercom and start pushing buttons!"

Gary now realized that Peter was no ordinary upset client; he was truly angry, and had caught Gary completely off guard. Gary felt a rush of adrenaline and looked around as if searching for help, or at least for the right words. Ms. Cooper had been very specific; she was with an important client and would not tolerate any interruptions. *Why does this have to happen now?* Gary wondered. "Um, I don't know, sir, I really don't think I can do that."

Peter pounded his fists on Gary's desk and stood upright, then walked behind the counter to confront Gary directly. "Maybe you don't understand me. I've got a serious problem and I need to speak with her—now!" he ordered through clenched teeth.

Gary avoided eye contact with Peter, not wanting to risk further antagonizing him. He was leaning so far back in his chair to put distance between himself and Peter that he felt he might tip over at any moment. He laughed nervously as he answered. "Sir, I'm just a receptionist here. I don't know what you expect me to do! It's not like they put me in a decision-making position here. Heh-heh. Heh."

Peter moved in even closer, standing over Gary like a vulture. He was so close that Gary could feel his breath. "What are you? A flippin' idiot?" he shouted.

Gary, paralyzed with indecision, managed to stutter, "Sir, I really think you should calm down—"

At that, Peter grabbed Gary by the collar of his shirt and pulled him to his feet. "You moron! Get her out here! Now!" he roared.

The Self-Deprecation Trap

Make no mistake about this situation: Peter broke the law by committing a physical assault, and Gary was by no stretch of the imagination responsible for that decision. Just because Gary didn't cause the physical attack, however, doesn't mean that he couldn't have prevented it. In fact, he made the three most common mistakes that encourage this type of assault:

- sacrificing boundaries
- self-deprecation
- assuming a submissive posture

We'll return to Gary's situation after a discussion of each mistake, in which we'll take a close look at where Gary went wrong and what he might have done differently.

Sacrificing Boundaries

Terri worked in a large office building and often traveled between floors by elevator. That's how she first met Jim, who also traveled between floors often. Their interactions on their first few shared elevator trips were normal enough.

Most of us know the "elevator rules" without being taught. Terri and Jim behaved accordingly: they stood facing the doors, eyes on the numbers, with a respectable amount of physical distance between them. Even their conversation was kept within the bounds of idle chatter.

But one day Terri began to notice a few things that seemed odd. She had probably been noticing them on some level for weeks, but on this day they became readily apparent to her. First, the timing of Jim's elevator trips was matching hers with increasing frequency. Second, the conversation had moved to a more personal level. He was asking questions about her personal life that just didn't seem appropriate—not necessarily out of bounds, but slightly inappropriate. Third, he had stood increasingly closer to her over the course of a few weeks, and had even brushed against her on occasion. Touching is hardly necessary when there are only two people in an elevator car.

Eventually Jim obviously and intentionally touched Terri. It was just a gentle pat on the shoulder during conversation, but it nevertheless felt inappropriate given the casual nature of their relationship, and it made her terribly uncomfortable. The fact that Jim had touched her in a closed elevator made the act even stranger.

After fretting over the situation for some time, Terri decided that she was overreacting. What was the harm in a simple touch? Sure, it was a bit creepy, and the guy had a poor sense of boundaries, but why make waves? It would pass, she told herself.

She began avoiding Jim whenever possible, but it seemed inevitable that eventually she would bump into him again. And so she did one afternoon: as the elevator doors opened, there he stood—grinning from ear to ear.

"Going down?" he beamed.

Terri had a bad feeling about the situation. She decided to listen to her intuition and wait for the next car.

"Oh, sorry, Jim. I must have pushed the wrong button. I'll wait for the next car."

"Nonsense," Jim answered. "Who knows when the next elevator will be along? No sense standing here all day!"

"No, really," she protested. "I'll be fine."

As she started to back away, Jim snatched her wrist and began pulling her into the elevator.

Terri was able to break away, and Jim was banned from the building when news of the incident reached management. Despite being understandably shaken, Terri was able to continue her life and work, none the worse for wear.

A Blessing in Disguise

The incident was a blessing in disguise for Terri. It forced her to assess her boundaries as well as her willingness to defend them.

What are boundaries? They're the understood, usually unspoken rules that govern the separation between two people. Sometimes they're stated, as when a person refuses assistance from a would-be helper; sometimes they're unstated, such as the "elevator rules" under which we rarely look at or touch another while the doors are closed.

We can't blame Terri for Jim's attack. She neither invited nor asked for the treatment he gave her. But had she addressed the problem during the weeks in which the situation was evolving, and the earlier the better, she might well have avoided being attacked. Part III will discuss this concept in much more detail.

Boundaries are important because many bullies and predators such as Jim will test our willingness to defend them. This presents several problems for us, the good guys. First, the tests can be too subtle to detect if we don't know what to look for—and even if we do know what to look for, tests are sometimes easy to ignore.

Next, it's difficult to know how to respond, and what level of assertiveness to use, because the nature of the test often disguises the predator's true intent. We may feel that we're being rude or overreacting if we respond in an assertive manner. We may also be overwhelmed by the nature and speed of the interaction.

Finally, it's easy to fall into the trap of wishful thinking. Most of us want to assume the best of others and avoid problems.

Gary, the receptionist in this chapter's scenario, had a very difficult time defending his boundaries with Peter. At every turn, Peter violated an unstated but obvious boundary, and Gary continually backed down. Peter interrupted Gary on the phone, stood over his desk in a threatening manner, raised his voice, stepped behind the desk, and so on. Each of these was an obvious transgression.

The failure to maintain boundaries with an aggressor like Peter sends a powerful message, or at least, the aggressor interprets it this way: "I won't defend my limits. Do with me what you will. Consider me an object for your abuse, not a person who deserves your respect."

Gary would have fared much better had he drawn a line early and tactfully; Chapter 14, "Early Response: The Bottom Line," explains how to do this. For now, let's examine the most common ways people unwittingly sacrifice boundaries: via self-deprecation and assuming a submissive posture. Some techniques to help you avoid these mistakes will follow the discussion.

Self-Deprecation

I once knew a Guardian Angel patrol leader who ridiculed himself during times of stress. Being new at the job of leading patrols, he wasn't yet certain that he could effectively manage the many stressful situations he and his patrol would encounter. As a result of his nervousness, during times of stress he was quick to denigrate himself with jokes about his lack of experience and ability. "I don't know whose bright idea it was to put me in charge," he would laugh.

Happily, he eventually became more confident and stopped saying such things. But until he did, he denied himself the respect of his patrol and almost everyone they encountered. As long as he considered himself a laughingstock, he was unable to perform his job well because his self-maligning behavior created an atmosphere of confusion and mistrust within his patrol. Each interaction with the public was clouded by the message that the leader couldn't be trusted. Until he stopped this behavior, he was putting himself and everyone around him in danger.

Gary, in this chapter's opening scenario, fell into the same trap when he joked, "I'm just a receptionist here. I don't know what you expect me to do! It's not like they put me in a decision-making position here." This type of comment, while an understandable expression of anxiety, can be exceptionally dangerous no matter what type of aggressor you're facing. If the aggressor feels cornered and is seeking help, this type of humor is actually a threat of sorts; it tells the person they won't be getting any help from you, likely increasing their desperation. If the aggressor is a predator, self-deprecation provides exactly what they're looking for: a sign of vulnerability.

That's not to say that humor should always be avoided. Even self-deprecating humor, if handled correctly, can bridge the perceived distance between people if it expresses confidence. Generally speaking, it's safe to joke about yourself if you think it will instill harmony, but never joke about your competence, your intelligence, or your abilities.

Assuming a Submissive Posture

Let's pick on Gary the receptionist for just a bit longer, this time for his completely passive response to Peter. It's been said that one shouldn't fight fire with fire, and this much is true. This doesn't mean, however, that one should lay down arms completely and be steamrolled.

From the moment Gary first encountered Peter and his overwhelming manner, Gary assumed a submissive posture by behaving as if he had no power.

Power comes from having options: to render assistance, to escape, to defend oneself if necessary. Because Gary assumed he had no options (read "power"), his only alternative was to surrender. His assumption was mistaken.

You always have *at least* one option: escape. Over, around, or through the attacker if necessary. It may be difficult; it may be terrifying. (Training helps make it less so.) But it's the ultimate option; you don't need to tolerate abuse.

In this case, Gary had not one but at least two options. Despite his overbearing manner, Peter came to Gary for help: he needed Gary in order to find his lawyer. And having the ability to help someone is a powerful bargaining chip.

The ability to help allows you, up to a point, to dictate conditions with someone like Peter. Gary might have used his bargaining chip by saying, "I can help you if you [lower your voice, take a step back from the counter, and so on]." By this statement, Gary communicates that if Peter truly wants his help, it will have to be on his terms.

This phrase can be remarkably powerful, especially when you have genuine empathy for the aggressor's situation. But if it fails, you still have your final option: escape.

The point is, Gary mistakenly assumed that Peter held all the cards. Had he been aware of the true nature of Peter's concern (fear) and of his own options (offering aid), he would have been much more able to reason with Peter. It was Gary, not Peter, who held the important cards.

Power phrase

"I can help you if you [your condition here]." Or, more to the point: "I want to help you, but I'll only do so if you . . ."

Confidence and Sturdiness

The ideal demeanor when dealing with most aggressors is one that conveys competence and sturdiness—the ability to solve problems and survive stressful situations. This Warrior's demeanor is enough to send a predatory aggressor hunting for new prey, and it offers calming reassurance to the desperate, angry, or frightened aggressor.

TECHNIQUES

Here are a few guidelines to keep in mind.

- **Maintain your boundaries.** As will be discussed later in the book, it's the small, seemingly insignificant boundaries that can be the most important.

- **No means no.** On several occasions throughout Gary's scenario, he told Peter no—at least in substance, if not literally: "No, I won't let you interrupt me on the phone"; "No, I won't discuss this with you now," and so on. But when Peter pressed onward, Gary continually gave ground rather than stand by his convictions or negotiate with Peter. This sent a powerful message to Peter that he could overstep Gary's boundaries without consequence.

- **Don't denigrate your competence, your intelligence, or your abilities.** If an aggressor is seeking your help, self-deprecation shows incompetence, which may cause the aggressor to panic. If, on the other hand, you're dealing with a predator who is searching for weakness, self-deprecation shows precisely that.

- **Use solid eye contact and body language.** When your mouth isn't speaking, your body should be, conveying competence and sturdiness, even if you don't really feel that way. Gary avoided eye contact with Peter and assumed a submissive body posture by leaning back in his chair; he probably also hid behind crossed arms and slumped his shoulders. He should have used the same body language he would use with any client: confident and friendly, not overbearing or threatening.

- **Avoid overcompensation.** Confidence doesn't mean cockiness—we all know this. But during times of stress, it's easy to overcompensate and send "tough-guy" signals. Doing so can display your fear and incite a hostile response, however. Practice is the best prevention; do the scenario training exercises in Appendix C, and ask for honest feedback from other participants about the verbal and nonverbal messages you're sending. In order to avoid a cocky slipup, err on the side of caution, as always: if you don't know whether what you're about to say is appropriate, don't say it.

• **Remember that you always have at least one option.** Escape is always an option, and this gives you power in any interaction. Also, the ability to help—on condition—is an often overlooked but very powerful bargaining chip.

No perfect opportunity to escape

If you ever decide that you must escape, the time to move is *now*. A perfect opportunity to escape rarely presents itself, so don't wait for one. Decorum should go out the window when you fear for your life or safety.

Let's revisit Gary's situation and see how things might have turned out had he been mindful of his boundaries and the options at his disposal.

SCENARIO: The Panicky Client— Version Two

Gary was sitting behind his plush reception desk talking to a client on the phone when Peter stormed into the law office, looking frustrated and nervous. He waited for a brief moment, hoping that Gary would conclude his phone conversation quickly.

"I'll let Ms. Cooper know that the package is in the mail," Gary said to the party on the other end of the line. "Yes. Is there anything you can fax us in the meantime?"

Unable to contain himself any longer, Peter interrupted. "Excuse me, I need to speak with Sandy Cooper."

Gary covered the phone with his hand and whispered to Peter that he would be finished in a moment, then returned to his phone call.

Peter wouldn't wait. "Excuse me!" he insisted. "I need to talk to Sandy!"

> *Peter is already testing boundaries by continuing to interrupt despite Gary's request that he stop. The little boundaries can be the most important.*

"I'm sorry, ma'am," Gary spoke into the phone. "May I put you on hold for a moment? Thanks."

> *Gary gave a little ground here by allowing Peter to interrupt. He could have insisted that Peter stop, but it's important to choose your battles wisely. In this case, he recognized Peter's urgency and decided to honor it.*

Gary turned to face Peter, who was leaning over the counter. "I'm sorry, sir, Ms. Cooper is in a meeting with a client at the moment. Is there anything I can help you with?"

Offering to help: a subtle but important expression of power.

"Yes. You can get me in there to see her," Peter countered. "I have a serious problem with my case. I need to talk to her."

Gary looked Peter directly in the eyes. It wasn't a challenging gesture, but one of confidence. "She specifically requested not to be disturbed. But I may be able to get you in, if you're willing to wait."

In the previous version of the scenario, this is the point at which Gary began to denigrate himself. He perceived himself as powerless, so it never occurred to him to offer assistance; instead, he joked about his ineptitude. Here he is expressing the power to offer assistance. It's a subtle expression, but an important one.

Peter raised his voice and leaned further over the counter. "I can't wait! Are you deaf or just stupid? I said I want to talk to Sandy!"

Feeling threatened by Peter, who was only inches from his face, Gary stood up and took a step back. "Sir, please don't stand so close to me," he said calmly but directly.

This is a bold expression of power on Gary's part. By standing up, he's saying, "I'm not a punching bag." Stepping back says, "I'm willing to leave." Most importantly, he made a direct statement of his boundaries. It can be intimidating to respond so directly. Obviously, Gary has had some practice.

Surprised, Peter leaned back and moved away from the counter slightly. Immediately, but calmly and while making good eye contact, Gary continued: "Thank you. Ms. Cooper has asked that she not be disturbed, but I can see that this is important. If you'll have a seat, I'll go talk to her. I don't know how long it will be, but I'll do my best."

Gary is listing consequences here, his main message being, "If you don't back off, you won't get in." However, instead of listing the negative consequence of bad behavior, Gary has listed the positive consequence of good behavior. This approach is less likely to put Peter further on the defensive.

Unfortunately, Peter was not yet ready to listen to reason. "I said, I need to see her. Now start pushing buttons!"

Gary made another attempt at addressing Peter's needs. "Sir, I can see that it's very urgent that you speak to her today. If you'll just have a seat . . ."

Peter paced for a moment, highly agitated, then stepped around and behind the desk. "Maybe you don't understand. I've got a serious problem and I need to talk to her *now!*"

At this point Gary was feeling trapped and physically threatened—and rightly so: Peter was blocking his exit. Gary was prepared to jump over the desk if necessary, but despite his rising anxiety, he maintained a steady voice, good eye contact, and a strong physical posture. He appeared as calm and confident as he could, given the circumstances (see the sidebar titled "Preparatory stance").

Gary continued in a measured tone, not wanting to appear panicked or aggressive. "Sir, I want to help you—I *can* help you—but I'll only continue this conversation if you go back to the other side of the counter."

> He's setting up boundaries for Peter's behavior. The unspoken message here: You need me, and I'll leave if you abuse me.

There was a long and uncomfortable pause while the two exchanged eye contact. Gary was ready to escape if Peter advanced further.

Fortunately, that proved unnecessary. Peter's angry expression softened into one of frustration. He sighed audibly, turned away, and rubbed his face with both hands as wandered toward the waiting area and plopped down in a large, padded chair.

Gary's fear subsided a bit. The break in tension allowed him to see that Peter was truly desperate and frightened. A note of pity found its way through the fear and anger.

"Thank you," Gary said as he picked up the phone. "I can see how important this is to you. I'll let her know that it's extremely urgent."

"Thanks," Peter mumbled.

A Country without Borders

Is Gary backing down by giving in to Peter's initial demand? Not really. Gary now understands how truly frightened and cornered Peter feels. Sometimes you don't know how desperate an aggressor is until you negotiate a bit.

Gary was able to avert a physical attack by maintaining his boundaries and remembering that he had power (that is, options). He was also able to address Peter's needs, which in this case further reduces the likelihood of attack. Peter doesn't appear to be a bully or predator, but rather someone who genuinely feels cornered. As long as his problem is being addressed actively, he's unlikely to continue being aggressive. (An aside: If Sandy chooses to meet with Peter, she should not do so alone, and she should arrange an escape route by sitting next to the door and positioning a buddy or two within earshot. Building security would be ideal.)

The act of shaming oneself—whether it be through sacrificing boundaries, self-deprecation, or feeling powerless—is one of the most common mistakes in stressful situations such as Gary's. Unabashedly submitting to an aggressor is often quite dangerous. Aggressors who are desperate, angry, or frightened may become that much more desperate when they find out you won't help, and predators will be thrilled to learn that you have no boundaries.

A country without borders is likely to be trampled on from all fronts. A person without boundaries is crippled when managing almost any hostile encounter.

Preparatory stance

In the situation involving Gary and Peter, Gary was rightfully concerned that Peter might become physically violent. At a time like that, proper physical stance can be as important as your mental stance.

You should always try to be at the same eye level as the aggressor. Sitting is best, but if the aggressor is standing, you should be, too. If they take a more aggressive stance, and if escape isn't an option, you must take a nonintimidating physical stance that will allow you to move and respond.

Relaxed, non-threatening, and ready to move

First, you should be at least an arm's length from the person so that you can see, and have a chance to respond to, any sudden movement they might make.

Your physical stance should be somewhat like a fighting stance, but with one vital difference: your hands should be open, not balled into fists. Alternatively, you might clasp your hands loosely in front of you at chest or waist level. In either position, your hands are ready to block and parry if necessary.

Your feet should be about a shoulder width apart, with one in front of the other, as if your heels are on the corners of a small square. Your knees should be slightly bent so that you are able to move quickly.

Avoid facing the aggressor head on, and never turn your back or block an escape route. Instead, move yourself to an angle at either side of them. This position lowers the chances that the other party will view you as an aggressor, provides them with the perception of an escape route, and shows respect for their boundaries. It's also less stressful for you—you won't have an angry aggressor breathing in your face.

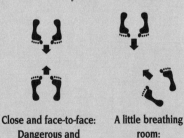

Close and face-to-face: Dangerous and undesirable   **A little breathing room: much safer**

A proper preparatory stance readies you to respond to a physical attack, and at the same time shows the aggressor that you mean no harm.

CHAPTER FOUR

Choose the Destination, but Be Flexible in the Path

JACKIE'S STORY IS REMARKABLE.

Rick, a coworker, had been harassing her for several weeks, making sexual remarks with increasing frequency and intensity. Jackie had asked him to stop, but to no avail.

As soon as Jackie's interactions with Rick began, she had become more security conscious. She no longer parked far from the elevator doors; instead, she would park close in and have an escort walk her to her car after work. But one day she came to work late and was forced to park in a dark corner. When she left, also at a late hour, almost all of the other spots were empty, and her car sat practically alone.

As she approached the car, she heard footsteps behind her, and her heart jumped. She knew who it was. Hoping she could make it to her car in time, she didn't look back. As she fiddled with the key, an arm reached in front of her, holding the door closed.

"Hey, gorgeous," Rick said in his smarmiest tone.

Jackie wasted no time with pleasantries. "Rick, get out of my way."

"Come on, hon. You and I both know we'll end up together. It might as well be now."

A shiver went up her spine. Jackie had been assaulted in the past. She knew the drill; she understood predators. She knew she couldn't fight her way past him; he was much larger than she. Nor could she reach for the pepper spray in her purse; he was too close and would stop her. She couldn't make a run for the exit; he would grab her before she got past him.

At this moment, more than anything in the world, Jackie wanted to be in her car, driving away. There had to be a way. She *had* to think of a way to get herself into that car.

Suddenly she heard herself talking, appalled at the words coming out of her mouth.

"Rick, hon, I know you're right."

She tilted her head seductively. "But you don't want it to be here in this smelly garage, do you? Besides, there are cameras everywhere and the cleaning crew will be coming through any minute. Let me freshen up and I'll call you tonight."

She felt as if she would retch. She didn't know where these words had come from or how she managed to utter them, but they seemed to be working. Rick was stunned. The woman he had been pursuing so aggressively was finally giving in! His persistence was paying off.

"Yeah, OK," he said reluctantly. "How about if I call you?"

That meant she would have to give Rick her number. She wasn't about to do that.

"What's the matter, stud?" She was feeling confident now. "Afraid of getting your heart broken? I have your number. You gave it to me, remember? Now go home, you." She smiled seductively and pointed at him as she whispered, "Don't tie up the line."

Rick smiled and leaned in for a kiss. She blocked his lips with a single index finger and smiled. "Not now," she whispered.

Rick returned her smile and held the car door open for her.

Jackie started her car and raced out of the garage, nearly knocking Rick over. She would never return to that job or see Rick again.

The Unfettered Mind

He thought with a kind of astonishment of the biological uselessness of pain and fear, the treachery of the human body which always freezes into inertia at exactly the moment when a special effort is needed. . . . It struck him that in moments of crisis one is never fighting against an external enemy but always against one's own body.[18]

—GEORGE ORWELL

What Jackie did may seem outrageous and reckless, and in a thousand other circumstances it may not have worked. For that reason, I would rarely recommend this type of strategy. But Jackie knew exactly what she wanted: an exit. Somehow she knew that this bluff would get her safely into her car, and she never took her mind off that goal.

By choosing her goal early in the crisis and being open to any strategy to achieve it, no matter how strange, she avoided two of the most dangerous pitfalls in responding to threats:

- developing tunnel vision
- being drawn into a fight

Both are the consequence of the same deadly error: becoming fixated on one escape route, one threat, even one word, and losing sight of the larger goal.

Choosing how you want a hostile encounter to end is absolutely vital. Otherwise you'll be adrift in a sea of possibilities, and you may not like the end result. And while a goal is important, it's equally important to be flexible in how you reach the goal. Jackie had a goal in mind, and she didn't much like the road she had to take to get there, but she was flexible enough to arrive safely.

Jackie's flexibility prevented her from developing tunnel vision, that condition of the mind that narrows our perception of the world around us. Imagine what would have happened had she simply fixated on getting into her car without considering the consequences. There's not much doubt that Rick would easily have stopped her, and she would have been drawn into a fight in which the odds were stacked heavily against her. While we can look at the situation with 20/20 hindsight and see the folly of that approach now, the error is much more difficult to see in the heat of the moment. Tunnel vision can be insidious and overpowering. It's an ancient problem that has been studied by many great minds, including a Buddhist monk named Takuan Soho.

Takuan lived in Japan around the year 1600. He was an advisor to statesmen and swordsmen alike, and is even rumored to have tutored Miyamoto Musashi, Japan's most infamous swordsman, on matters of mental control during times of stress. Musashi had *plenty* of combat-related stress.

Takuan had much to say on the topic of successfully concluding conflicts without developing tunnel vision. In one of his most famous essays, he warns us against the perils of fixating the mind on any one thing.

> When you first notice the sword that is moving to strike you, if you think of meeting that sword just as it is, your mind will stop at the sword in just that position, your own movements will be undone, and you will be cut down by your opponent.[19]

Takuan calls anything that the mind fixates upon a "stopping point." As soon as the mind comes to rest on a stopping point during an attack, all other considerations disappear from perception. Suppose, for example, that a customer approaches a service counter employee to register a complaint. Their conversation becomes so heated that the customer utters a racial epithet. The employee begins thinking, *Did he just call me that? He did! I can't believe it! I hate that word!*

The employee's mind has been captured by a single word. If unable to pass over that word, they'll be drawn into a pointless fight that is unlikely to have a positive outcome. (A point of clarification: I am not suggesting that the employee should tolerate the epithet, just that they shouldn't become defeated by one word.)

It's a terribly easy mistake to make, and it can be very costly. But there is hope. Takuan advises us:

If the instant you see the swinging sword your mind is not the least bit detained and you move straight in and wrench the sword away from him; the sword that was going to cut you down will become your own.[20]

In other words, if your mind doesn't stop, you remain open to possibilities. You are able to pursue a goal much larger than a simple counterattack. You aren't drawn into a pointless battle of escalation:

"You're a jerk!"
"Oh yeah? Well, you're a jerk!"
"No, *you're* a jerk!"

And so forth. Takuan calls fixating on any one point "the affliction of abiding in ignorance"—ignorance of one's surroundings and options. When we focus intensely on one thing, all others become obscured. A skydiving instructor once told me, "Don't stare at power lines or oil rigs, or that's exactly where you'll land." Talk about an unpleasant stopping point.

The mind can be taken by the sword. If you put your mind in the rhythm of the contest, your mind can be taken by that as well. If you place your mind in your own sword, your mind can be taken by your own sword. Your mind stopping at any of these places, you become an empty shell. You surely recall such situations yourself.[21]

Had Jackie focused exclusively on the distant elevator, the car door, the pepper spray in her purse, or any other of a thousand possibilities, she would have lost control of the interaction. Instead, she kept a broad focus. She was able to pursue her goal with flexibility, finesse, and an impressive degree of creativity.

TECHNIQUES

Jackie, our parking garage hero, had no formal training in Zen philosophy or psychology. She was able to maintain a broad focus and avoid being drawn into a fight simply because she'd had past experience handling crises. She'd been

A word about panic

You've no doubt heard that you should "remain calm" during a conflict. In reality, your body isn't designed to do so. A heightened mental and physical state is an important survival skill that shouldn't be suppressed. Can you imagine a gazelle remaining calm as he's being stalked by a cheetah?

However, it's helpful to *appear* calm and in control even if you don't feel that way. Working toward a goal, whether the goal is escape or solving a problem, is a particularly useful and effective way to calm yourself and avoid panic.

Panic is an extreme state of indecision and helplessness; it's the opposite of tunnel vision. Whereas a person suffering from tunnel vision sees only one option and only one method, the panicked person doesn't know which way to go. He may start in one direction, then inexplicably switch to another direction, over and over.

If you're busy pursuing a goal, you won't have time to panic. The downside is that developing this type of focus takes practice; see Appendix C for some helpful exercises.

assaulted in the past, and as a result had obtained training in self-defense and crisis management. As any Warrior knows, lack of training is perhaps the biggest cause of tunnel vision, panic, and pointless fights.

Here are a few guidelines for pursuing a successful end to a crisis without fixating, fighting, or floundering.

- **Take a breath.** When you notice extreme emotions such as fear, panic, anger, or confusion creeping up on you, stop to take a breath and ask yourself why you feel that way. This will broaden your focus and free your mind from any stopping point that may have seized it. It "resets the system." You probably won't ever be in a situation so immediately threatening that you can't afford a brief moment to take a breath and make a quick assessment. Not doing so can cause you to become sidetracked by a stopping point.

- **Avoid being drawn into a fight.** Remember that wounded and desperate souls can say very hurtful things. They may even try to provoke you into a fight because they don't know how else to respond to the situation. Threatening or manipulative language is another matter; see the sidebar titled "Hurtful versus abusive language."

- **Choose your battles wisely.** An old military expression helps put most conflicts in perspective: "Is this the hill you want to die on?" Sometimes—very rarely—the answer is yes; usually it's no. It's terribly easy to be distracted by petty battles; if you feel yourself being drawn into one, stop and take a breath.

- **Experience adrenaline.** The stress hormone adrenaline can cause unexpected side effects during times of conflict, including tunnel vision. Part of your training in managing hostile conflict should include experiencing adrenaline in a stressful but safe atmosphere so that you can become accustomed to its effects and learn to act in spite of them.

- **Choose the destination, but be flexible in the path.** Jackie knew that she wanted her interaction to end in one way, and only one way: with her in her car, driving away. Similarly, you should as quickly as possible decide how you would like a conflict to end. Keep a broad focus and be prepared to adjust your goal as new information comes in.

- **Polish your technique.** The principles of responding are useless without sound and well-polished technique. Practice is the only way to perfect techniques. Takuan knew this well, and so did Jackie.

Hurtful versus abusive language

Hurtful language and abusive language are two very different things, and require different responses.

Hurtful language is generally the attempt of a desperate individual to assert some dominance when feeling cornered. Often this name-calling is nothing more than blowing off steam, and it's not necessarily the same as an attack.

Abusive language, on the other hand, is a verbal attack. It's a threat or intimidation designed to manipulate or frighten you into compliance, and it may be followed by a more serious assault. When you sense that the interaction has turned manipulative or threatening, it's time to seek an escape. Part Four discusses the subject of recognizing threats in greater depth.

The Affliction of Abiding in Ignorance

Pursuing a goal during conflict is absolutely vital, but approach it as you would approach driving a car. When you first get into a car, you generally have a destination in mind: home, work, the grocery store, or the like. But that goal doesn't consume your consciousness. You don't drive down the street staring at the pavement immediately in front of the car and chanting, "Must get to work, must get to work, must get to work." You must deal with many other considerations along the way: traffic signs, other cars, pedestrians, and an infinite number of surprises. You may even change your destination midtrip.

Because your focus when driving is much broader than simply reaching the destination, you're able to manage unforeseeable challenges along the way. And the more you drive, the better you become at handling unpredictability.

Here are a few guidelines for broadening your focus while pursuing an overall goal.

- **Take a breath.** It's so important, it's worth saying twice.

- **Stall.** Let the other person talk, and ask them questions to keep them talking. You can use this time to learn what's going through the aggressor's mind, to make decisions, to broaden your focus, and to devise an escape plan.

- **Switch perspectives.** If you have the time and opportunity, switch your perspective and try to see the situation from the other person's point of view, just for a moment. You may see options and opportunities that you would otherwise miss.

- **Listen to your intuition.** You're never alone when facing a conflict. Your intuition is like a little helper that constantly watches out for you and keeps a broad focus, even when your mind seems stuck on a stopping point. Jackie's intuition told her to use a very unconventional strategy in order to escape her pursuer in the parking garage. As is almost always the case, her intuition led her to safety. The next chapter explores the power of this little helper we all possess.

CHAPTER FIVE

Listen to Your Intuition

Intuition is widely used by successful people. But they treat it like a black-market com-modity: It is rarely discussed, acknowledged, or given much credit. Since the Age of Reason, intuition has fallen into such disrepute that most ordinary people are a little ashamed of using it and won't admit to it even to themselves. It is as though they had decided to work with only one hand, when two hands are available.[22]

—MILTON FISHER

I HAD ONE OF THE BEST CHILDHOODS anyone could ask for, spending my form-ative years working in my father's bar. That experience helped set me on the path of studying aggression. Time and again I watched various interactions turn hos-tile, and sometimes violent. But my father had a knack for handling people, and whenever he mediated a potentially violent situation, he was almost always able to bring it to a peaceful conclusion. One night in particular has always stood out in my memory.

It was a typical Saturday night. The place was packed, which made for a hectic evening. Part of the nightly chores included closing the restaurant around 11 P.M. and herding the remaining customers into the "front bar," which remained open to serve drinks until 2 A.M. (The restaurant was then dark and empty—an ideal hid-ing place for criminals and malefactors.) As on most Saturday nights, my father was forced to "eighty-six" (kick out) a couple of rowdies, who, as usual, left loudly but peacefully. My father never seemed to mind the rowdies' backtalk and name-calling, as long as they were headed toward the door while they were doing it.

The night wound down in its usual fashion: last call, then the ritual cleaning of the bar while the few lingering customers nursed their drinks and waxed philosophical. At 2 A.M. my father said goodnight to the last customer, locked the door, took the cash drawer from the register, and began to walk through the darkened restaurant to the office in the back of the building.

When he reached the threshold of the restaurant, he took a few steps into the darkness. But something didn't feel right, so he stopped.

For several moments he stood in one spot holding the cash drawer. He didn't know *what* was wrong; he simply knew not to go any farther. As his eyes adjusted to the darkness, he noticed the slightest detail: on the floor behind the corner of the waitress's station, barely visible, was the tip of a tennis shoe.

He reversed course and discreetly called the police. They promptly arrived and arrested a man hiding in the restaurant, whose tennis shoe my father had seen. He was one of the men my father had chased out of the bar earlier in the evening. He had planned to club my father as he walked by, and presumably steal the cash as revenge for being ejected from the bar.

My father was saved by his intuition—and his willingness to listen to it.

Making the Most of Our Senses

Intuition isn't ESP. It doesn't give us the ability to read people's minds or see the future—at least not directly, although we can make forecasts based on past and current events. Intuition isn't a sixth sense or a window into another dimension. It's simply a subconscious process that makes the most of the information gathered by our senses of hearing, sight, touch, taste, and smell.

We humans appear to process information on at least two separate levels: the conscious level, in which we attempt to follow specific rules of logic, language, and problem-solving, and the subconscious level, in which we use another set of rules. We can learn without being consciously aware that we're learning[23] and, interestingly, we can possess knowledge of which we're consciously unaware.[24]

For example, imagine that you see a friend walking toward you on the street. At first glance she seems happy; she's smiling, and she greets you warmly. But you get the sense that something is wrong, although you don't know *why* you feel this way. And indeed, your intuition is confirmed when your friend tells you of a problem. You knew before being told because, at some time in your life, you learned to sense when this particular person is upset, in spite of her attempts to hide it. You may not know how or when you learned this skill, but you did learn it.

Every waking moment, the brain gathers much more information from the five senses than we're consciously aware of. One portion of our brain—the reticular system—is specifically devoted to filtering out extraneous information so that, through selective attention, we can concentrate on a single task. Think of the reticular system as the mind's coffee filter: it removes chunks of information that might otherwise overwhelm us.

This is no simple task. Think of the wondrous complexity of the brain functions involved in holding a conversation in a crowded room. Through the marvels of the reticular system, we're able to pay attention to one person even when the din of other conversations grows loud. Yet if our name is uttered in an adjacent conversation—a conversation we're consciously ignoring—we instantly tune in.

Sound like a complicated process? That's not the half of it. Our minds are constantly receiving data from the senses, constantly sorting, constantly prioritizing. Wherever you are right now, take a moment to notice all of the stimuli that your brain is automatically filtering out as you read this: perhaps the refrigerator humming in the background, or the sound of traffic outside, or a conversation in another room, or birds singing, or lights buzzing, or clouds changing the level of sunlight, or the slightest itch on your left arm, or the mildly unpleasant odor of a dog overdue for a bath.

The amount of information our brain receives at any given time would be absolutely overwhelming if we weren't equipped with a supercomputer to filter out that which we're not consciously interested in. Yet all of that information is analyzed: sorted, measured, and prioritized. Some of it is sent onward into our immediate consciousness: the things we choose to pay attention to, or that grab our attention, such as when we hear our name in an adjacent conversation. The bulk of it, however, is filtered out by the reticular system and remains behind in our subconscious. If what was left behind is important to our well-being, our subconscious will find a way to let us know through the language of intuition: emotions, physical sensations, and symbolic acts.

"I Had a Feeling That Would Happen"

Learn to see everything accurately. . . . Be aware of what is not obvious.[25]

—MIYAMOTO MUSASHI

"May I borrow your gun?" Joanne asked her husband, a police officer.

It was a lazy Saturday afternoon and he had nearly dozed off while reading a book. The question caught him off guard. He had never heard his wife say such a thing.

He hesitated. "Well . . . why?"

"I have to make a sales call on the north side of town tonight, and I'm just not comfortable going into that neighborhood," she answered.

A cosmetics sales representative, Joanne sometimes attended parties organized around her product line. This evening's gathering was hosted by a sales rep who had specifically requested Joanne's help. There was money to be made.

Joanne's husband usually granted her any favor she asked, as she would for him, and he almost said yes to this one. After all, he had trained her in the use of the weapon, and he certainly didn't want her to get hurt. But something just didn't add up. His wife was normally a level-headed person, and yet here she was planning to take a *gun* to a cosmetics party.

"Is there any *other* reason you want to borrow it?" he asked.

She looked aghast. "Of course not! I just don't like the neighborhood. You know as well as anybody the amount of crime that goes on around there."

It was true. He had told her on many occasions about the criminal element on that side of town. Still, he couldn't bring himself to simply say yes.

"Well," he mused, "if you're so uncomfortable that you won't go without a gun, then maybe you shouldn't go at all. Your intuition may be trying to tell you something."

Joanne paused for a moment, surprised. "You know, you're right," she said. "I'm so busy right now that it never even occurred to me."

Joanne stayed home that night and was relieved to do so.

Perhaps we'd all be more willing to listen to intuition if it spoke to us in the direct language that Joanne's husband used. Unfortunately the language of intuition is more subtle. It speaks to us through feelings and symbols.

Most of us have experienced the "I knew that would happen" phenomenon. We had a feeling that some course of action would have unfortunate consequences, but we let our conscious minds override what our subconscious was trying to tell us.

"Intuition" has a number of synonyms, none of them relating to logic: "gut feeling," "instinct," "hunch," "premonition," "insight," and even "educated guesswork." The insight born of intuition often comes to us as a feeling or an emotion. We might experience physical sensations such as butterflies in the stomach, skin tingling, or even nausea or headache. We might experience emotions such as a vague sense of sadness or depression. We might feel confused, as if we're missing some crucial piece of information.

Intuition can also express itself through symbolic acts. For instance, during an uncomfortable job interview you may notice that you're turning your body—ever so slightly—toward the door. Or you might find your true feelings expressed through an accidental slip of the tongue. You may have dreams that express your concerns. Or you may unwittingly commit a powerfully symbolic act, as Joanne did when she asked to borrow her husband's gun.

The point is, intuition feels and looks different to everyone. The only commonality we share regarding intuition is its vagueness, and its vagueness is one of the main reasons intuition is so easy for us to ignore. As logical creatures accustomed to expressing ideas through language, we often find subtle, intuitive messages too delicate to notice, especially when we're busy or preoccupied, as Joanne was in preparing for the cosmetics party.

Even if we recognize our intuition, many of us ignore it because it seems rude or flies in the face of social convention. We allow others to talk us out of following our "gut feelings," like the teenager who is goaded into accepting a ride with friends despite the fact that the driver is tipsy. When I was teaching a defense skills class for women, many participants told me about past problems they could have avoided had they only listened to their intuition. Usually they had ignored it, they said, because they didn't want to seem rude.

It doesn't need to be this way. We need not ever again admonish ourselves because we knew something bad would happen, but proceeded anyway. Each of us can reacquaint ourselves with the ancient power of intuition if we're willing to do a bit of work.

Step One: Willing Heart and Open Mind

Think back to the last time you regretted not following your intuition and reproached yourself with "I knew that was going to happen." Now is your chance to make sure that doesn't happen again. Instincts sometimes seem out of place, but rarely are they incorrect.

An old legend tells of a sword master who was napping against a cherry tree in an orchard near his school. Suddenly he snapped awake, jumped to his feet, and drew his sword. He searched the orchard, angry and agitated, convinced that someone nearby was plotting to attack him while he napped. There was no one to be found, save for a couple of his students who stood chatting in the distance. Eventually he decided that he was safe, and returned to his nap.

Only later did he discover the reason he had become upset. The two students he saw chatting in the distance were in fact talking about him. One of the students had remarked, quite innocently, "Master certainly looks vulnerable right now."

That single, barely audible comment was enough to trip the teacher's internal alarm. In spite of the fact that the orchard appeared empty, he didn't question his intuition. He searched the orchard until he was satisfied that he was safe.

The moral of the story: avoid falling into the trap of believing that your intuitive messages are illogical. Intuition may in fact be illogical by some standards, but that doesn't necessarily make it incorrect.

Your subconscious, intuitive thought processes are privy to much more information than your conscious mind. The last time you had to scold yourself for ignoring intuition, you were probably able to look back on the event and reconstruct the cause and effect with perfect logic. Your subconscious mind had already beaten you to the same conclusion and tried to warn you.

Pollyannas and paranoia

One of a police officer's greatest fears is that one day they will have to draw their gun and fire it at a person. Some officers will boast with great pride, "I've gone twenty years and never drawn my gun!"

It's said that an officer will typically adopt one of three mind-sets concerning the subject.

Some officers adopt a Pollyannaish attitude, persuading themselves that it will never happen: "Other cops draw their guns, not me." These officers become complacent and reckless and will probably have to draw their gun eventually as a result of their carelessness.

Others become paranoid and persuaded that they'll eventually have to fire on someone: "The way my luck goes, I just know it'll happen to me." Because we often find what we look for, these officers' worst nightmare will likely come true.

Still others take a more realistic approach. They recognize that it *might* happen to them, and regularly make time to train and sharpen their skills, never becoming complacent or paranoid. These officers have the greatest likelihood of never having to draw their weapon.

While some people resist their intuition for the sake of manners, others simply aren't comfortable or familiar enough with it to use it effectively. Most of us are taught from an early age to value reason and logic over emotion. This causes us to reject perceptions that seem to be based solely on emotion. The vague nature of intuition can be disquieting in a world that demands logic and order. The truth is, intuition is often more accurate and faster to appear than our conscious decisions.

Strengthening your intuition is like strengthening any other skill. It takes practice, and nothing less will do. The more we use our intuition, the more success we enjoy with it, and the more open our hearts and minds become. The good news is, you don't have to wait until you're in a life-or-death situation to strengthen your intuition, if you're willing to do your "pushups" now.

Step Two: Do Your Pushups Every Day

"Stay centered."

Every day, instructors in the martial arts and other sports admonish their students to "stay centered" during a challenging activity. Rarely do they explain what they mean, though: that the students' perception of themselves, their opponent or the other people involved, and their environment should be as close to reality as possible. Their perception of the scene should closely match the perception of an objective, all-seeing observer watching from a distance. In other words, the mind and body should be in the same place at the same time.

THE HIDDEN RAZOR BLADE

One Saturday night I was patrolling with the New York City chapter of the Guardian Angels when I made the dangerous mistake of not staying centered during an angry encounter. My mind and body weren't in the same place at the same time.

Our patrol leader came upon a known prostitute who was extremely agitated and angry. He stopped the patrol and began to talk with her, but she became hostile toward him. I felt he should have moved on at that point, and was perplexed as to why he continued to talk with her when there was clearly nothing to be gained.

Nevertheless, I supported his decision and "posted up" (a normal procedure in which the patrol members, usually about four people, position themselves to watch the surroundings while the patrol leader is otherwise occupied). I stood about arm's length from the woman's right side, but although I was trying to pay attention to the situation, I was nevertheless distracted by my puzzlement regarding the patrol leader's course of action, and my mind began to wander.

The conversation was reaching a fever pitch when suddenly, with the deftness of a cat, the patrol leader grabbed the woman's right wrist and extracted a razor blade that she had palmed between two fingers. If she had chosen to slap me, the nearest target, I could have been severely injured.

The patrol leader dropped the blade down the sewer, and we were on our way. The reason he hadn't left sooner was that he hadn't wanted to turn his back and expose the rest of us to a danger we weren't aware of.

Awareness doesn't simply mean *looking* for things; I probably wouldn't have seen the razor blade no matter how hard I looked. But had I not been so distracted by my own chattering thoughts, I might have picked up on any of a dozen other clues, such as the patrol leader's stance, the way the woman cupped her hand, or the worried looks on her friends' faces. Had I been "centered" and paying attention, my intuition would have told me that I was in danger.

If intuition is like a car, then awareness is the fuel that makes it run. Intuition functions on information from the environment, and staying centered allows you to pay attention, which in turn provides your intuition with as much accurate information as possible.

Staying centered involves three types of awareness: awareness of the environment, of others, and of yourself. The best way to improve your awareness is simply to exercise it every day. The following are three exercises I've offered to almost everyone who has participated in my training sessions. They take a bit of discipline, but they become easier with practice and will greatly increase your perceptiveness.

- **Awareness of your surroundings.** Whenever you enter a new environment, even a familiar one, take a brief moment to look around and notice a few specific things—three or four items are enough. They don't need to be particularly important, and you don't need to name them or apply a label like "door" or "pencil sharpener." In fact, it's better if you don't apply a word or label to them—let the nonverbal part of your brain speak to you in its own language. Simply notice and move on.

- **Awareness of others.** This exercise is similar to the first. Whenever you encounter a new person, take a brief moment to notice their general demeanor. If you encounter many people in a typical day, this can be a tiring exercise. Don't take it too far by trying to analyze each person's mood; ease off when you've had enough. As with the previous exercise, don't waste energy applying a label like "sullen" or "chipper" to their demeanor. Just notice and move on.

- **Awareness of self.** Three to five times a day to start, take a moment to assess yourself. Notice your emotional state. If you feel at all uncomfortable and don't know why, analyze the situation briefly.

You can also imagine viewing yourself from another's perspective. What does the expression on your face say? Do your words and body language match, or are you saying, "Glad to meet you" while your crossed arms are sending the opposite message? This is a challenging but particularly insightful exercise, especially if you do it discreetly while interacting with others.

These simple exercises are really nothing more than techniques for paying attention. Their beauty is this: no matter how good you are at noticing the small things, you can always be a little better.

You may find it difficult to remember the exercises at first. Place a reminder where you'll regularly see it—on the dashboard of your car, on your computer monitor, or the like.

Here are a few other techniques to help you improve your intuition.

- **Allow your curiosity to flourish.** Our world isn't generally geared for the use of intuition, and the people around you may not respond well to the idea of "gut feelings." Don't let that stop you. We are, by nature, curious animals, and curiosity is the seed of intuition. Too often, we give up our curiosity in pursuit of the many tasks we must complete each and every day. Worse, we give up intuition because it doesn't appear to be "logical." The exercises above, if performed regularly, will reacquaint you with curiosity.

- **Alter your routines.** Habits and routines can save time and mental resources. Buttoning our shirts the same way every day saves us from having to figure it out anew each time we get dressed; taking the same route to work every day saves us the trouble of finding a new route each morning.

    Of course, there's a downside: practiced too long, habits can rob us of our awareness of the world. How many times have you suddenly realized, when driving, that you don't remember anything about the last several blocks?

    If we learn to think habitually, always using the same arguments and appraisals, then we become mentally lazy and deprive ourselves of new information—the fuel for intuition. Robert Spencer observes in *The Craft of the Warrior*:

    > By your habits you restrict the range of possibilities of experience, and all the other possibilities—the rich range of actions and responses— are not available and sometimes cannot even be imagined. This poses a great restriction in a person's versatility of functioning, and restricting choice is inconsistent with the warrior's way.[26]

Here's an easy cure for this condition: simply alter your routines on occasion. Take a new route to work occasionally, or argue the other side of an issue once in a while. Perform your daily tasks in a different sequence. Occasionally reverse your usual route in the grocery store, or order something new at your favorite restaurant. These small changes force you to consciously interact with the world rather than function on autopilot. They provide a smorgasbord of new information for your intuition, and you may be pleasantly surprised by what you discover in your own backyard. Spencer offers this example:

> At areas where rock climbers practice, they soon become familiar with the holds necessary to complete any particular practice climb. To increase the challenge and make the familiar unfamiliar, they put the key hold of the crux move out of bounds and then climb the pitch. You can do this not only with actions, but with habitual points of view, emotional responses,

and problem-solving strategies. You also can imitate how other people respond or act, putting your own way on hold. This is an incredibly rich source of variations.[27]

- **Play the "what if" game.** This simple exercise helps you become consciously aware of your environment, the others around you, and the world of possibilities available to you at any given time. Simply ask yourself "what if [fill in the blank] happened right now?" For instance, on a recent hike with family I asked myself, "What if someone twisted their ankle right now?" I then spent a few minutes mentally exploring ways of seeking assistance or helping them back to the car. In the process I was forced to review all of the resources at hand, the strengths of the people around me, the shortest route to the car, and the items that I had forgotten but would bring next time.
This game is perfect for idle times—when standing in line at the store, for instance, or waiting for an appointment at work.
  Be sure, however, that the game doesn't evolve into paranoia. It should be an enjoyable, awareness-building activity that helps you feel stronger and more capable, and it should feed your intuition the information it craves; it shouldn't make you feel consistently vulnerable or frightened. Please see the sidebar titled "Pollyannas and paranoia" for a bit of perspective on preparation.

- **Don't dismiss your emotions.** Intuition communicates through feelings, physical sensations, and symbolic acts. Avoid dismissing your emotions and feelings by criticizing yourself (*I'm just being silly—nothing's going to happen if I let this guy into the house to use the phone*), making excuses for something that makes you nervous (*She's not really going to hurt me—she's just blowing off steam*), or giving in to social convention (*I know I shouldn't stand here and let the boss stare at me like that, but I don't want to be rude*).
  Just as importantly, avoid assuming that intuition is illogical. Hindsight almost always proves that our intuition was, in fact, correct and impeccably logical.

- **Balance goals with awareness.** The previous chapter advised you to choose how you want a given situation to end and to pursue that goal. But goals must be balanced with awareness; it doesn't do any good to run away if you run into the path of an oncoming bus. Goals must not be pursued at the expense of awareness of environment, others, and self. If you're too goal-oriented and unable to adjust, you may not discover that "hidden razor blade."

- **Read.** A library or Internet search on the subject of "intuition" will reveal many books that can help you improve your intuition. Their tone ranges from touchy-feely to scientific, so browse before you buy; there's sure to be at least one that appeals to your sensibilities.

- **Stop.** When you get that funny feeling and you don't know why, *stop*. Take a moment to assess the situation, just as my father did that evening when the thug lay in wait for him. Slowing down could save your life.

- **Ask "why?"** This is probably the most important question you can learn to ask yourself. Did the person you met at that party make you nervous? Ask yourself why. Do you have a funny feeling about driving to the store today? Why? Did the last interaction with a certain customer give you a vaguely nervous sensation? Why? Are you apprehensive about closing the bar this evening? Ask yourself why. The Warrior looks for what is not obvious.

Your intuition is like an angel tugging at your shirtsleeve. The angel's message may not always be obvious, but when it tries to speak to you, it almost always has something important to say.

We Americans go to great lengths to prevent violence in our lives. We fortify our homes and workplaces with alarm systems, security measures, and guards. We write complex workplace violence policies, and we have the most high-tech police force in the world.

Yet when violence occurs, it almost always begins with a conflict between two individuals. During those moments that precede an attack, policy and security measures are mostly useless. Even our well-armed police force must, by their very nature, arrive *after* an incident, not before. With these profound and inherent weaknesses in our defenses, what can we rely on? Training, knowledge, and skill.

In the first five chapters of this book, we've discussed five ground rules to help you through the formative moments of conflict:

1. Establish common ground.
2. Don't shame the attacker.
3. Don't shame yourself.
4. Choose the destination, but be flexible in the path.
5. Listen to your intuition.

Following these ground rules will often be enough to discourage an attack. But although they form a good foundation, much more knowledge is necessary to complete the structure. In the following chapters, we'll examine two types of hostility: Desperate Aggression and Expert Aggression.

PART II
DESPERATE
AGGRESSION

Never fight back against anyone who has nothing to lose. Find another way out.[28]
— TERRY DOBSON AND VICTOR MILLER

IF YOU HAD ASKED A PATRIOTIC British citizen, around the time of the American Revolution, which party had started the war, he likely would have blamed the colonists: "It's the Americans who consistently draw first blood," he might have said. "Remember the riot that ensued after our soldiers seized a ship that was in clear violation of trade laws? The Americans should have shown gratitude for the support and structure offered by the British crown. Instead, the surly bastards spat in our faces!"

Ask the same question of an American colonist, and you might get a very different answer: "Those Brits are really chafing our hides. We aren't allowed to expand westward beyond the control of the throne. We're forced to quarter their soldiers in our own homes. And that "trade law"? It amounts to nothing more than taxation without representation! Sure, we might have thrown the first stone in that little Boston tiff, but we had no choice!"

Which perspective is correct? For our purposes, it doesn't matter. All that matters is that the colonists *perceived* no alternative to war. It's been said that in politics, perception is reality; the same principle holds true when dealing with a panicked or angry individual. People will act on what they perceive. If they see no option other than hostility, even if other options do exist, then hostility is exactly what they'll deliver.

Even with nonhumans, perception of desperation matters more than the reality of the situation. An animal that *feels* it is threatened will lash out, whether in fact it's truly threatened.[29]

Like a cornered animal, a Desperate Aggressor perceives no options other than violence. That, in essence, is the definition of Desperate Aggression. When dealing with Desperate Aggressors, it's absolutely necessary to understand some of the challenges they're facing:[*]

- **They're at the end of their rope.** You may be encountering them for the first time, but their problem probably has a lengthy history. They may have already made unsuccessful attempts to solve it.

- **They don't want to listen.** Desperate Aggressors are often not in the mood to hear what you have to offer. They may feel they've already tried every option, and nothing works. To make matters worse, if you do have a magic solution, they may feel foolish for not having thought of it.

- **They're pessimistic.** Desperate Aggressors didn't become desperate because things were working out well for them. They may see no reason to expect that matters will now start going their way. This poses an extra challenge for you.

- **It's easy to say the wrong thing and make matters worse.** Desperate Aggressors feel frightened and cornered. They're hypersensitive and hypervigilant, which makes it easy to say or do something—with the best intentions—that further inflames them.

- **They have little concern for consequences.** Desperate Aggressors are generally not *completely* immune to the concept of consequences, but they're much less likely to consider consequences due to their highly emotional state of mind. Millions of "crimes of passion" are committed each year in America by otherwise level-headed people caught up in the throes of emotion.

Dealing with a Desperate Aggressor is like walking in a minefield: one false step and your world suddenly becomes a much worse place to be.

---

[*] While the two categories of aggressor discussed in this book cover the majority of violent incidents, there are some aggressors who simply don't respond to the sorts of verbal techniques offered in this book: those suffering from mental illness, intoxication or impairment, or a severe level of desperation (aggressors who break into homes to commit crimes, for example, can become extremely desperate and dangerous if cornered). Sometimes escape is the best option, and words only waste time. Let your intuition be your guide: if your gut says it's time to go, then head for the door.

Discouraged? Don't be. You may hold the answer to their problem, even if you don't know it. Approach the situation correctly, and Desperate Aggressors are likely to see you as a friend rather than an enemy. Helping them in spite of all the challenges involved can be a very rewarding experience.*

---

* It can be reasonably argued that almost all aggressors, including those that we'll later refer to as Expert Aggressors, have turned to aggression and violence as a result of desperation. One might argue that even those who profit by aggression, plan their attacks, and use hostility to solve problems that the rest of us would address in a more constructive manner are doing so because they have been unable to develop reasonable problem-solving abilities. There is a substantial degree of truth in these arguments. The purpose of this book, however, is not to analyze habitual aggressors, but to provide basic response skills for people who may find themselves the target of aggression. In that limited context, it matters whether the attack was planned or spontaneous, hence the division between Desperate and Expert Aggressors.

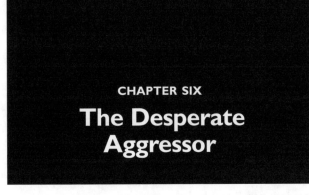

CHAPTER SIX

The Desperate Aggressor

Be kind, for everyone you meet is fighting a harder battle.

—PLATO

SCENARIO: The Dismissed Employee—Version One

KIM AND LAURA SAT IN THE conference room, waiting.

"She's late, as usual," Kim sighed. "Thanks for coming, Laura. I'm not looking forward to this. Firing someone is hard enough, but frankly, Molly worries me. I don't know how she'll react."

"Why is that?" asked Laura. "She seems nice enough—I mean, in spite of her work record."

Kim leaned back in her chair and sighed. "She's a nice person, and that's what makes this tough. Besides, word has it she's been under a lot of stress lately. Her husband just left her, and she has to take care of the kids. She's on the phone with her lawyer a lot. Sometimes she just gets so sullen and withdrawn." Kim gazed out the window. "I guess I worry about what might be going through her head."

"Kim, you've done everything you can to keep her. Unfortunately, it's just time for her to move on to something else. It's not like she hasn't seen this coming. Take it from me, letting someone go is never easy. But I'm sure it'll all work out fine."

Kim and Laura worked in a midsized insurance company. Kim, a manager, had been having disciplinary problems with Molly, a claims processor, for some time. Molly increasingly arrived late, failed to meet deadlines, and rarely attended required meetings. Kim had spoken to Molly several times and had offered the services of the company's Employee Assistance Program (a free, confidential counseling service contracted by many employers) to help her work out her personal problems.

It was all to no avail. After months of documenting problems and meeting with Molly to address them, Kim had exhausted her options. The situation was getting worse and the work simply wasn't getting done. Kim was starting to feel pressure from her superiors, who saw that the quality of her department's work was falling, and from her employees, who resented Molly's lack of performance. It was time to let Molly go. Besides, Kim reasoned, Molly was clearly unhappy; she would be better off somewhere else.

Now Kim sat waiting with Laura, one of the company's human resources representatives. Laura was new to the company and fresh out of college. Her lack of experience was disquieting to Kim. She knew this was going to be a stressful meeting.

Finally Molly arrived. She was more than fifteen minutes late and looked haggard, as if she had just rolled out of bed.

Kim and Laura stood to greet her. "Hi, Molly," Kim said with the same tone she would use to greet someone at a funeral.

Molly avoided eye contact and seemed to already know the purpose of the meeting. "Hi," she said quietly.

Kim wanted to get things moving as quickly as possible. "I think you've met Laura from Human Resources."

"Yeah," Molly answered. "Hi."

Laura returned the greeting almost apologetically. "Hi, Molly."

The three of them sat down around the conference table. Molly continued to avoid eye contact and looked terribly troubled. Kim wished she could leave and suddenly realized that Molly sat between her and the door, blocking her only exit. Nor was there a phone in the room. She wished she'd planned better.

Kim began. "Well, Molly, I'll get straight to the point. The reason we've called this meeting is to let you know that the company has decided to terminate our working relationship with you."

Molly made eye contact for the first time. She was shocked. "What?"

Kim fidgeted in her seat. "Molly, you know we like you here, but I'm afraid that it just isn't working out. The higher-ups have decided to let you go."

There was a long, uncomfortable silence. Molly was genuinely shocked. She'd known that this would be a disciplinary meeting, but she had no idea she'd be fired. After what felt like ages, Laura finally spoke up. "Molly, I have a final check here, along with some information on your health insurance and—"

Molly leaned forward in her chair and stared directly at Kim. "Oh my God! How could you do this to me?"

Kim didn't know how to answer. "Molly, this—this wasn't my decision. The higher-ups—"

"Don't talk to me about the 'higher-ups'!" Molly was beginning to shout. Her brow was furrowed, and she leaned far forward in her chair. "*You're* my supervisor, Kim! *You're* the one who talks to them. *You're* the one firing me!" There was another uncomfortable pause. Molly leaned back in her chair and looked out the window while she tried to suppress her tears. "I can't believe you're doing this! I thought you were my friend."

That last, stabbing comment hurt and angered Kim. "Molly, please try to calm down," she pleaded.

Molly looked horrified. She stood up. "Calm down? What the hell are you talking about? Do you have any idea what I have to face at home? Do you?" She was visibly agitated now. Tears streamed down her reddened face, and she was beginning to pace back and forth with her arms crossed tightly in front of her.

Kim was becoming terribly nervous and wished she could leave to call security. She was kicking herself for sitting so far from the door. She didn't know what to do. Ending the meeting was the first and only thing that crossed her mind. "Molly," she said, "I think it's time to end this meeting."

Molly was astonished. She continued to weep, but quickly her astonishment turned to fury. "That's it? You bitch! I can't believe this!" She picked up a notepad and threw it at Kim, then began to pace frantically. She knocked over first one chair and then another as she sobbed and shouted at the two women.

Kim and Laura were dumbfounded. They were afraid to say anything for fear that it might make the situation worse, and they feared standing up and leaving, as that might provoke Molly into further physical violence.

Kim had no idea what to do. She would have given anything not to be there.

Critical Reaction

Kim and Laura are right to be worried. We'll discuss shortly some of the disturbing signs that Molly is displaying, as well as the completely understandable mistakes that Kim made. As is so often the case, she simply wasn't prepared to handle the situation.

Before we can respond to Desperate Aggression, we must be able to recognize it and distinguish it from other types of aggression. We must know when a person is likely to turn to Desperate Aggression, what the behavior is meant to accomplish, and what the early warning signs look like.

Characteristics

Sun Tsu tells us that if we know our enemies as we know ourselves, then even in a thousand battles we will never be in peril.

The Desperate Aggressor isn't necessarily an enemy, and we shouldn't set out to do battle. But Sun Tsu's notion still stands. When we understand the aggressor, we can address the problem rather than being caught off guard and floundering like Kim.

Here are some traits of Desperate Aggressors.

- **They feel they have run out of options.** This is one of the most important concepts in the entire book. Violent crime in America is often spontaneous: somebody loses their temper, and the results are tragic. When an otherwise rational person reaches a high enough level of emotion, when they perceive no solution to their problem, then violence—normally not something they would ever consider—may seem to them like their only option.[30]

- **They seek to regain control.** Humans are willful creatures, and we don't like to feel helpless. Take a moment to imagine how helpless Molly must have felt at her meeting. She has kids to support, no partner to lean on, and now no source of income. If we were to ask her, during a calm, rational moment, "Is violence a way to solve these problems?" she would say no. Violence will not put food on the table or restore tranquility to her home.

  But she isn't rational at the moment. She's having difficulty distinguishing small problems from large ones, and at least temporarily, she's incapable of tackling one problem at a time. She is being led by the emotions of fear and helplessness. Those emotions demand that order be restored and that the threat be eliminated; those emotions know nothing of problem-solving other than an attempt to annihilate the perceived source of the problem.

- **They display verbal and physical indicators of stress.** When our rational minds step aside and emotions take over, our words, deeds, and appearance can change. During her meeting Molly must have felt cornered, panicked, and ashamed. These types of emotions are often reflected in physical and verbal indicators of stress, which can be the most direct means for recognizing the Desperate Aggressor. The next chapter explores these indicators in detail.

CHAPTER SEVEN

Early Warning Signs of Desperate Aggression

MELISSA AND CANDACE LIVED IN A residential treatment facility for teenage girls. They slept in adjacent rooms in a dormitory with about twenty other girls. Candace, an African-American girl, had been raised on the mean streets of Los Angeles. Melissa, a white girl, had been raised by an uneducated white-supremacist uncle.

Given their respective backgrounds and the proximity of their rooms, Melissa and Candace had bumped heads on many occasions. From the beginning they had disliked each other intensely, so they had learned to avoid each other. But one morning Melissa and Candace ran into each other—literally—and Melissa insulted Candace using a cruel racial epithet.

Candace had worked hard with her counselors at developing responses other than violence when confronted by disagreements. But, in this instance, she could feel the eyes of the entire dorm on her. Pride prevented her from backing down or laughing it off. She felt forced to save face, and so the two girls stood nose to nose in defiant challenge of one another.

The three staff members present were quick to intervene and separate the girls, and Candace was instructed to wait in the living room. There was too much going on for the staff to deal with the problem immediately, she was told, but they promised to help her shortly.

For about five minutes, Candace waited impatiently for a staff member to return and offer a solution. She paced about the living room, muttered to herself, and was unresponsive to the other girls. Unfortunately, the staff was overwhelmed and distracted by a dozen other problems.

Finally, Candace could wait no longer. She marched back into the dorm, found Melissa, and resumed the physical confrontation. Counselors were forced to restrain the girls.

The intent here isn't to implicate the staff for ignoring Candace; they were understaffed and overwhelmed. That said, Candace's actions prior to returning to the dorm are highly instructive. She did not simply wait patiently, then at random decide to resume the fight. She showed signs of distress while her mind chewed on the problem: she had been publicly humiliated, and the people who promised her an alternative to violence were not honoring their word. The five minutes that she waited must have seemed like an eternity, and as her sense of desperation increased, so did her signs of distress.

The signs were, to a certain extent, unique to her personality and perhaps even subtle, but they represent a pattern that applies to nearly anyone who feels the desperation of running out of options.

Physical Warning Signs

On the outside, Candace may have appeared to be waiting in relative calm for a staff member to help her. She was not throwing things, sobbing, or knocking over furniture. But on the inside was a tempest, and the signs would have been evident to anyone who took the time to look for them.

For instance, she paced around the living room and made several false starts toward the dorm. Her arms were tightly crossed. She stared at the ground and muttered. Her breathing was rapid and shallow. At one point she wiped away a small, single tear. All are signs of a body ready to fight; all are signs of the effects of adrenaline.

Most of us have experienced these effects—what's commonly called the "fight or flight" response, a momentary burst of energy that can come from fear, anger, or exhilaration. Think back to the last time you experienced a rush of adrenaline: Perhaps your heart raced, or your muscles suddenly felt so powerful that they shook. Perhaps you were nauseated or felt butterflies in your stomach.* All were effects of the powerful hormones that were suddenly released into your bloodstream. These effects include

- increased heart rate
- increased rate of breathing
- heightened acuity of the senses, such as that resulting from pupil dilation
- increased sugar metabolism, leading to greater strength and alertness
- dilation of the small arteries in muscles, allowing greater blood flow and increasing strength

---

* Adrenaline is made up of two neurotransmitters, epinephrine and norepinephrine. In times of stress the central nervous system signals the adrenal glands, which sit atop the kidneys, to release adrenaline into the bloodstream. The immediate "adrenaline rush" is the result of the effect that these chemicals have on our tissues.

- inhibited digestive activity, diverting resources to the muscles
- relaxed bladder

The biological purpose of these effects is to ready the body for action—although we have to question Mother Nature's wisdom on that last item.

The effects of adrenaline are important to us because they can cause visible changes in an aggressor. Even if they haven't yet reached the critical and dangerous point of "fight or flight," the adrenal response can provide a clue to the aggressor's psychological state. The effects listed above are internal changes (meaning we can't necessarily see them). The effects listed below are often visible:

- changes in breathing
- shaking
- fidgeting and restlessness
- vocal changes, such a raising or lowering of their normal pitch and volume, or a change in the rate of speech
- a defensive or offensive physical posture—that is, looking as if they want to either fight or run away (clenched fists, body half-turned away, head lowered, hands and arms crossed or placed in front of the body)
- protective facial gestures such as clenched jaw, squinted eyes, furrowed brows, and tensed facial muscles (all instinctive preparatory measures designed to protect the face during combat)
- flushed or reddened face (or, in some people, color appearing to drain from the face)

These physical indicators of adrenaline are the most immediate and obvious signs that a person is extremely angry, frightened, or panicked. But there are other signs of stress as well.

Everybody's engine revs once in a while

Adrenaline, like yawning, seems to be contagious. When the person you are dealing with loses their temper, you may find yourself suddenly under the influence of adrenaline as well.

Adrenaline affects each person in a slightly different way. Some people notice "butterflies in the stomach" or nausea, or feel extreme emotions such as panic or rage. Others enjoy the sensation that adrenaline offers, and notice an increase in physical and emotional energy.

Adrenaline can greatly affect your ability to respond to stressful situations—in both positive and negative ways.

It can increase the speed at which you think and respond, particularly if you've trained your mind to use it correctly. It also increases your physical strength and agility in case you must escape.

But adrenaline, especially if you're unaccustomed to its effects, may more likely have the effect of limiting your mental resources. You may experience tunnel vision; time distortion; extreme fear, anger, or elation; inability to think logically; and plain old confusion.

It may cause you to panic, to say things you'll truly regret, and, as Takuan Soho so vehemently warns, to freeze.

The best way to overcome these potential problems is to learn how to think and act in spite of adrenaline. This is a key lesson on the Warrior's path. Safe but stressful activities such as martial arts training, competitive sports, and even public speaking can help you become familiar with its particular effects on you. Martial arts training is especially useful, as it's specifically geared toward teaching students how to overcome the negative effects of adrenaline and capitalize on the positive effects. Add scenario training exercises (see Appendix C) and you have a recipe for success in almost any crisis.

Everybody's engine revs once in a while. The trick is to not do or say something, while your engine is roaring, that will haunt you for the rest of your life.

As you grow familiar with adrenaline, it will become a powerful tool. With practice, you'll be able to think and act quickly and accurately through what is, quite literally, an altered state of mind.

Verbal and Behavioral Warning Signs

Knowing the physical signs of stress can give us clues about the emotional state of a Desperate Aggressor, who is typically reacting to an increased level of stress during a state of reduced options. Along with the physical indicators of stress come a host of verbal and behavioral indicators.

AGITATION

Stressed-out, adrenaline-impaired individuals may find it difficult to sit still, and equally difficult to mentally focus on any one course of action. Their attention span is often short.

Signs to watch for are physical restlessness and a lack of patience.

UNCHARACTERISTIC OR POOR JUDGMENT

As stress increases, courses of action that seem outrageous during a normal state of mind become acceptable. Candace, for example, clearly didn't *want* to assault her dorm-mate Melissa, or she would have done so immediately. As time went by, and as tension evolved into crisis, that option became not only acceptable but seemingly the only course of action.

The Desperate Aggressor may also have trouble distinguishing small problems from large ones. What seems a fairly small problem to you may seem insurmountable to them. And if it seems insurmountable to them, then for all intents and purposes it *is* insurmountable, until you can change their perspective.

Signs to watch for are unrealistic or heat-of-the-moment statements, such as name calling or outrageous demands. The aggressor may make an unrealistic appraisal of the scope of a problem—that is, make a mountain out of a mole-hill. They may also make poor decisions, such as Candace's decision to march back into the dorm.

PARANOIA AND DEFENSIVENESS

Desperate Aggressors are desperate because things aren't going their way. This in itself causes a certain amount of defensiveness. Add to that the fact that adrenaline impairs judgment and awakens the most primitive part of our minds (the emotion-based limbic system), and you have a person who may perceive threats in the most innocuous statements or actions.

Signs to watch for are defensive statements such as "What's that supposed to mean?" or "I knew you'd take their side." The aggressor may also have selective memory, recalling only past wrongs. They may paint the target of their aggression as a longtime enemy, using statements such as "You always . . ." or "You never . . ." even when that's clearly not the case.

For a bit more on recognizing defensiveness, see the sidebar titled "Big talk."

EXTREME PESSIMISM

Desperate Aggressors wear a dark cloud over their head and are quick to shoot down suggestions. Their state of reduced options seems to create the ideal condition for pessimism.

Signs to watch for are statements such as "That will never work" or "I knew this would happen to me."

NERVOUS CONFUSION

The tunnel vision and time distortion that often accompany adrenaline can lead a person in a dozen different directions at once; it can lead them to commit false starts; and it can cause them to forget important information. The person may behave as if they don't know which way to turn. They may pace, their eyes may dart, and their speech may seem unrelated to the matter at hand.

WITHDRAWAL

Candace, while she was displaying signs of adrenaline's effects, was at the same time withdrawing from the rest of the group in her dormitory. She closed her arms tightly on herself, stared at the ground, and was unreceptive to others. A person who feels cornered will often turn inward and ultimately find the justification to lash out.[*]

Withdrawal is one of the most insidious warning signs of Desperate Aggression because it makes the Desperate Aggressor difficult to detect. You might think of all Desperate Aggressors as storming about, shouting and cursing, but this isn't always the case. An employee of a detox unit I worked at, for example, once lost control of his temper and choked a client into unconsciousness. The employee was suffering an unbearable level of stress at work and at home, and had run out of ways to manage that stress.

---

[*] Some might argue that Candace did not truly withdraw; instead, she was separated from the rest of the group involuntarily. That's a reasonable observation, but not especially pertinent here. Whether or not she withdrew voluntarily, she displayed effects of adrenaline, although they were masked and subtle. She was withdrawn and highly agitated, regardless of how she got that way.

You might wonder why his coworkers didn't detect his desperation before he attacked. They didn't fail to do so out of any lack of concern; it was simply that his response to stress did not appear to be aggressive. Rather, he became sullen, brooding, and withdrawn, sitting in a corner with his arms crossed. In the meantime, his coworkers had a dozen other matters to attend to. It's easy to see how they missed the warning signs; in a passing glance, he probably appeared to be the calm amid the storm.

The nature and consequences of withdrawal in the Desperate Aggressor offer us yet another reason to heighten awareness and welcome intuition. Signs to watch for include physical isolation, closed body language (crossed arms, furrowed brow, and the like), avoidance of eye contact, silence, muttering under one's breath, and other signs of withdrawal.

HURTFUL LANGUAGE

Hurtful language consists mainly of insults, such as when Molly (in the previous chapter's scenario) said to her supervisor, "I thought you were my friend," or when an angry citizen says to a police officer, "Why don't you leave me alone and go catch the real criminals."

Hurtful language is meant to belittle or cause pain, to draw you into a fight. It's not necessarily a warning of bad things to come, and that's the vital distinction between hurtful language and threats or abusive language. Hurtful language is usually best ignored; of course, it's entirely up to you how much you're willing to tolerate before you draw the line or end the interaction.

As difficult as it may be, it's important to keep in mind that Desperate Aggressors are trying to inflict pain because they feel victimized. Like injured animals, they're lashing out at anyone who gets close enough to pose a threat. Reacting to hurtful language by allowing yourself to be sidetracked and drawn into a fight may cause you to say or do something that you'll forever regret. And of course, it causes you to forget the true nature of the problem. Recognize hurtful language for what it truly is, and stay on track.

THREATS AND ABUSIVE LANGUAGE

Hurtful language is usually best ignored, but threats and abusive language are a different story. Let's define our terms:

- **Hurtful language** is designed to inflict pain or draw you into a fight. Examples: "I can't believe you would do this to me! I thought you were my friend!" or "At least I'm not sleeping with the boss."

- **A threat** is any expressed or implied warning of harm, such as "I'm going to cut you" or "We'd all be better off if you weren't around."

- **Abusive language** is any attempt to intimidate or manipulate someone into compliance: "If you don't give me a good evaluation, I swear you'll pay" or "If you know what's good for you, you'll do it my way."

Threats and abusive language should never be tolerated or ignored. When threatened, get to a safe environment and report the threat to the proper authorities.

Early Response, Early Detection

Think back for a moment to Candace's situation in the dormitory. Imagine that you had walked into the living room as Candace was pacing and muttering. You don't know what's going on; you simply see a girl who doesn't bother to greet you.

The untrained observer might ignore this situation. "She must be having a bad morning," they might think. "She doesn't want to be bothered. I'd better leave her alone so she can work through it."

Fortunately, you're not untrained. That approach, while understandable, can lead to disaster. The ability to understand warning signs is the first step toward an early and safe response.

The second step in preventing violence is a willingness to recognize the danger in the situation without succumbing to wishful thinking or avoidance. This step requires two things: the willingness to listen to your intuition, and the ability to respond. When you know you have the ability to respond, situations like Candace's or Molly's no longer seem unmanageable. When you have the appropriate skills, wishful thinking is no longer a necessity.

Big talk

Fear doesn't always look like fear. Just ask any bartender. Most people who spend time around drunks become familiar with one of the most interesting indicators of fear and insecurity. Some psychologists call it "compensating behavior." The rest of us know it as "big talk."

For some unfortunate souls, insecurity and drunkenness are intertwined; alcohol helps them blunt the pain of fear and uncertainty. Rarely, however, are they willing to wear their vulnerability on their sleeve, and some choose to mask it with hostility.

A drunk's compensating behavior is as magnified as any other aspect of their behavior. They speak louder, their opinions are stronger, and their big talk is often very, very big.

The drunk who becomes angry at someone may make outlandish claims. For instance, they may threaten to have a person fired, claiming to be best friends with their employer. They may threaten to have the person arrested because, of course, they know the chief of police. They may brag about the $150,000 Ferrari that their ex-spouse won in the divorce settlement. I've heard all these, and more.

Because the drunk's behavior is so flamboyant, it's usually easy to maintain proper perspective. They act big because they feel small. It's obvious.

That perspective is difficult to maintain, however, when we're faced with a sober person who is engaging in the same behavior, but on a much less obvious level. Many's the time an irate customer has threatened to "write a letter," or a rookie cop, not knowing how to handle a resistant citizen, has resorted to threats they could never legally carry out.

A sober person's idle threats are more subtle and realistic than those of the drunk, and this can blind us to the true nature of the situation: like the drunk, people who make idle threats are usually acting big because they feel threatened.

Genuine threats are a different matter, but big talk and compensating behavior are almost always a sign of fear and should be treated as such. Assuming that the person *is not threatening your safety or the safety of others*, the best policy is to recognize big talk as a defensive maneuver and continue problem-solving as you normally would.

CHAPTER EIGHT

Listening, Empathizing, and Providing Options (LEO)

No fight, no blame.
—TAO TE CHING

IN HOMER'S THE ODYSSEY, ONE OF the perils that Odysseus faced on his journey was navigating his ship through the narrow passage between Scylla and Charybdis. He would perish if he came too close to either one. Scylla was a six-headed snakelike monster that would snatch sailors from passing boats. Charybdis was a whirlpool that three times daily would engulf any vessel whose timing was off. Resourceful Odysseus made the passage, of course, but just barely.

Responding to the Desperate Aggressor is a bit like navigating between Scylla and Charybdis. It poses two dangers:

- **Being drawn into a fight.** Desperate Aggressors generally feel that they're under attack, and this perception awakens the most primitive part of the brain, what some psychologists refer to as the "reptilian brain" because it's similar in structure and chemistry to a lizard's brain.[31] We rely on the reptilian brain very little, but when we feel that we're under attack, the reptilian brain wants nothing more than to take over and protect us from danger.

  The good news is that the reptilian brain acts quickly and decisively. The bad news is that it knows no mediation skills; "friend" and "enemy" are the extent of its relationship repertoire. Anyone who isn't a friend is by default an enemy, and this is why the Desperate Aggressor is so adept at hurtful language, abuse, and threats.

  When faced with the reptilian brain hurling insults and abuse, as when faced with the monster that sucks up entire ships, it's easy to be distracted and drawn into a fight. But to do so is to never complete the mission. It takes a steady hand to navigate these waters.

- **Making the aggressor feel that he has no options.** Desperate Aggressors may appear dangerous, and may in fact be. But keep this in mind: as long as Desperate Aggressors are talking, they're not attacking. If they're talking, that means they haven't yet reached a state of complete desperation, which is when they feel they have no options other than violence. Once aggressors reach that level of desperation, they become like the six-headed monster, ready to devour anyone in sight.

   Desperate Aggressors usually don't have the words to describe their problem, and in any case they aren't in a problem-solving mood. If either were the case, they would cease to be an aggressor, let alone a desperate one. The job of presenting options to a Desperate Aggressor isn't always simple, but it can be done.

Your response to a Desperate Aggressor must accomplish two goals:

- **Focus on solutions.** You must transform the aggressor from someone who simply wants to fight into someone who is willing to discuss solutions to their problem.

- **Return a sense of power to the aggressor.** Trying to control a Desperate Aggressor is like trying to wrestle a rhinoceros to the ground. Unless your safety is threatened, a softer touch is in order. Lack of power is what brought this aggressor to their current condition; returning a sense of power is most often the best remedy.

Most importantly, the strategy must be one of compassion. Desperate Aggressors feel cornered, and they probably don't want a fight any more than you do. Presenting options, however, isn't always as easy as "Hey, why don't we try this. . . ." First you must establish trust. Remember, the reptilian brain sees only friends and enemies—"If you ain't for me, you must be against me." Desperate Aggressors won't work with you unless they're certain that you're on their side.

Recall the first ground rule, establishing common ground. That rule stems from the aggressor's belief, however misguided, that the target of their aggression is an enemy. The best strategy against this misinformed mind-set is to establish trust by creating common ground, and that takes time: you must demonstrate trustworthy intent through trustworthy actions.

The most direct route to establishing trust (however rudimentary or shallow that trust may be) is Listening, Empathizing, and, ultimately, providing Options

(LEO)—a strategy that demonstrates trustworthiness, helps you understand the aggressor's problem, and allows the aggressor to begin taking control of the situation so that violence isn't necessary. This strategy calms the reptilian brain.

LEO is a starting point. Often it's enough to solve the problem by itself; however, there will be times when, halfway through the formula, you discover that you're dealing not with a Desperate Aggressor, but with an aggressor of the more opportunistic type—an Expert Aggressor. (That's the topic of Part Three.) Other times you may execute the formula flawlessly, only to be frustrated by stubborn resistance. We'll discuss how to handle that in Chapter 9, "What if LEO doesn't work?" But for now, let's begin with the basics.

Listening

"Old school" isn't necessarily the best school. Many psychologists once considered aggression to be a simple, almost automatic response to frustration or danger. Newer research perspectives view it as a means of solving a problem; it's much more than a blind reaction.[32]

Aggression between animals, for example, could be either defensive, as when a foreign critter invades the home front, or offensive, as when one critter attacks another to obtain sorely needed territory. In either case, aggression is addressing the problem of obtaining territory that's necessary for survival.

This viewpoint goes well beyond the simple stimulus-reaction model from the days of old. It supports what becomes obvious simply by observing others: aggression is generally a response to a grand problem such as survival, territory, or pride. (That last one, pride, is uniquely human, and there are times when it's more important than survival itself.)

Let's take a moment to review the scenario in which Kim fired Molly.

The Dismissed Employee, revisited

Kim, Laura, and Molly sat down around the conference table. Molly avoided eye contact and looked terribly troubled. Kim wished she could leave and suddenly realized that Molly sat between her and the door, blocking her only exit. Nor was there a phone in the room. She wished she had planned better.

Kim began. "Well, Molly, I'll get straight to the point. The reason we've called this meeting is to let you know that the company has decided to terminate our working relationship with you."

Molly made eye contact for the first time. She was shocked. "What?"

Kim fidgeted in her seat. "Molly, you know we like you here, but I'm afraid that it just isn't working out. The higher-ups have decided to let you go."

There was a long, uncomfortable silence. Molly was genuinely shocked. She'd known that this would be a disciplinary meeting, but she had no idea she'd be fired. After what felt like ages, Laura finally spoke up. "Molly, I have a final check here, along with some information on your health insurance and . . ."

Molly leaned forward in her chair and stared directly at Kim. "Oh my God! How could you do this to me?"

Kim didn't know how to answer. "Molly, this—this wasn't my decision. The higher-ups—"

"Don't talk to me about the 'higher-ups'!" Molly was beginning to shout. Her brow was furrowed and she leaned far forward in her chair. "*You're* my supervisor, Kim! *You're* the one who talks to them. *You're* the one firing me!" There was another uncomfortable pause. Molly leaned back in her chair and looked out the window while she tried to suppress her tears. "I can't believe you're doing this! I thought you were my friend."

That last, stabbing comment hurt and angered Kim. "Molly, please try to calm down," she pleaded.

Molly looked horrified. She stood up. "Calm down? What the hell are you talking about? Do you have any idea what I have to face at home? *Do you*?"

Molly was visibly agitated now. Tears were streaming down her reddened face, and she was beginning to pace back and forth with her arms crossed tightly in front of her.

Kim was becoming terribly nervous and wished she could leave to call security. She was kicking herself for sitting so far from the door. She didn't know what to do. Ending the meeting was the first and only thing that crossed her mind. "Molly," she said, "I think it's time to end this meeting."

If Molly's aggression was in response to a problem, then what was the problem? Obviously, she's being fired and that constitutes a problem, but that doesn't seem sufficient to explain her actions. People are fired every day without turning to violence. Assuming that Molly is an otherwise reasonable person, some other factor must be leading her toward violence.

We know from an earlier bit of conversation between Kim and Laura that Molly was having problems at home. Was that the motivation behind her behavior?

Maybe. We simply don't know because Kim never took time to discover the true nature of the problem. Kim dismissed any possibility of allowing Molly to discuss her problem with the statement "I think it's time to end this meeting."

Kim and Laura went into this meeting knowing that it would be tense. They probably wanted it to be over as quickly as possible, so they rushed it along in order to avoid having a "scene" on their hands. In so doing, they made a common mistake: they confused *escape* with *avoidance*. Escape means to extricate oneself from a situation, forcibly if necessary. Avoidance means hoping that the problem will magically go away—for instance, by calling an end to the meeting. The result of Kim's attempt to avoid was being trapped in a closed conference room with a woman who was becoming physically violent.

Kim's not a bad supervisor or a bad person. She's simply and understandably unfamiliar with heightened conflict. The listening phase is for many people the most difficult and counterintuitive portion of responding to a Desperate Aggressor. There are a couple of legitimate reasons why listening can be such a challenge.

La-la-la, I Can't Hear You!

First, listening can be terribly uncomfortable. Few of us are accustomed to dealing with irate individuals, nor should we be. Voices are louder, actions are exaggerated, and judgment is impaired. Nobody likes being yelled at.

Next, you may feel pressure to solve the problem *now*. The aggressor may be discussing their problem with such volume, animation, and urgency that you fear you must act immediately or face immediate consequences. This isn't necessarily true. Listening seems too passive when it feels like we ought to be doing something—*anything*.

We may be physically stuck with the person, as was Kim, and it's natural to feel that the sooner we calm them down, the safer we are. It's also natural to assume that in order to help, we must talk and they must listen. Don't fall into this trap. Listening is powerful. How many times have you heard someone say, "I just need someone to talk to, someone to listen to me"? I have yet to hear someone say, "I just need someone to talk at me."

The Costs of Not Listening

Failure to listen comes with an exorbitant price tag.

First, if you don't take time to listen, you probably won't understand the true nature of the problem. This means that all of your interactions with the

Desperate Aggressor will be based on a shaky foundation. Worse yet, the aggressor may feel that you are working at cross-purposes. You may think you're helping, only to find out that you've inadvertently supplied the last straw. Such tragedies are usually characterized by post-incident statements such as "He just blew up without any warning at all! I don't know what went wrong!"

Second, despite your best intentions, you may inadvertently confirm the aggressor's belief that no one is listening. This, as you might guess, reduces their perceived options. When the act of listening gets uncomfortable, just remember what we already know: as long as they're talking, they're not attacking.

Finally, failure to listen robs you of time, which is generally on your side. You can use that time to take a breath, to let them expend energy, and to gather information and plan a strategy for escape or for helping the person.

You can't control a Desperate Aggressor any more than you can control the tide. Dealing with a Desperate Aggressor requires a soft touch and a willing ear. Ultimately you may want to help the person, but that simply won't happen until they're ready, and they generally won't be ready until they've been heard.

TECHNIQUES

Imagine yourself sitting on Andy Griffith's front porch in Mayberry, USA. He begins to regale you with stories of Barney, Opie, and Floyd the barber. His easy manner and down-home humor are like a backrub for the soul. You find yourself simply sitting and listening. It seems to come naturally.

Now imagine yourself in a conference room faced with the likes of Molly—irate, emotional, and headed toward physical violence. Sitting and listening suddenly doesn't seem so appealing, or so natural. It's going to take some effort.

It's difficult to discuss listening without sounding sanctimonious, but knowing when and how to listen under stress doesn't come naturally. It can be a harrowing experience, especially when you're cornered, and listening to an angry aggressor is the last thing you feel like doing.

A few tips and tricks are in order:

- **Don't fear breaks in the conversation.** As we saw with Candace in her dormitory, the aggressor who withdraws can be on the verge of becoming violent. However, irate individuals who are in the process of expressing their problems and frustrations may at times need to pause and gather their thoughts. This "awkward silence" can be uncomfortable, but it's not to be feared. Let aggressors gather their thoughts and continue. Unless you sense that it's

The ear can be mightier than the word

At first glance, it looked as if it would be like any other Saturday morning at the detox facility where I spent my weekends working as a counselor. It seemed normal, that is, until I caught wind—literally—of Harvey's predicament.

Harvey had soiled himself during his drunken stupor the evening before. The next morning, as the unpleasant light of reality overcame the fog of drunkenness, he was becoming increasingly embarrassed and agitated. He constantly moved from one location to another in the facility, contaminating everything he came into contact with and creating a very unsavory environment.

Several counselors in the facility had asked, ordered, and begged Harvey to take a shower and wear the clean pants that the staff had gladly donated. But his shame was too great. He no doubt feared that a shower would only bring a harsher light to the reality of his situation—it would be an admission that he had a serious problem on his hands—so the harder the staff pushed him, the more resolute he became, until he flatly refused to take a shower: "No way, no how."

But in an act of selfless heroism, and in the face of adverse olfactory conditions, I was able to persuade Harvey to take a shower where all others before me had failed.

What magic did I perform? None, really. I simply took Harvey aside to talk privately, affording him some much-needed dignity, and asked him why he didn't want to take a shower.

For nearly ten harrowing, smelly minutes I listened to Harvey. His thoughts weren't well organized, nor did they lead toward any particular conclusion. He simply needed to talk, however indirectly, about the overwhelming embarrassment of his situation. After a good dose of listening and a few words of encouragement, Harvey was ready for his shower.

The lesson in all this? Listening isn't always pleasant or easy, but if I can do it, so can you.

time to move on to the empathy stage (more on that shortly), the most you should say at this point is "Go on" or "Take your time."

- **Ask open-ended questions.** If the conversation needs a jump-start or a gentle push in one direction or another, use the opportunity to gather information. Ask open-ended questions that require some elaboration, such as "What has made you angry?" or "What would you like to happen next?"

   Sometimes aggressors want to talk but don't know what to say. Your job is to steer them toward discussing their problem so that together you can devise a solution.

- **Offer responses that encourage talking.** Reward aggressors for talking. Phrases such as "That must have been difficult," "Thanks for sharing this with me," and "Is there anything else?" encourage talking and discourage violence. And of course, don't forget your nonverbal messages of encouragement, such as eye contact, nodding, and open body language (facing them in your open prepara-tory stance, arms and legs uncrossed, hands in a nonthreatening position).

- **Give them plenty of room.** Make sure you don't invade their personal physi-cal boundaries, and don't rush them. If you tend to comfort others with a gentle touch, avoid doing so with Desperate Aggressors. They're probably under the influence of adrenaline and may be highly defensive. Any invasion of their personal space might be misconstrued as a threatening gesture. Maintain a distance of at *least* an arm's length, and refer to the sidebar titled "Preparatory stance" on page 40.

- **Suspend judgment.** You may not agree with Desperate Aggressors; you may not be able to sympathize with them; you may even detest them. Your defenses may be up and your emotions may be high. But it's absolutely imperative that you approach their situation as objectively as possible, because their problem is very real to them, and that makes it very real to you. As difficult as it may be, keep yourself firmly geared toward information gath-ering rather than opinion forming.

- **Suspend premature solutions.** If they haven't yet finished their story, keep your ideas to yourself until you feel they're ready to listen. It's tempting to begin offering solutions prematurely out of discomfort, fear, or the desire to help.

Timing is important, however. Offer solutions too soon, and you may aggravate the situation. The upcoming section on empathy will help you know when an aggressor is most receptive to your input.

- **Emulate good listeners.** If you know someone who is a particularly good listener, study them. Find out how they do it.

The audience effect

One of the most important things you as a listener can do to comfort the aggressor and reduce the chance of a violent crisis is to *isolate the incident*.

Onlookers, friends, subordinates, peers, and superiors standing in the wings can all have a profoundly negative impact on the aggressor's behavior.

When dealing with a single aggressor, try to move them to a more private, neutral location. For instance, if an employee becomes verbally aggressive in the boss's office where other employees can hear and observe the confrontation, move the person to a conference room that doesn't carry the same sense of subordination as the boss's office. It should go without saying that you should not go alone or allow yourself to be cornered in the room. Keep control over the exit at all times, and keep law enforcement, security, or a buddy ready at a moment's notice to help you escape.

Moving to a neutral environment isn't always possible, but you may be able to create one by clearing the area as quickly as possible. Remove all unnecessary onlookers and establish some privacy (again, not isolating yourself with the aggressor).

When multiple aggressors are involved, intervening can be tricky. These matters are usually best left to law enforcement, *especially* where domestic matters are concerned. If it's absolutely necessary to intervene between two combatants, however, never do so alone. Create as much distance as possible between the people—simple separation isn't enough. Hostilities will most likely resume if the parties can see or speak to one another. As always, don't isolate yourself with either combatant.

FOUR POINTS TO KEEP IN MIND

The listening phase should last only as long as necessary to take the edge off the aggressor's anger and provide you with useful information. The success of the listening phase is partially up to you. Aggressors are by definition not highly skilled at communication, or their behavior would not be bordering on violence. They may be relying on you to take the lead. Here are four basic requirements for good listening during times of crisis.

- **Keep your emotional armor well oiled.** Study well the distinction between hurtful language and abusive language or threats. Clinical detachment will help you stay on track when the aggressor is being hurtful out of fear or frustration, and it will help you know when to stop talking and focus on escape, which you should do when the aggressor becomes genuinely abusive or threatening.

- **Avoid sarcasm or dry humor.** Humor, especially gallows humor and sarcasm, is a common and useful survival skill. For some of us, making wisecracks under stress comes naturally. Unfortunately, well-crafted sarcasm may be lost on someone who is functioning at a more survival-based level. If you decide to use humor to calm an aggressor, be sure that your humor is easily understood and not even remotely—even by misinterpretation—directed at the aggressor. If in doubt, bite your tongue.

- **As always, follow the ground rules when dealing with the Desperate Aggressor.** Of particular importance are "Establish common ground" and "Don't shame the aggressor." Share your own experiences that are similar to the aggressor's (but keep it brief), and avoid messages that implicate them, even if they've made obvious mistakes.

- **Don't overlook those who withdraw.** Some aggressors withdraw rather than expend great amounts of energy as they enter a crisis, like Candace after her dorm-mate hurled the racial epithet. Whether a person's behavior becomes loud and demonstrative or sullen and withdrawn, each is an important change. Your goal with a withdrawn aggressor is to get them to expend some of the emotional energy they've built up. Encourage them to talk, if they're willing. You can't force it—nor should you try—but you can ask questions and let them know that you're willing to listen.

The purpose of the listening phase is to gather information—ammunition, if you will—that will help you get yourself away from this dangerous situation. It's a crucial part of the LEO strategy that requires an artful touch. Sometimes an aggressor doesn't know what to say, or their thoughts are all over the map because they're confused or overwhelmed. Your job is to keep them focused, gather information, and at the same time offer the comfort of *truly* being listened to.

When the listening phase is over and you have the information you need, it's time for you to start taking more of an active role. How do you know when the listening phase is over? Read on.

Are you listening?

Have you ever found yourself planning your reply instead of listening to another person? Or waiting for them to stop talking so you can talk? How about organizing your day or planning your grocery list while they chatter away?

There are a myriad of things to think about when facing a hostile person—looking for escape routes, creating options, measuring their demeanor, and so on. To complicate matters, it's vital that you actually listen to the aggressor. Empathy cannot exist without listening, nor will you be able to provide options if you don't truly understand their problem.

In fact, a failed attempt at empathy can make the situation worse. So when you find your mind wandering to other matters, as it inevitably will during a crisis, stay focused. You *don't* want to ask aggressors to repeat themselves.

Empathizing

The word *empathy* is sometimes confused with *sympathy*, but the two have very different meanings. *Sympathy* means to feel what someone else feels. If my friends' puppy becomes ill, they're sad and I'm sad along with them. I like puppies, so I'm personally affected.

Empathy means to understand what someone else feels, but not necessarily to share the emotion. If my friend kicks a puppy because the puppy soiled the carpet, I understand that he is mad and I might know the reason why, but I don't share the emotion or support the action.

Empathizing with a Desperate Aggressor may at times seem like this latter example. You may find their behavior distasteful or even repugnant, but it's still necessary to examine why they're acting that way, and what problem brought them to their present condition.

The timing of the three LEO stages—Listening, Empathizing, and providing Options—is dictated almost entirely by the aggressor's current state of mind. We can't move from one LEO stage to the next until the aggressor shows that they're ready. Unfortunately, aggressors seldom announce, "Okay, the listening phase is over. It's time for you to provide empathy." We need to know when, why, and how to use this stage of the strategy.

WHEN

During the listening phase, you—the target—utter only enough words to keep the person talking. As you enter the empathy stage, however, it's time to take a more active role in the conversation.

Timing is critical. Speak up too early, and you run the risk of aggravating the aggressor. They may feel that you're not listening or, worse, that you're arguing with them. Wait too long and the opportunity can be lost, leaving the aggressor to assume that you don't care. Either case can trigger the "If you ain't for me, you must be against me" reptilian response.

I once watched four motorcycle riders race around the inside of a spherical metal cage about fifteen feet in diameter. They all rode at once, very fast, and in different directions. That took precise timing. The good news is that the timing here isn't nearly that critical. Another bit of good news is that the aggressor will show you, through their words and actions, when it's time to begin the empathy stage.

As people enter a crisis, their rationality wanes and their behavior typically changes dramatically. As Molly was being fired, for example, she stood up, raised her voice, and kicked over a chair—not her normal behavior. Candace, normally an outgoing and happy girl, paced, muttered, and eventually became so irrational that she returned to her dorm for a physical confrontation.

As people enter a crisis, their energy output typically increases—although often, as with Candace, the person seems to withdraw. This change in energy level defines for us the listening phase. As long as they're talking, we should be listening. We want them to expend in a safe way some of the emotional energy they're experiencing. Eventually their energy output will begin to wane, and that's when we enter the empathy stage.

The level of energy that people expend during a crisis is difficult to maintain for extended periods of time. Even people like Candace, although they may not show it externally, are seething with emotional energy on the inside. Once you

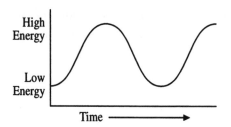
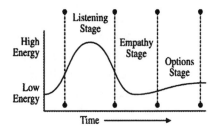

get an aggressor talking, they'll usually let loose and expend great amounts of energy. Doing so is tiring, and eventually a person runs out of steam.

If you choose to take part in scenario training exercises (see Appendix C), you'll quickly discover that it's tiring to be the aggressor. No matter how good your acting is, you can only rant and rave for so long before you get just plain worn out. Even aggression in animals tends to occur in distinct bursts of energy followed by quieter periods.[33]

If we were to plot a graph of an aggressor's energy output, including the fuming, self-contained energy spent by those who withdraw, it would look something like this:

The first upswing in activity is the crisis phase, the period of time when rationality wanes and behavior changes dramatically. This period is also the listening stage.

The downswing in activity indicates a return to rationality, however slight, and a return to a more normal level of activity, however tenuous. This downswing marks the beginning of the empathy stage. As the aggressor begins to lose momentum, this is your opportunity to enter the conversation.

WHY

Verbally empathizing with the aggressor benefits you as well as them. Empathizing ensures that you understand the problem from their point of view so that you can move into the options phase on solid ground. Understanding the problem keeps you from solving the wrong problem and inadvertently making matters worse.

The empathy stage serves several purposes:

- It lets aggressors know that you'll act in their best interest and are therefore not an enemy.
- It ensures that you are addressing the true problem, from their point of view.

- It introduces you as a problem solver, a director, an authority rather than a victim. A gentle show of competence and strength can be very comforting to the Desperate Aggressor.
- It lays the groundwork for presenting options.
- It helps you meet the all-important requirement of establishing common ground.

How

Entering the conversation can, all by itself, present quite a challenge. The Desperate Aggressor may not willingly yield the floor. Although you shouldn't resist if they need to continue talking, eventually their words will become repetitive, or other considerations will require you to move the interaction along.

One of the most basic and effective techniques for entering the conversation is to restate the aggressor's problem in your own words. In addition to providing a fairly simple entry, this technique helps you ensure that you actually understand the problem. Most people will listen to you restate their problem, if only to make sure that you get it right. The steps are as follows:

1. Recount the aggressor's thoughts or feelings.
2. Define the problem.
3. Ask for confirmation.

The goal is to demonstrate that you're focused on them and their problem. Examples:

> *"You feel/think _____ because _____. Is that correct?"* *

> *"You're angry because your future seems to depend on this performance review, and you feel that it's unfair. Is that accurate?"*

> *"You think that if the staff here doesn't respond to this situation, others will begin to see you as a 'chump.' Is that right?"*

---

* An important part of mirroring an aggressor's message is mirroring their cognitive state, meaning that you should echo their preference for either "feeling" words or "thinking" words. If an aggressor tends to use words that describe emotions, such as "angry" or "pissed off," then it's probably safe to use similar words: "You're angry because you didn't get the promotion." However, if an aggressor tends to use analytical descriptions, omitting emotional labels, then you should do the same: "You think it's unreasonable that you weren't promoted." When in doubt, it's safest to use analytical rather than emotional labels. Many people resent being told how they feel.

"Without your paycheck, you can't feed your kids, and you're worried you won't find another job. Is that a fair statement?"

"You believe your supervisor is acting as if he's out to get you. Do I have that right?"

The reason for requesting confirmation is that the highly agitated individual may not respond well to being *told* how they feel. By asking them to confirm your statement, you allow them the opportunity to correct you without feeling that they need to argue about it. You also show a genuine desire to understand. If they agree with your interpretation, or if they disagree but take the time to correct you, you have gone a long way toward establishing trust.

Unlike some of the open-ended questions you asked during the listening phase, this is a direct, yes-or-no question (with room for elaboration). At this point in the conversation it's helpful to keep the ball in your court, so that you can begin directing the conversation toward a goal. If they need to correct you, or if they begin offering new information, then listen. When the opportunity arises and their energy level once again decreases, repeat the empathy process:

"Thanks for setting me straight. Let me try again. You're frustrated because your supervisor and team leader seem to want you to fail. Is that correct?"

Of course, some aggressors won't stop talking long enough for you to speak, or won't pay attention to you. In that event, use this magic phrase, which almost always captures people's attention and allows you to interrupt, but to do so in a way that the aggressor approves of:

"Tell me if I've got this right."

You're asking them to correct you if you're wrong, but in order to do so they must first listen. This allows you to enter the conversation while maintaining the notion that they're in complete control. It might look like this:

"Wait. . . Tell me if I've got this right. [short pause to get their attention] You're frustrated because your supervisor and team leader act like they want you to fail. Is that correct?"

As soon as you understand their problem

Power phrase

How to interrupt a broken record: "Tell me if I've got this right," "Tell me if I understand you correctly," or "Let me be sure I heard you correctly."

and have described it accurately, move directly into the options phase. There may be some discussion and some fine-tuning in describing the problem, but this isn't the time for extended psychoanalysis; this is crisis management. Further, you don't want to be drawn into a discussion about whether or not the person's perception is correct. In the example above, it doesn't matter whether the Desperate Aggressor's boss is really out to get him. If they believe it to be true, then that is the premise from which you begin. You don't have to agree; you just have to move forward and discover what solution soothes the aggressor. Trying to convince an aggressor to buy your point of view is a pointless battle.

TECHNIQUES

The empathy stage can be difficult, especially when you feel that you are under attack or when you find the aggressor's behavior offensive. Here are a few techniques that will make the empathy stage a bit easier.

- **Reflect feelings.** You may completely understand how the aggressor feels and why. But they won't know that until you say so. Use reflecting phrases such as "You feel ___ because ___." If you need to clarify their position, don't be afraid to do so. Most aggressors won't escalate when asked clarifying questions such as "Are you saying that you feel ___ because ___?"

- **Keep a clinical detachment.** Don't take the harsh words and bad manners of the Desperate Aggressor personally. You need to think clearly; being drawn into an emotional morass will cloud your judgment and could lead to a dangerous crisis. Staying objective will be much easier if you look for the precursors to the aggressor's behavior during the listening phase. Precursors are those problems that existed long before the aggressive episode.

    In Kim's situation, for example, she knew that Molly was having trouble in her marriage, and surmised that this was probably a major contributor to Molly's violent outburst. Even though Molly used some harsh and hurtful words, Kim must bear in mind that Molly's problem is deeper than anything Kim alone could have created. Knowing that the aggressor is indeed facing some difficulties makes it easier to remain objective, as long as you measure those difficulties by *the aggressor's* standards, not yours.

Precursors may include
- unmet physical needs (hunger, lack of housing, illness, and the like)
- fear for safety or welfare of self or loved ones
- loss of personal power and control over job, home life, and so on
- damage to self-respect
- depression or other clinical conditions
- problems in marriage or home life
- addictions or impairment
- inexperience or inability to handle crises

It may help you maintain a sense of objectivity to realize that you weren't the cause of these precursors, so there's no sense in taking personally the harsh words that stem from them.

- **Model the desired behavior.** Try to appear calm and in control, even if you don't feel that way. Behavior is contagious, and demonstrating control will help the aggressor reach a controlled state more quickly.

  Modeling behavior isn't a one-way street, however; the aggressor's behavior may be affecting you without your knowledge. As we already know, adrenaline is contagious. You may, without realizing it, be speaking much more loudly, quickly, and forcefully than you intend to. Empathizing simply doesn't carry the same weight when it's shouted rapid-fire at the top of your lungs:

  "LET ME SEE IF I UNDERSTAND [*no pause*] YOU'RE ANGRY BECAUSE THIS IS THE THIRD TIME YOUR PAYCHECK HAS BOUNCED!! IS THAT CORRECT?!"

- **Avoid verbal pitfalls.** During the empathy stage, it's tempting, but rarely productive, to say such things as "Calm down," "I understand," or "Don't panic." Avoid these kinds of statements. If you don't know what to say, keep the aggressor talking.

- **Maintain contact.** Make eye contact with the aggressor, and use body language that says "I'm listening" and verbal acknowledgments—not physical contact. This helps prevent you from mentally drifting off, and it puts you on the aggressor's team by demonstrating concern.

- **Observe.** Remember that much of communication is nonverbal. Pay attention to an aggressor's body and facial expressions as well as their words. You may gain important clues about the problem and their state of mind.

PREPARING FOR RESISTANCE

The Desperate Aggressor may not respond politely and peacefully to your attempts at empathy. In addition to hurtful language, which we've already discussed, your words may be met with questions or challenges. There are two types of questions: legitimate ones, and those designed to draw you into a fight or distract you from your purpose. Legitimate information-seeking questions deserve legitimate answers, as in this example:

TARGET: "You're angry because your future seems to depend on this performance review, and you feel that it's unfair. Is that accurate?"

AGGRESSOR: "Well, so what if I am? Does it make a difference?" (Here the aggressor is genuinely concerned that his opinion doesn't matter.)

TARGET: "Your opinion absolutely makes a difference. If you think that the review is unfair, then we need to discuss it."

Or this:

TARGET: "You're worried that if you fix the report, then upper management will blame the mistake entirely on you. Is that correct?"

AGGRESSOR: "Well, won't they?"

TARGET: "You're not a department of one, and you won't take the fall for the rest of us."

Each of these questions could have been interpreted as a challenge, had the listener not maintained a sense of detachment. Depending on the tone, the phrases "Well, what if I am? Will it make a difference?" and "Well, won't they?" could be interpreted as insults—i.e., "my opinion *doesn't* matter to you," and "upper management *is* a bunch of narrow-minded henchmen."

But the listeners knew this not to be the case. Even if spoken with a harsh tone, these questions contain a kernel of genuine concern. Compare them to these questions:

TARGET: "You're angry because your future seems to depend on this performance review, and you feel that it's unfair. Is that accurate?"

AGGRESSOR: "Who are you, Sigmund Freakin' Roid? I'm not here to have my head examined!"

Or this:

TARGET: "You're worried that if you fix the report, then upper management will blame the mistake entirely on you. Is that correct?"

AGGRESSOR: "Are you telling me they're not a bunch of jackasses up there?"

Not a grain of concern in either of these questions. They're pure challenges, designed to start a fight and distract you from your purpose. There's no way to answer this type of question without being drawn off track. Stay focused:

TARGET: "You're angry because your future seems to depend on this performance review, and you feel that it's unfair. Is that accurate?"

AGGRESSOR: "Who are you, Sigmund Freakin' Roid? I'm not here to have my head examined!"

TARGET: "That's not my intent. The issue is your performance review. Are you willing to discuss it with me?"

Or this:

TARGET: "You're worried that if you fix the report, then upper management will blame the mistake entirely on you. Is that correct?"

AGGRESSOR: "Are you telling me they're not a bunch of jackasses up there?"

TARGET: "I'm telling you that we have a problem to correct and that you won't be the fall guy. Are you willing to discuss the report with me?"

The final purpose of the empathy stage is to get the aggressor's attention and begin steering them toward a rational discussion of options. Once you have their attention—once you get an affirmative response to the questions listed above ("Am I correct?" "Are you willing to discuss this with me?")—then waste no time. Begin providing options so that you can both be on your way.

Providing Options

Moving from the empathy stage to providing options is a bit like moving from the listening stage to empathy, in that it requires good timing. At the end of the empathy stage, you were engaging the aggressor in conversation, reflecting their feelings along with the nature of the problem, with such statements as

"You're afraid that without your paycheck you won't be able to support your family and it will be difficult to find another job that pays this well. Is that a fair statement?"

and

"You feel hopeless because your supervisor seems to be out to get you. Is that an accurate statement?"

If you're successful in the empathy stage, you'll see a slight return to rationality. Take that as your cue to gently transition into providing options. Sometimes the closest thing to rationality you'll receive is the lack of a negative response. That can work just as well.

There's no race to beat the clock in providing options, particularly when the aggressor feels like talking. Let them do so if they like. There may even be some give-and-take, some negotiation. Any discussion that borders on rationality is good. Nevertheless, you should move with purpose in this stage. You want to return to the aggressor a sense of power, a sense that they're solving problems and making progress.

As you move through the stages of LEO—particularly the options stage—in scenario training and in real life, keep this truth in mind at all times: you can't force anyone to cooperate. Knowing this, strategic warriors don't *take* control, they *give* it.

Providing options isn't simply a matter of listing alternatives as if reading a grocery list. The aggressor must be involved in the entire process, and you must develop an atmosphere of cooperation—even reluctant cooperation will do—before committing to a course of action.

The following is a four-step process—a recipe, if you will—for providing the Desperate Aggressor with options.

GET THEIR ATTENTION

In an old *Saturday Night Live* skit, a man is repeatedly asked for directions to various locations. He answers each question with "'Fraid ya can't get there from here." This is the mind-set of the Desperate Aggressor. Solutions that the rest of the world plainly sees aren't at all obvious to this person. Even when solutions are offered, the aggressor may shoot them down out of pure frustration at failed previous attempts. Provided that you can't escape, you must somehow convince them, in spite of their innate pessimism, that they *can* get there from here.

Fortunately, during the previous two stages you've gone to great pains to "prepare" the aggressor for the process of discussing options. Now you begin a subtle transition from reflecting feelings and problems to moving toward a solution.

Take another look at this empathetic statement:

TARGET: "You're angry because your future seems to depend on this performance review, and you feel that the review is unfair. Is that accurate?"

If you get a negative response, then ask for clarification:

AGGRESSOR: "No, that's not it at all! My God, I can't believe how dense you are!"

TARGET: "Help me understand why you're angry."

At that point you start over with the listening phase. Remember, as long as they're talking, they're not attacking.

If you eventually restate the conclusion and get the desired positive response—or lack of a negative response—then build upon the original empathetic statement, putting forth a goal or a desired outcome. Again, ask a direct question in order to keep the aggressor on track and to confirm that you are addressing the right problem.

TARGET: "You're angry because your future seems to depend on this performance review, and you feel that the review is unfair. Is that accurate?"

AGGRESSOR: "Yeah, I guess."

TARGET: "And you'd like to be able to present your case on a more level playing field. Is that correct?"

Here again, the response can be either positive or negative. If it's negative, seek clarification; let the aggressor talk. If it's positive, continue to build on the foundation that the two of you are building.

Power phrase "I see some options. Would you like to hear them?"	TARGET: "You're angry because your future seems to depend on this performance review, and you feel that the review is unfair. Is that accurate?" AGGRESSOR: "Yeah, I guess."

TARGET: "And you'd like to be able to present your case on a more level playing field. Is that correct?"

AGGRESSOR: "Wouldn't you?"

TARGET: "Sounds reasonable to me. I see some options here. Would you like to hear them?"

If you've gotten this far, the aggressor will probably answer this last question with a simple *yes*.

You've gotten their attention, and you've defined an abstract goal (presenting the aggressor's case on a more level playing field). Now it's time to introduce specific options.

OFFER OPTIONS

How do you begin to provide options? Start small:

TARGET: "You're angry because your future seems to depend on this performance review, and you feel that the review is unfair. Is that accurate?"

AGGRESSOR: "Yeah, I guess."

TARGET: "And you'd like to be able to present your case on a more level playing field. Is that correct?"

AGGRESSOR: "Wouldn't you?"

TARGET: "Sounds reasonable to me. I see some options here. Would you like to hear them?"

AGGRESSOR: "Sure. Whatever."

TARGET: "Well, first, you could sit down with your supervisor and an out-side mediator to discuss the specific points you feel are unfair. That would ensure a level playing field. Are you willing to schedule a meeting?"

This bit of interaction ended with a specific question and an intermediate goal: *Would you be willing to schedule a meeting?* Intermediate goals are always more palatable than larger, more overwhelming ones. *Schedule a meeting? Sure. Fight the entire corporation in a battle for my future? Probably not.*

You also ended this interaction by stating positive consequences: *scheduling a meeting with a mediator will result in a level playing field.* Stating positive consequences is much more motivating than listing negative consequences. Compare that statement to this: *You should schedule a meeting, otherwise the report will go into your file for good.* Technically, it's the same information, but the first rendition is much more palatable.

You've offered an option, so at this point you'll need to be flexible. You may be met with an affirmative response, a negative, or a host of legitimate information-seeking questions.

If the answer is no, try other options. (Continued resistance is the topic of the next chapter.) If the answer is yes, it's time to make plans.

PLOT A COURSE

Having made it this far, the aggressor has returned to some level of rationality. That doesn't mean they're primed and ready for big-time problem solving, though; they're probably exhausted, embarrassed, and overwhelmed. They'll need your help in formulating a strategy, and you want to keep them moving toward a solution.

Pursue a course of their choosing—even though you may have steered them in that direction. It's time to take them by the hand and form a simple plan. Starting with the empathy stage, it might look like this:

TARGET: "You're angry because your future seems to depend on this per-formance review, and you feel that the review is unfair. Is that accurate?"

AGGRESSOR: "Yeah, I guess."

TARGET: "And you'd like to be able to present your case on a more level playing field. Is that correct?"

AGGRESSOR: "Wouldn't you?"

TARGET: "Sounds reasonable to me. I see some options here. Would you like to hear them?"

AGGRESSOR: "Sure. Whatever."

TARGET: "Well, first, you could sit down with your supervisor and an outside mediator to discuss the specific points you feel are unfair. That would ensure a level playing field. Are you willing to schedule a meeting?"

AGGRESSOR: "Yeah, I guess."

TARGET: "OK, here's what's involved: we need to contact the HR department and have them find an outside consultant. I can do that for you. From there, HR will schedule a meeting between you, your supervisor, and the mediator in a neutral location. Does that sound good?"

Having made it this far, you probably won't be met with much resistance, just legitimate information-seeking questions. Once the questions are settled, summarize the strategy and get the plan rolling.

INITIATE

You're in the home stretch now. You've presented an option, the aggressor has agreed to it, and some degree of rationality reigns once again. In order to keep the situation from flaring up again, you need to initiate action.

TARGET: "OK, here's what's involved: we need to contact the HR department and have them find an outside consultant. I can do that for you. From there, HR will schedule a meeting between you, your supervisor, and the mediator in a neutral location. Does that sound good?"

AGGRESSOR: "Yeah. OK."

TARGET: "Great. We can start by contacting Sandra in HR right now."

Congratulations. You've averted a crisis. Now try it in scenario training.

What About the Larger Goal?

In the example above, we didn't solve the aggressor's overall problem of an unfair performance review. That wasn't our purpose; our purpose was to return an irrational, aggressive individual to a more level-headed state of mind and thereby avert a crisis.

> **Power phrase**
>
> "We can start by . . ."

When you're confronted by a Desperate Aggressor, it's important to realize that you can't fix all of their problems. The best you may be able to hope for in that heated moment is to create a safe atmosphere. You can help them up to a point and provide resources, but eventually it's up to them.

TECHNIQUES

Here are a few tips and tricks to help you along.

- **Take a break, if possible.** When things seem to be going downhill, taking a break allows you to center yourself and search for options. State simply and honestly to the aggressor that you would like to take a break to explore options, and that you'll meet again at a designated time. Make the break as quick as is feasible. If ten minutes would help, then ask for that. If you need a day, ask for a day. Set a specific time and place in which you'll resume the conversation. If you can't take a break, then at least take a breath.

    Of course, taking a break can be used as a ruse to help you escape. There's absolutely no shame in deception when you fear for your safety.

- **Rehearse the steps.** When you and the aggressor decide to follow a specific course of action, don't assume that they'll know how to proceed. List the steps and help them get started.

- **Develop an intermediate goal.** Remember, your purpose is to avoid a crisis, not necessarily to solve the aggressor's central problem (e.g., unmet physical needs, fear for safety, loss of personal control, or the like). It's often helpful to create intermediate goals, like scheduling a meeting, rather than trying to solve the problem then and there. Short aims are far more palatable than massive, life-altering objectives.

- **Help the aggressor initiate action.** As will be evident when we replay The Dismissed Employee in a moment, the aggressor is often exhausted, embarrassed, and overwhelmed as they begin to return to rationality. They may need a jump-start to get moving.

- **List positive consequences first.** You're much more likely to get a positive response by listing positive consequences rather than negative ones. Compare the following phrases:

  - ◆ "If you don't put that chair down, I'll have to call security."

  - ◆ "As soon as you set the chair down, we can get on the phone with the boss and find out what we're going to do about your paycheck."

  - ◆ **Don't lose sight of your goal.** In helping the aggressor address their problem, don't lose sight of *your* goal, which is to avert a crisis and get yourself to a safe place. Don't hesitate to abandon the aggressor's goal if your safety is threatened.

Putting It All Together

Listening, Empathizing, and providing Options: these are the keys to helping a Desperate Aggressor return to rationality. If all goes as planned, these three stages should blend smoothly together, easing the aggressor toward rationality. If things don't go as planned and you fear for your safety, don't hesitate to force an escape. The next chapter discusses what to do in the event that escape isn't possible.

Let's return to the situation involving Molly and her supervisor, Kim, to see how the interaction *could* have gone. Kim and Laura are in the conference room discussing how to approach the meeting, and Molly has not yet arrived.

SCENARIO: The Dismissed Employee—Version Two

"We need to talk about what we're going to do here, Laura," Kim said. "I don't foresee any major problems, but I do want to be prepared. I've notified Jim the receptionist to keep his eyes and ears open for signs of trouble. He's working right outside. I've also notified security that this meeting may be an emotional one, so Jim's got them on standby in case Molly gets too agitated."

This time, Kim is taking time to prepare the environment.

"Do you really think it will come to that?" Laura asked. She looked concerned.

"I don't think so, Laura. At least I hope not. But I'm nervous, and it's best to be prepared."

Kim continued, "I'd like to have Molly sit over here so that you and I are closest to the door and she's not blocking our exit. I also think it would be wise for one of us to take the lead in talking to her so she doesn't think she's being double-teamed. Would you like to do that, or shall I?"

"You seem to know what you're doing," Laura answered. "Why don't you do it?"

"OK," Kim answered. "I'll just need you to be ready to discuss the severance package, her insurance, and the like. I'll break the news as gently as possible and answer whatever questions she has as to why we're letting her go."

After more than fifteen minutes had gone by, Molly finally arrived. She looked haggard, as if she had just rolled out of bed.

Kim and Laura stood to greet her. "Hi, Molly," Kim said as cheerfully as possible, given the circumstances.

Molly avoided eye contact and seemed to already know what this meeting was about. "Hi," she said quietly.

"Molly, I think you've met Laura from HR."

"Yeah," Molly answered. "Hi."

"Hi, Molly."

"Molly, why don't you have a seat over here," Kim stated, directing Molly to the seat they had reserved for her. The three of them sat down.

Kim began. "Well, Molly, as painful as it is, I'll get to the reason we've asked you here. We've called this meeting to let you know that after a great deal of soul-searching, we've decided to let you go."

Molly made eye contact for the first time. She was shocked. "What?"

"Molly, you know we like you here, but—well, you know what the problems are. This company just doesn't seem like the right fit for you."

> To truly prepare for this meeting, Kim would have given Molly plenty of written warnings about her performance. She should also have all of Molly's final pay, unused vacation pay, and other benefits at this meeting.

Kim wanted to keep the meeting rolling. She looked at Laura, who took the cue. "Molly, I have a final check here, along with some information on your health insurance," Laura said. "We can go over that now if you—"

Molly interrupted as if she hadn't heard Laura talking. She leaned forward in her chair and looked directly at Kim, aghast. "Oh my God! How could you do this to me?"

"I know the timing is bad, Molly," Kim said with a concerned look.

"You're damn right, it's terrible!"

Molly fell silent. Kim allowed her a moment to process the situation.

> *Kim is giving Molly an opportunity to gather her thoughts. It was apparent that she was thinking, and Kim didn't want to interrupt.*

After several seconds, Molly spoke again, this time in a shout. "You bitch! Do you have any idea what I'm going through?"

Kim answered calmly and with empathy, as if inviting Molly to continue. "No, I don't." She waited for a response.

> *An invitation to begin talking; the beginning of the listening phase.*

Molly paused for another moment, and tears began to well up in her eyes. Her face was becoming red, she sat bolt upright in her chair, and her voice broke as she answered. "Try two kids and a husband who left with everything! Do you know he stuck me with a house payment I can't afford? And do you think he's sending child support? You people are all the same! Two months now I've had to beg, borrow, and steal to buy groceries. My so-called family is even avoiding me now. And tonight I have to go talk to Matt's teacher because he's failing. I guess it runs in the family."

Kim felt terrible. She wanted to speak up, to say something—anything—that would calm Molly down. But she knew that the best thing she could do for Molly just then was to simply listen. "I had no idea," she said softly, as if inviting Molly to continue.

Molly sobbed, then went on. "Best part is, I don't even have enough gas in the tank to get to his school. And now you're sitting here telling me that on top of all that I don't get a paycheck anymore! Thanks, Kim. I just don't understand how you could do this to me! I thought you were my friend."

Molly flopped back into her chair, arms crossed, tears streaming, looking exhausted, but still clearly furious and frightened. Kim waited a few seconds to be sure that Molly had finished. She sensed that Molly was beginning to withdraw, and if she didn't speak up now she might lose her opportunity.

"Molly, I'd like to help, if you'll let me."

> *Kim's decided it's time to enter the empathy stage. She will be wise to keep things moving along so that this meeting lasts no longer than necessary.*

Molly shot Kim a spiteful look. "Oh, right. You've just destroyed my life! What are *you* going to do to fix it?"

The horrible guilt that Kim felt was beginning to turn to anger. How could Molly say such hateful things, she wondered. She felt her own blood starting to boil. Nevertheless, she kept her emotions in check and forced herself to remember that it was Molly who was feeling genuinely and justifiably threatened. With this in mind, she continued in a normal tone—the tone she wished Molly were using.

"Tell me if I understand, Molly. You're feeling cornered because you don't know how you're going to care for your kids without a paycheck. Is that the situation?"

"No shit, Sherlock. Wouldn't you?"

"And you'd like to know where the next meal is coming from; who's going to provide insurance; who's going to provide some stability for the kids. Is that right?"

"Yeah." Molly began to cry, but tried desperately to hide her tears.

"Well, Molly, I think you're handling this quite well given the circumstances. I have some ideas, and there are some options here if you'd like to hear them."

> *A word of encouragement followed by a smooth transition to the options phase.*

Molly said nothing. She simply sat in her chair, arms crossed, with the look of a frightened and angry child on her face. But she didn't say no, and so Kim proceeded.

"Well, first of all, you're not completely without money. I'll let Laura describe our severance package and outplacement service in a minute, but you should know that we've already begun arranging for the weeks to come so that you won't be caught without the resources to take care of your kids."

Laura sat stunned by the words that had been exchanged and the level of emotion in the room. Nonetheless, she followed Kim's lead and explained the company's severance package as succinctly and calmly as she could. Molly was cynical and bitter, but she did listen. When Laura was finished, Kim resumed.

"Molly, we have a check for you here, including severance pay. And if you're willing, I'd like to have you meet with the outplacement service as soon as possible so that they can help you find something. Would you be willing set up a meeting?"

Molly huffed. "Sure, like it's gonna do any good."

> *A bitter yes is still a yes.*

The response was cynical, but Kim knew that, cynical or not, it was an affirmative answer and that was what counted. She continued. "I'm glad you're willing to give it a try. We can start by setting up a time to meet. Laura will call you at home and set that up. Molly, the sooner we get the ball rolling, the better. Anything I can do to help along the way, please let me know."

Kim is getting Molly to start acting.

With that, Kim and Laura stood up. As was company policy, security personnel met them outside the conference room and helped Molly box up her possessions and carry them to her car, without incident.

Later that day, Kim and Laura met to discuss and document the meeting. It had not been pleasant, but no one had been hurt or arrested, and that made it a success.

> *It's always important to have a debriefing to discuss, learn, and plan for the next encounter. Unfortunately, this is often overlooked.*

What Makes a Success?

As I've stressed all along, you may not be able to solve a Desperate Aggressor's overall problem, and you probably won't be able to make them like you. In many cases such as Molly's, the aggressor has gone on to sue the company, and Molly might take that route. The bottom line, though, is that Kim successfully averted a violent crisis: no one got hurt, and she moved Molly safely out of the building. Future events can't sully that victory.

CHAPTER NINE

What If LEO
Doesn't Work?

IF LEO WORKS PERFECTLY, THEN CONGRATULATIONS; you've averted a crisis. Sometimes, however, perfect planning and flawless execution simply aren't enough, for a number of reasons:

- The aggressor may not have the experience or emotional maturity necessary to cooperate.
- You may not be dealing with a Desperate Aggressor, but with the more predatory type of aggressor that will be discussed in Part Three.
- The solution you offered may not address the problem.
- The aggressor may not be capable of rationality (e.g., they are impaired, are too overcome with fear or anger, or lack the faculty to weigh outcomes).
- Environmental factors or the aggressor's history may make it impossible to communicate effectively.

There are three basic responses to a failed attempt at providing options:

- repeat
- set alternatives
- escape

The appropriateness of each depends on the aggressor's behavior and the reason for the failure.

Repeat

If you get to the options stage and suddenly the aggressor begins to resist your ideas, you may have misinterpreted the problem and may need to start over, as in this example:

TARGET: "You're scared that if the staff here doesn't respond to this situation, others will begin to see you as a chump. Is that correct?"

AGGRESSOR: "Yeah, I guess."

TARGET: "And you would like us to help you reestablish your reputation. Is that right?"

AGGRESSOR: "What? No! Aren't you listening to me?"

TARGET: "I guess I don't completely understand. Walk me through it again."

The options stage can sometimes involve a bit of negotiation and clarification, and that's okay. After all, if they're talking, they're not . . . well, you know the rest. Some aggressors may not agree to anything, as in this example:

TARGET: (after a second attempt at defining a goal) "So tell me if I have it straight now. You're worried that the staff has shown favoritism toward you and that the other clients are going to gang up on you."

AGGRESSOR: "Yeah."

TARGET: " . . . and you want to . . ."

AGGRESSOR: "Look, man, I ain't working with you people. You can go screw yourselves."

TARGET: "I'd like to think we can find an answer. Is there anything I can do to help you?"

The target here either has run out of options or feels that the conversation has gone on too long. Not wanting to repeat the same strategy over and over again (which can be dangerous and should be avoided), he has used a phrase equivalent to the used-car salesman's popular pitch, "What do I have to do to put you in this beauty today?" Our version is "I'd like to think we can find an answer. Is there *anything* I can do to help you?"

Using the phrase "Is there *anything* I can do to help you?" serves two purposes. First, it's a last-ditch attempt to focus the aggressor on finding a solution. Although this technique rarely elicits a flash of insight in the aggressor, it's sometimes enough to jump-start a stalled conversation. Second, their response educates you about their willingness to solve the problem. If the answer is "no," it's probably time to find a hasty escape.

> **Power phrase**
>
> When running out of options with a resistant aggressor: "I'd like to think we can find an answer. Is there *anything* I can do to help you?"

This last-ditch effort may prompt an answer that tells you the aggressor is

- having a hard time expressing himself, or having difficulty finding a solution
- immature or inexperienced in solving problems or handling crises
- impaired by substance abuse, mental concerns, extreme level of emotion, or other problems that make logic difficult

If your attempts to move toward a solution are met with increased frustration, take a more active role. Rather than asking the aggressor to choose, take the lead by setting alternatives.

Setting Alternatives

Setting alternatives means helping the aggressor choose a course of action; it means steering them toward a solution when they can't seem to find their own way. It takes a bit of skill and diplomacy, but it can be very useful with the right type of aggressor. Used incorrectly, however, it can cause the situation to degrade very quickly, so it's important to observe the aggressor closely for signs of a negative reaction to this technique.

An aggressor may fail to cooperate due to immaturity, inexperience, impairment, confusion, or even extreme levels of emotion. When you are faced with an aggressor who, by all appearances, wants to improve their condition but doesn't respond to any of the options you've provided through the LEO formula, offer some guidance by setting alternatives and asking them to choose one.

This technique provides a framework for an aggressor who needs or craves structure, and it's a somewhat different approach from LEO. With LEO, you are placing responsibility on the aggressor, essentially saying, "How does this option sound to you?" You are putting all the power in their hands.

When you begin to set alternatives, however, the message is "Here are your choices. Which one do you prefer?" You're still providing the aggressor with power and options, but you're also providing structure and limits. To an aggressor who is having a hard time making decisions, structure can be very comforting. This technique is especially useful with children and adolescents.

If the aggressor still fails to respond, you can further reduce the scope of the problem and provide even more structure by offering two alternatives and stating that you'll be acting on one of them—"Would you like to [option A] or shall we [option B]?" The implication here is that if the aggressor doesn't choose option A, you'll act on option B. As always, list positive consequences first: "If you choose to [option A], we can [positive consequence B]."

If the situation continues to degrade and you feel threatened by the aggressor, you may be forced to bring out the "big stick": an option with negative consequences, such as calling the police. This should be an absolute last resort, used only when a peaceful escape isn't an option and all other methods have been exhausted. Once you bring out the "big stick" by stating negative consequences, you are essentially threatening the aggressor. It might look like this: "If you will please [preferred option A], we can avoid [unpleasant consequence B]."

We'll look at an example of these techniques shortly. To review, the steps for setting alternatives with a resistant Desperate Aggressor are:

1. **LEO.** Begin with this basic formula. They can't resist until you try to solve the problem.

2. **Set alternatives.** If the options you provide are shot down or refuted due to an apparent inability to choose, pick the best options and ask the aggressor which one they prefer. Be prepared to follow up with "We can start by . . ."

3. **Set limits.** If resistance continues, inform the aggressor that you will choose one course of action unless they choose something different. Bring out the "big stick" only as a last resort.

Let's take a look at an example of setting alternatives.

In this example, Mike has been notified that he is being audited by the IRS. He has gone to the office of Michelle, his accountant, without notice. He demands to see her, but she is out of town. Overwhelmed by fear and panic, he is harried and upset.

RECEPTIONIST: "Hi. Can I help you?"

MIKE: (frantic) "I need to talk to Michelle."

RECEPTIONIST: "I'm sorry, sir, Michelle is out of town for the week. Is there anything I can help you with?"

MIKE: "No! I need to see her! Right now!"

RECEPTIONIST: "There's clearly a problem here. Do you mind if I ask why it's so urgent?"

—*entering* LEO *phase*—

MIKE: "Michelle screwed up! I'm being audited! Do you know what that means? My God, woman! I can't go to jail! I have a wife and kids to take care of! I need to talk to Michelle and find out what to do about this! (pounds desk) Get her on the phone!"

RECEPTIONIST: "Sir, tell me if I understand correctly. You're upset because you feel that we're responsible for your audit, and you'd like to know how we're going to handle it. Is that correct?"

MIKE: "Yes! I want to know how Michelle is going to handle it!"

RECEPTIONIST: "I'm afraid we don't have a way to reach her, but there are a few options here. Would you like to hear them?"

MIKE: (no response)

RECEPTIONIST: "Well, first, I could have you sit down with one of the other accountants–"

MIKE: (interrupts) "No, that won't work! I need to talk to Michelle!"

RECEPTIONIST: "We could schedule an appointment when Michelle returns next week."

MIKE: "Dammit! How is that going to help me now?"

RECEPTIONIST: "I could also have you sit down with one of the partners to discuss the audit process and map out a–"

MIKE: "(expletive deleted)! Aren't you listening? I need to talk to Michelle. I know you can call her! So do it!"

—*entering alternatives phase*—

RECEPTIONIST: "Sir, I want to help you. We can do one of two things here. I can schedule an appointment with Michelle as soon as she returns, or I can have you talk to one of the partners this morning and we can start solving the problem today. Which would you prefer?"

The receptionist is drawing the line with Mike and setting alternatives. At this point Mike will either agree to one of the options or continue to resist. If he chooses one of the options, the receptionist should immediately respond with "Great, we can begin by . . ." Let's assume that Mike continues to resist.

MIKE: "I said, I-WANT-TO-TALK-TO-[expletive]-MICHELLE!"

—*entering limits phase*—

RECEPTIONIST: "Sir, I'm very uncomfortable with your tone. I want to avoid having security escort you out. I have to ask you to choose. Please tell me if you're willing to discuss this with one of our partners this morning so we can solve the problem."

Mike is not only resisting, he's escalating. The receptionist has run out of options and brought out the "big stick" by threatening to call security. (We can only assume that an easy escape wasn't available, hence the threat.) If Mike presses on, the receptionist must be willing to immediately escape and call security. For an ending with a bit more finesse, see the sidebar titled "Milk or juice with that?"

Setting alternatives carries with it an inherent danger. As you move through these steps, you are systematically reducing the aggressor's level of personal power and assuming a dominant posture. If by chance you've read the aggressor incorrectly and they are *not* craving structure but simply being inflexible, a power struggle may result.

As you begin to use the technique of setting alternatives, watch for signs of increased anxiety—the same verbal and physical signs of desperation that we discussed in Chapter 7, "Early Warning Signs of Desperate Aggression," especially insults and challenges. If you sense increased tension, go no further and

Milk or juice with that?

Parents of small children have long been aware of this powerful persuasive technique. If a person is avoiding an unpleasant task—say, a child avoiding taking medicine—you can get what you want *and* avoid the inevitable power struggle by letting the person choose how or when they want to perform the dreaded task. A phrase such as "Would you like to take your medicine with milk or with juice?" grants the person a bit of power over their circumstance. Everybody wins.

In the above situation, the receptionist might have ended the limits phase this way:

"Sir, I'm very uncomfortable with your tone right now. I have to ask you to choose. Shall I schedule an appointment for this morning or this afternoon? Which is better for you?"

The man is thereby led to make a choice rather than to continue arguing.

consider reverting to the phrase "Is there *anything* I can do to help you out of this situation?"

If at any point you reach an impasse with the aggressor, it's time to find an escape.

A Few Words About Escaping

Escaping is your privilege at any point during any interaction. You're under no obligation to remain with an aggressor and go through the LEO stages if you feel that your safety is threatened. The LEO techniques are provided for use when escape isn't feasible or possible. Escape should always be one of the first things you consider.

Sometimes escape may be a simple matter of walking away. At other times you may need to physically defend yourself. As always, it's best to know your options *before* you need to use them.

Your Use-of-Force Continuum

It goes without saying that police officers often deal with dangerous people. They must make difficult decisions about detaining or restraining hostile individuals. As a result, the profession has devised a mental device called the *use-of-*

Bluffing: mistake or strategy?

Bluffing (issuing an unenforceable threat) can be a dangerous mistake. It's easy to do, particularly when you're having trouble devising options or understanding the cause of the aggression. The phrase "Do this or else. . . ." is spoken far too easily when we're under stress. Unfortunately, this approach severely limits the aggressor's options and may force them to escalate their hostility. It also limits your options if they fail to cooperate, which is highly likely. Once you've issued a threat, you must either follow through with something you probably don't want to do, or back down. Neither is appealing.

Bluffing can be a worthwhile gamble when you have nothing left to lose, but it should be used only as a last resort.

A police officer friend once told me of the time he bumped into an ex-convict at the grocery store while off duty. This large and menacing man recognized my friend and, after an angry exchange of words, began to charge at him. Knowing that a physical fight was imminent and there was no escape, my friend decided to bluff. He reached behind his back and, without showing what he had in his hand, said, "Please don't make me shoot you."

Of course, he had nothing in his hand. But the ex-con didn't know that; he stopped his advance and was eventually arrested after being held at bay by an imaginary gun. The gamble paid off for my friend. The crucial point in this strategy is that he would have been no worse off if the bluff had failed.

Bluffing doesn't have to involve threats. Think back to Jackie's encounter in the parking garage. Her bluff was to feign interest in the aggressor. She, too, would have been no worse off had the bluff failed.

A sample use-of-force continuum used by law enforcement

Minimum force, lowest risk

- verbal persuasion
- verbal force (ultimatums and threats)
- physical force (restraint)
- incapacitating force (baton, pepper spray, and so on)
- deadly force

Maximum force, highest risk

force continuum to help officers determine the appropriate level of force to use when subduing people who pose different levels of threat. The continuum is simply a list of options ranging in intensity from the most benign to the most deadly.

During their training, police officers are taught a variety of persuasion and control techniques (both verbal and physical), each falling somewhere on this continuum. When trying to control or subdue a suspect, an officer is to select the most appropriate tool from this continuum and go no higher than absolutely necessary. For instance, an officer shouldn't use pepper spray when verbal persuasion will do.

Most of us, not being police officers, have no interest in controlling or subduing others. But we may one day have the need to escape from a potentially dangerous aggressor. Like the police officer, we have a wide range of options available to us. And as with the police officer, it's our responsibility to go no higher on the continuum than absolutely necessary. That's not just a moral responsibility, but a legal one as well. For those of us who aren't police officers, our use-of-force continuum contains many more options, since we're not responsible for upholding the law or protecting justice. Unlike the police, if we don't like a situation, we can simply walk away and be done with it.

A sample use-of-force continuum for the rest of us

Minimum force, lowest risk

- "taking a break"
- walking away
- summoning outside help
- verbal persuasion
- distraction, deception, and misdirection
- verbal force (demanding that the aggressor let you leave)
- bluffing
- physical force (forcing your way past the aggressor)
- incapacitating force (harming an aggressor en route to exit)
- deadly force

Maximum force, highest risk

Obviously, the least amount of force is the most desirable, and the only reason for using any force at all is to allow you to escape. One of the easiest ways to ensure a minimal use of force is to plan the environment whenever possible.

Recall the two versions of The Dismissed Employee, in which Kim had to fire Molly. In the second version, Kim planned her environment and created a couple of important options. First, she was near the exit. She probably could have simply walked out had she felt the need. Second, she notified others in advance that she might need assistance. If you can't get to a safe environment, bring the safe environment to you.

Even when you don't have as much control over the environment as Kim did, you can almost always prepare yourself and your environment to some extent through verbal and physical training, along with awareness of your surroundings. Training provides response options that the untrained don't possess; awareness alerts you to exit routes and danger zones.

Think of planning as cheap insurance. It sometimes takes a bit of extra work, but it could save you a lot of trouble in the long run.

Knowing When to Escape

Knowing when to say "when" can present a challenge all by itself. In the heat of the moment, your mind may be floating a thousand miles away because you're distracted by a dozen different things, or you may be suffering "the affliction of abiding in ignorance" by fixating on a triviality. It's easy to get caught up in a conflict and lose sight of the larger goal, so here are some guidelines. In general, you should start looking for an escape when

> **Plan the environment**
>
> Whenever possible, take the time to plan your environment, just as Kim did in the second version of her scenario.

- you fear for your safety
- your attempts at providing options seem to be going nowhere or, worse, moving in a negative direction
- your intuition says so

Once you decide to escape, don't wait for an ideal opportunity, because there probably won't be one. Go immediately.

Self-Defense

Imagine this worst-case situation: like Kim in the first version of The Dismissed Employee, you are cornered, and the person blocking your exit has demonstrated violent intent through threatening gestures and language.

Suddenly you find yourself bolting for the exit. The aggressor blocks your path, and now you're in a physical fight. Not exactly how you planned to spend your day. Is this self-defense, or have you just committed an assault? Let's take a look at the generally accepted definition of self-defense.

Self-defense is a common legal defense asserted by people charged with a crime of violence, such as battery (striking someone), assault with a deadly weapon, or murder. In essence, the defendant admits committing the crime, but claims that it was justified by the other person's threatening actions. Here are the three core issues in most self-defense cases:

- Which party was the aggressor?
- Was the defendant reasonable in believing that they were in danger and that self-defense was necessary?
- If so, was the force used by the defendant also reasonable given the circumstances?

Self-defense is rooted in the belief that people should be allowed to protect themselves from physical harm. This means that a person doesn't have to wait until actually being struck in order to act in self-defense. If a reasonable person would think that they are about to be physically attacked, they have the right to strike first in an attempt to prevent the attack. But they cannot legally use more force than is reasonable (a term fraught with complications), and they cannot legally use force when other means of escape are available. If they do, they may be guilty of a crime.

Thus, it's terribly important to remember that when you fight, you fight for only one thing: *escape*. If you find yourself in any kind of physical altercation, break off the fight as soon as you possibly can and head for populated areas. Keep going until you know you are safe. Believe it or not, it can be easy to forget to leave as soon as possible.

If your escape attempt turns physical, have no illusions. Don't expect weapons or self-defense gimmicks to disable an assailant. Don't expect your self-defense training to work like it did in class. Expect things to move surprisingly quickly; expect to get hurt; expect to see blood. But also expect to withstand injury in a way you would never have imagined. Your body and mind are designed to tolerate great amounts of stress, and in the end, this is your ultimate weapon: spirit. As Winston Churchill told his countrymen, "Never, never, never, never give in."[34]

A Different Kind of Power Struggle

Imagine that you are hiking through the mountains on a crisp spring day. All is going well, and you are enjoying the sights and sounds of nature, when suddenly you hear a low growl. You turn to the left to see a mother mountain lion with her cubs. Behind her is a rock wall that prevents her from leaving. Her only escape route is right where you are standing.

What do you do? Do you crowd the mountain lion further, insisting all the while that you pose no threat? Or do you back away and provide her with escape routes? The answer is obvious: you wouldn't crowd the lion. Yet it's easy to do just that with a Desperate Aggressor by trying to take control of the situation, by being drawn into a power struggle, by issuing threats and bluffs, or by falling into any of the other pitfalls we've discussed.

Dealing with a Desperate Aggressor is truly a different kind of power struggle—one in which we try to *give* power rather than take it. To Desperate Aggressors, perception is reality. If they think they're under attack, they will act as if they're under attack. The best remedy is to remove the perceived threat and replace it with options and personal power.

Dealing with a Desperate Aggressor

LEO:

- **L**isten
- **E**mpathize
- provide **O**ptions

When LEO *doesn't work*:

- **R**epeat
- set **A**lternatives
- **E**scape

How to Become a Master Peacemaker

By now we've discussed many tips and techniques. We've covered the five ground rules (Part One), discussed the early warning signs of Desperate Aggression, trained in the ways of LEO, and discussed what to do when LEO doesn't work. It's a lot to remember, especially considering that you may need to recall this information in the heat of the moment, when emotions and adrenaline are running high.

Sounds like a lot of pressure, you say? Not to worry. There's an answer both ancient and effective: scenario training.

Scenario training is basically a dress rehearsal in which you and a few friends or coworkers play-act and put to use what you've learned. You begin with a pre-arranged situation in which one person plays the aggressor and another plays the defender, or the target. There are also a mediator and onlookers. Once the target has had a chance to respond to an unexpected situation, that same scenario can be practiced and repeated until ideal responses become ingrained.

Scenario training is nothing new. It's used by police, medical personnel, counselors, and emergency workers, and it's been used by armies for centuries. Of course, the reason that it's such a popular learning tool is that it causes knowledge to become reflexive and automatic. Scenario training quite simply leads to quicker and better responses.

Appendix C offers some guidelines for effective scenario training as well as a few sample scenarios. The first two relate specifically to the skills we've discussed up to this point. You can also make up your own scenarios, or use any of the case studies or scenarios in this book.

Scenario training may be a bit more work than you bargained for when you picked up this book, but I can't overstate its benefits. Studying these skills is one thing; *owning* them is another matter entirely. Before going on to Part Three, please turn to Appendix C.

If scenario training isn't possible for you, at least run through the scenarios in your mind. You can also play the "what-if" game presented earlier. This little bit of mental exercise will be far better than none at all.

PART III
EXPERT
AGGRESSION

"Your words always give you away."

—George Carlin

Remember Molly, the Desperate Aggressor? She was having one of the worst days of her life. She had lost her husband, her kids were doing poorly in school, and she was having serious money problems. On top of all that, she was losing her job. Nothing seemed to be going her way.

In the first version of this scenario, Molly turned to violence, throwing a notepad at Kim, her supervisor, and kicking over several chairs. While we can't condone Molly's actions, we can appreciate the frustration and powerlessness she must have felt.

In the second version, Kim learned to manage powerlessness by returning power. Kim knew that for Molly, violence was the only remaining alternative, so she provided other options. They weren't perfect solutions, but they were good enough to change the outcome.

Now we switch gears and discuss a completely different type of aggressor. Not every aggressor resorts to violence because they've run out of options or reached a state of panic. As you may have learned from personal experience, some people use hostility for profit, the way a carpenter uses a hammer. To them, hostility is a skill, a solution to a problem, a means to an end. Their violence isn't a spur-of-the-moment act of passion; it's calculated and planned to meet a specific need.

While the Desperate Aggressor is searching for a way out of conflict, this person is searching for a way in—if he can find a suitable victim. Meet the Expert Aggressor.

CHAPTER TEN

The Expert Aggressor

The criminal values people only insofar as they bend to his will or can be coerced or manipulated into doing what he wants. He has been this way since childhood, and by the time he is an adult, he has a self-centered view of the world in which he believes that he's entitled to whatever he wants. Constantly, he is sizing up his prospects for exploiting people and situations. To him the world is a chessboard, with other people serving as pawns to gratify his desires.[35]

—STANTON SAMENOW

PREDATORS, HARASSERS, CRIMINALS—WE'VE PROBABLY ALL known at least one or two in our lifetimes. They're the childhood intimidators who use threats and physical force to subordinate others. They're the office snakes who use manipulation, coercion, and vague threats to advance their careers. They're the confidence men, the muggers, and the rapists we've become all too accustomed to hearing about on the news and in frightening stories told by our friends and coworkers. They're the ones who would use those around them as "pawns to gratify [their] desires." They'll take what they want, not through fair and open competition, but through trickery, intimidation, and violence. They're experts at using aggression for profit. They are, in a word, bullies.

It's easy to assume that bullies and predators arrive at their methods because they lack other skills. There may be a grain of truth in this, but it doesn't mean they aren't skillful. Make no mistake: bullying is a science. The most refined predators pose a real threat to their victim, and they have practiced their science for years. Bullying is usually learned early in life—in the schoolyard, at home, or on the streets.*

---

* Researchers have cited many different reasons why a child may develop a penchant for bullying, including an abusive home environment, lack of stimulation, failure to learn social bonding, and so on. We won't delve into the quagmire of why bullying begins early; we'll simply acknowledge that many researchers, on many sides of the argument, agree that bullying behavior generally begins in childhood.

We can't begin to understand bullies and criminals without looking at the victims they choose, because their choice of victim is a direct reflection of what they hope to gain. Research has made telling discoveries about the type of childhood victims who unwittingly attract and reward bullies. They often possess the following qualities:[36]

- They're more likely than their nonbullied counterparts to acquiesce to the demands of the bully. They have a history of giving in, or resemble in manner and bearing others who typically give in.
- They tend to radiate anxiousness or vulnerability. They may have a meek manner, avoid eye contact, and appear openly nervous during social situations.
- They have an appeasing or "shrinking" demeanor. They're quick to mollify others in an attempt to avoid conflict.
- They tend to be socially isolated. Having few friends to come to their defense makes these children attractive targets for bullies, who seek the path of least resistance.
- They typically fail to defend themselves.

Young bullies can gain quite a bit by intimidating and harassing others. They stand to reap material gain (milk money belonging to others), social elevation (the company of lackeys and tag-alongs), and the respect of others (kids who fear them and give them a wide berth). Regardless of why they became bullies, it's easy to see how this system of rewards confirms the usefulness of, and strengthens their resolve to engage in, their bad habits.

Unless childhood bullies manage to overcome their abusive behavior, they'll carry these habits into adulthood. They'll increasingly view those around them as resources rather than people, and their abusive methods will become more firmly ingrained until they come to almost depend on them to get what they want, be it social or material gain.

Their childhood motives may remain the same through adulthood, but their methods, while remaining essentially the same, will become more refined. With time and practice they'll become an Expert Aggressor. By adulthood they'll be highly skilled at their trade and will be adept at picking "good" victims. And as they mature, their transgressions can become more serious and their demands greater, and they can become much more dangerous. The habitual bully can easily evolve into the criminal.

We, the good guys, need to understand how bullies operate in order to detect them from a safe distance. Fortunately, bullies and predators often telegraph their intent through telltale warning signs. The process of identifying a victim generally has two steps:

1. searching for signs of vulnerability
2. testing the victim

Why They Attack, What They Want, and the Warning Signs

In Part Two we discussed Desperate Aggressors. We looked at why they attack (perceived lack of options), what they hope to gain (a return of personal power), and the physical and behavioral warning signs of an impending attack.

Asking the same questions about the Expert Aggressor yields very different answers. The Desperate Aggressor chooses violence as a last resort, while the Expert Aggressor chooses violence as the preferred option.

Why do Expert Aggressors attack? Expert Aggressors are interested in social or material gain, in taking something that doesn't belong to them. Sometimes what they want is material, as with muggers, burglars, and confidence men. But the object of their desire is often less tangible. Many times after a training session, a participant has told me of some workplace bully whose sole purpose seemed to be to make the victim's life a living hell through intimidation and subjugation.

Others have told me stories of rape and sexual assault in which the sole object was humiliation and the gratification of causing another to suffer. No property was stolen; no materials exchanged hands. What was ripped from the victim was a sense of being. The predator was attempting to elevate himself by lowering someone else. Crimes of social gain can be every bit as brutal as crimes of material gain—often, more so.

Who do Expert Aggressors attack? Expert Aggressors tend to attack those whom they find to be suitable victims. They choose victims who offer the greatest chance of success. This isn't necessarily an easy task, as willing victims can sometimes be difficult to identify. To compensate for this, bullies and predators often use rituals to test the "willingness" of a victim. Chapter 12, "Testing Rituals," discusses these rituals at length.

Of course, no one *wants* to be attacked. But some of us will *tolerate* an attack more than others, like the pliable child whom the schoolyard bully chooses in favor of more savvy classmates. The mark of a victim is one who'll let the testing rituals of the Expert Aggressor proceed too far. It's an easy trap to fall into, and it doesn't mean that you're weak, stupid, or naive. In fact, the more trusting, kind, or loving we are, the more vulnerable we can be to the overtures of a predator.

With knowledge in our corner, we don't need to succumb to bullies' tests and tricks. But even with knowledge on our side, the most experienced of us can still make less than ideal choices because our character is good and we assume the best of others. When this happens, don't let it get you down. Bullies and predators are highly skilled in their trade. Study their methods and learn from your mistakes. Add your newfound knowledge to your arsenal of wisdom. There's no value in maligning yourself.

The "mark of a victim"

A "suitable victim" is one who knowingly lets aggression progress too far.

What are the early warning signs of Expert Aggression? Imagine the life of a big cat living on the African savannah. When it's time to eat, she gets precious few chances to capture a meal. If she tries to chase down prey and loses, she has just spent a remarkable amount of energy and gained nothing. She will have to rest and regenerate for several hours before she can try again. If she fails a second time, it may well mean her demise, as she may not have enough energy remaining for a meaningful third attempt. It's therefore terribly important that she choose her prey carefully by studying the entire herd and finding the one who will offer the least resistance.

The same logic holds true for Expert Aggressors. If they choose a victim who'll fight back, they stand to get hurt, arrested, or worse, so they must choose carefully. This requires them to search from a safe distance for vulnerability, then usually to test the victim prior to an attack—to interact with the target in some way. These testing rituals, which we will dissect, are the mark of a predator. They're the early warning signs of a possible attack.

The following scenario showcases the methods of an Expert Aggressor. Watch for signs of vulnerability in the victim, as well as of manipulation and testing from the aggressor.

Desperate versus Expert Aggression:
Different reasons require different responses

Desperate Aggression

- Likely to occur when the aggressor has run out of options
- Generally an attempt to regain control
- Characterized by signs of stress

Expert Aggression

- Likely to occur when the aggressor finds a suitable "victim"
- Generally an attempt to profit
- Characterized by testing rituals

SCENARIO: The Bullying Client—Version One

Luanne was new at her job. She had just graduated from college and had eagerly accepted a position in her hometown unemployment office as a benefits administrator.

During her first few weeks on the job, Luanne had encountered many challenging clients. Some had been manipulators, trying to lie and cheat their way into benefits they didn't deserve. Others were truly hard-luck stories who earned her deepest sympathy. Young and idealistic, she sometimes lay awake at night wondering how she could help her most challenging clients.

But none of her clients were as challenging as the one she was about to meet.

As she sat busily ordering papers on the new desk of her new office, she was startled by the terse ring of the intercom. "Luanne, James Taggart is here to see you."

"Thanks, Mike. Send him in, please."

After several moments James appeared. He had clearly taken his time, giving Luanne an uneasy feeling she couldn't quite explain. Tall and lanky, James had shoulder-length dishwater blond hair and wore a tattered denim jacket over a plaid shirt and blue jeans. Luanne noticed that his least worn articles of clothing were his work boots. She stood to greet him as he ambled into the room.

"Good morning, James!" she said with a smile. "At last we meet!" After reviewing James's lengthy case file, which she'd inherited from her predecessor, she'd called him in to discuss the fact that his benefits would be ending if he didn't meet the terms of the work contract he'd signed earlier in the year. The contract specified that certain conditions, such as participating in training and interviewing for jobs, must be met in order to receive benefits.

James looked at her with a smile that bordered on a sneer and returned her greeting. "Mornin'," he answered, then plopped into a chair before being invited. Luanne's vaguely uneasy feeling increased.

Luanne seated herself. "Well, how are things going for you, James?"

James huffed disdainfully as he reached for a folded letter in his shirt pocket. "You oughta know. You're the one who sent me this damn letter." He held up the letter as if displaying the physical manifestation of a profound injustice that had been perpetrated against him.

"What letter is that?" Luanne asked with artificial curiosity.

"It says my benefits are ending. What the hell is that about?"

Luanne was flustered by James's directness. "Well, um, James, when I took over your case file from Sandy, she and I went over the requirements that you need to meet in order to continue benefits. And we found that you've come up short in a few areas."

James stared at her, an indignant look on his lean face. The source of Luanne's discomfort was becoming clearer with each passing moment. James seemed to be ever so subtly violating the rules of social convention. Uncomfortable with the silence, she continued.

"Like you were supposed to complete coursework at our career center. . . . Um, you haven't been there once since I took over your case last month."

James leaned forward in his chair, an indignant look on his face. "This is *crap*! Sandy knew I didn't need to take those stupid classes."

Luanne answered with sincere politeness. "James, it clearly states in your contract—"

James stood up. "I can't believe you're gonna hold me to a contract I didn't even want to sign! This is such B.S.!"

Luanne was growing very uneasy. "Um, James, will you please have a seat?"

Defiantly, James spun the chair around so that its back was facing Luanne. He sat down, straddling the back of the chair, his arms crossed in front of him in an insolent manner. He stared at Luanne with disdain.

Luanne was visibly shaken. "Thank you. Well, um, as I was saying, you haven't met your training requirements, and Sandy never said anything to me about—"

James interrupted her. "Listen, kid, I know you're new here, so let me explain it to you. Sandy and I had an understanding. Do I have to spell it out?"

Luanne laughed nervously. "But Mr. Taggart, you signed a contract, and . . . and . . . What are you saying?" She was astonished and frightened at the implication of James's tone and posture.

James stood up, planted both hands on her desk, crossed his legs behind him, and stood over Luanne. "Do you know what it's like to have kids to feed?"

Luanne stuttered. "Well, I—"

"Do you have any idea what it's like to look for a job out there? Of course you don't. Your mommy and daddy probably sent you to a perfect little college. Where'd you go, Berkeley? Go to a lot of parties there?" James straightened up and put his hands on his hips. Luanne sat slack-jawed.

"Well, my life's not like that. I don't have time for stupid classes, you know? Why don't you try my life for a while, then maybe we could skip this stupid red tape. My life's hard enough." James spun around so that his back was to Luanne. "*God*, why don't you just cut me some slack!"

Luanne didn't know what to say, but she felt as though she must say something, and she was frightened by James. She simply hadn't encountered anything like this outside of TV soap operas, and she didn't know how James was going to react. "Well, I don't know. . . . Maybe we can talk about it."

James dropped his hands to his sides and turned to face Luanne. "Yeah, we can talk about it. Just give me the credit on this one course, OK? You look like a nice enough kid. What do you say?" James flashed a saccharine smile.

Luanne was nervous and angry all at the same time. She felt as though she had just been manipulated by a master. Still, she was frightened by James's display of passion and didn't want to aggravate him further. "OK," she said reluctantly, "but just this once."

James smiled. "Sure, kid. Thanks." With that, he shook her hand, smiled contemptuously, and left.

Luanne sat at her desk for several moments, stupefied. She didn't know how she would explain this to her supervisor.

CHAPTER ELEVEN

Early Warning Signs of Expert Aggression

HAVE YOU EVER WONDERED WHY PEOPLE like James Taggart are so adept at finding victims? And why they seem so sure of themselves? He was taking a risk in treating Luanne the way he did. She had the power to punish him by taking away his source of income, and yet he persisted, seeming to know exactly which buttons to push.

Clearly this wasn't a case of Desperate Aggression. The signs of stress weren't there, and the sense of being cornered wasn't present, at least not in a genuine sense. Indeed, James seemed to have the upper hand from the beginning of the scenario to the end, unlike Molly in the previous scenario. Given his situation and his apparent need to appease Luanne, one might expect him to be contrite and cooperative. Instead, he was overbearing, as if he knew that such an approach would be profitable. Experience, and a keen eye for a victim, probably told him that it would be.[37]

How did James know that Luanne would respond the way she did? How did he know that his plan wouldn't backfire? Like most Expert Aggressors, he tested the waters before he dove in. His first step was to decide whether or not Luanne would be a suitable victim. He had to watch her, as a hunter watches the herd.

Step 1: Watching the Herd

Nick arrived at detox one sunny Saturday morning, bruised, beaten, and very drunk. Dozens of blood and dirt stains covered his torn jeans and T-shirt. His arms were scratched and bloody, his face was filthy, and he sported a brand-new black eye and a rapidly forming lump on his head. He looked as if he had crossed paths with a band of angry wildcats.

It's never appropriate to blame the victim for his crime, but if ever a person's behavior constituted a foil-stamped invitation to predators, it was Nick's behavior the night before. Being the adventurous type, he'd hopped a bus to Denver, a town he'd never visited, and planned to spend a few days of his vacation exploring what it had to offer.

He arrived at the downtown bus station late in the day. Without knowing the lay of the land, and traveling alone, he set out to find quarters for the evening. Almost immediately, he was mugged by several of the ruffians who typically loiter around the station. They attacked him from behind, beat him into submission, and took his money. Nick, however, had outsmarted them—at least somewhat. Knowing that he might encounter trouble, he'd split his cash into two piles. The smaller of the two he pulled from his pocket and gave to the muggers; the larger stash was hidden elsewhere on his person.

Feeling as though his troubles were over, Nick began to wander westward. He found himself in a suburb of Denver, where he was befriended by a group of men well known to those of us who worked at detox. Friendly faces were a welcome sight to Nick, and the men made him feel instantly at home. When they asked where his bruises had come from, Nick told them of his earlier encounter and bragged how he had outsmarted the men who jumped him.

Out of apparent kindness, his new friends offered Nick a drink. Then another. And another. When he could barely stand, they took him behind a grocery store and beat every remaining dime out of him. He spent the rest of the night in the emergency room, followed by a lengthy stay in detox. Physically he was okay, but this was hardly how he'd planned to spend his vacation.

THE SEARCH FOR VULNERABILITY

The first step Expert Aggressors must take in finding a victim is to search for vulnerability—for a victim who looks as though they won't be able to resist. At this point, the aggressor hasn't invested much time or effort in cornering the prey; they're simply sizing up potential victims and searching for chinks in their armor. (Their lack of investment means they'll be easily discouraged by strength and savvy.) They're like a tiger circling a herd in secrecy, searching for the most vulnerable member.

It may seem difficult to imagine putting yourself in a position as vulnerable as Nick's. In retrospect, it seems ridiculous to accept a drink with strangers when alone in a strange city. But how many times have you known someone to drink a bit too much and walk home alone? Or jog after dark while wearing headphones? Or simply refuse an escort to their car when leaving work after hours? Situations like these can make a person just as isolated and vulnerable as Nick. It's at these moments that predators are watching and waiting.

Expert Aggressors search for vulnerability in both security and demeanor. They'll choose a house that's not well fortified; they'll choose a victim who, like Nick, appears unable to escape or defend themselves. The most attractive targets, like Nick, are isolated and inattentive and appear vulnerable.

- **Isolation.** Predators prefer isolated victims for the obvious reason that there's strength in numbers. One of the simplest and most effective ways for us good guys to avoid isolation is the buddy system. Use it at work, on first dates, when out on the town. The buddy system has only one rule: don't split up—under any circumstances—until both parties are satisfied that everyone is safe. Had Nick been traveling with a partner, his assaults would have been much less likely.

- **Inattention.** Predators love to see a victim who is inattentive, unaware, and complacent. This person is like a gazelle wearing blinders and earmuffs while big cats lurk behind rocks and trees. Predators can approach at their leisure, undetected. The good news is, it's easy to banish inattention from your life through awareness (see Chapter 5, "Listen to Your Intuition").

- **Appearance of vulnerability.** Here's where matters become a bit more nebulous. The appearance of vulnerability is something that you and I may not be accustomed to looking for, simply because we don't seek to exploit others. Those who are inclined toward abusiveness and manipulation, however, are experts at detecting subtle behaviors that betray vulnerability.

We already know that childhood bullies have a laundry list of preferred traits in their victims: they tend to easily give in, radiate anxiousness, have a shrinking demeanor, and be socially isolated. As the childhood bully matures into a full-grown predator, additional factors come to signal a "good" victim. These include the failure to establish and follow one's own safety rules (such as never accompanying a stranger to an isolated area under any circumstances) and gullibility (such as willingness to engage in conversation or other interaction against one's better judgment).

Once Expert Aggressors identify vulnerability in a potential victim, they begin to move in for the attack. This can be a dangerous proposition for aggressors, as they still don't know how the prey will react. In the interest of safety, aggressors will often rely on subtle tests to determine whether they should proceed, and they may use tricks and ruses in order to isolate the victim, as did Nick's second set of attackers when they feigned friendship.

Step 2: Habit, Ritual, and Magic

The heading of this section is borrowed from a chapter title in one of the classics in aggression research, Konrad Lorenz's 1963 book, *On Aggression*. In it, Lorenz painstakingly catalogued the aggressive behaviors of ducks, fish, dogs, and rats, offering a bit of insight into our own methods of aggression in the process. A staunch behaviorist, Lorenz believed that all activity is, at its core, biologically hard-wired: that aggression is always an automatic response to some external stimulus, rather than a tool to be used, at least somewhat judiciously, to solve problems.

Many now consider Lorenz's work unfashionable, probably because of the unyielding nature of his argument that all behavior is automatic and reflexive.[38] In spite of his inflexible approach to behavior, however, his work can make several important contributions to this discussion.

First, Lorenz noted several healthy outcomes of aggression between members of the same species. It serves the purpose of mediation and settling disputes; for instance, competitive aggression helps ensure the equitable distribution of territory.[39] It also provides the herd with strong and able protectors. Lorenz observes:

> This interaction [rivalries and conflict within a group of animals] has produced impressive fighters such as bull bison or the males of the large baboon species; at every threat to the community, these [baboons] valiantly surround and protect the weaker members of the herd.[40]

Aggression between members of the same species is useful, however, only insofar as the competitors don't kill each other, which would be bad for the species as a whole. That brings us to Lorenz's second area of contribution to this discussion: ritual, one of the mechanisms Mother Nature has given the animal kingdom in order to avoid serious, deadly conflict between members of the same species. Lorenz discusses at great length how ducks, for example, settle territorial disputes with ritualized combat in which blows are rarely exchanged. As long as each duck plays by the same rules, no one gets hurt and the matter is resolved.

You don't need to hide in the duck blind in order to see animal rituals at work. You've likely been awakened in the middle of the night by two cats resolving a property issue. As noisy and tumultuous as that struggle appears to be, it's still merely a ritual.

We can look at the ritualized nature of kitty conflict by contrasting it to *true* cat aggression. When a cat is stalking its prey—an act of true aggression designed to solve the problem of hunger—its ears are low, its mouth is silent, and it moves quietly, with stealth and gracefulness. If it catches its prey, the cat will kill it and eat it.

When two cats fight with one another, their behavior is very different. Rather than trying to look as small as possible, each cat tries to look as large and frightening as possible. The noise they make is enough to wake the dead. Any cat who relied on this type of flamboyant behavior when hunting would soon starve to death.

What does this noisy, frightening behavior accomplish? It settles the dispute without either cat getting truly hurt. Granted, they may come away with a few nicks and scratches, but when was the last time you saw a chalk outline of a cat who had been murdered by another cat? Cats rarely let the conflict go that far, because they each know the rules of the ritual. When one cat is mutually deemed the winner, the other will slink off to greener pastures, leaving the spoils to the victor. While it looks and sounds brutal, in reality the cat fight is a relatively peaceful mediation mechanism.

We humans have our rituals as well. Consider the apology, for example. In the grand scheme of things, the words "I'm sorry" are nothing more than a series of sounds uttered by one person in the hopes of persuading the other person that no offense was meant. It's just a simple ritual, but it's an extremely important one. It satisfies the sense of honor that was trampled upon, and it prevents an ugly confrontation.

Humans also have more complex and aggressive rituals for settling conflict. For example, imagine this scene: You are at the neighborhood pub when you spy two men about to engage in a brawl. As with most such conflicts, this one doesn't begin with one person marching over to the other and punching him in the nose. Instead, a precise and delicate "dance" takes place between the two men prior to any physical hostility. Nearly all of us are familiar with this ritual. Before you read my description of it, think back to your childhood days on the playground, when you may have watched two boys settle a score.

First, they contact each other indirectly through comments and innuendo among their friends and associates. This is meant to get the other's attention and rally support for the cause. We might call this initial strike "psychological contact."

Next, they stare each other down. They catch one another's glance and hold it for too long. This is the evil eye, the stink eye, the hook eye, the crook eye— or, if you prefer, "eye contact."

Following eye contact comes verbal contact: some thoughtful assertion of the problem at hand, such as "Whatta you lookin' at?" to which the opponent replies, "I'm lookin' at *you*, punk!"

After verbal contact comes physical contact. The two boys (or men at the pub, as the case may be) begin to push and shove one another. Note that they do not generally attempt to severely injure one another by breaking knees, gouging eyes, or choking one another. Most likely, they're simply pushing each other around rather harmlessly and hoping—*praying*—that someone will step in and separate them, or that the other will back down.

It's all quite a show, but rarely is it anything more than a ritual—although sometimes, to be sure, the dispute gets out of hand. As long as everyone plays by the same rules, no one gets seriously hurt, and territorial disputes are settled. Some people—the Expert Aggressors of the world—have elevated this type of testing ritual into a survival skill; people like James Taggart, in our most recent scenario, have even learned to profit by it.

As you read the scenario, you probably noticed early in the interaction that James was playing a game of vague intimidation. From the moment he greeted Luanne until the time he issued a veiled threat, his actions were consistently inappropriate, but not openly aggressive.

Why did James need to go to this much effort? If he truly wanted to assault or threaten Luanne, why not simply do so without wasting time?

The answer—and this is a crucial point—is that he didn't know how Luanne would respond to direct threat or verbal assault. He needed to test her willingness to defend herself, while maintaining a position from which he could retreat. If at any point she had ordered him to back down, or if she had sought the help of coworkers, James could have refuted the accusation in his most convincing voice: "Hey, I was just kidding around. Lighten up, will ya?" After all, James may be a hunter, but he is no Warrior.

Testing rituals are the mark of Expert Aggressors. They use them subtly, and sometimes brilliantly, to discover, with minimal risk to themselves, which of their potential targets will be most cooperative and give them what they want. If at any point during the procedure they sense that the target has strong defenses, they can back down before they have committed themselves too far.

The first step in an Expert Aggressor's assault is the search for outward signs of vulnerability. These signs can range from a person simply traveling alone in an isolated environment, to a sullen and withdrawn appearance that seems to signal, "I won't defend myself." We can endeavor to avoid displaying these signs, but no matter how many precautions we take, none of us can be completely invulnerable all the time. Thus we must all be prepared for the overtures of a predator. The best weapon is knowledge: if we can see the attack coming, we have a better chance of stepping out of the way.

A word about sexual assault in the workplace

Each year the U.S. Bureau of Justice records hundreds of thousands of rapes and sexual assaults in America.[41] According to these and other statistics, more than 85 percent of the victims knew their aggressors beforehand, meaning they had had some verbal or nonverbal interaction prior to the assault. This raises special concerns for the workplace.

Employees are often called upon to interact with many people they would not otherwise encounter, to travel in unfamiliar territory, and to stick to highly predictable routines that are easily tracked by sexual predators. These vulnerabilities create an ideal hunting ground for the Expert Aggressor. Teaching employees how to recognize and respond to predators is one of the most valuable benefits an employer can offer.

CHAPTER TWELVE

Testing Rituals

JAMES TAGGART, AND PEOPLE LIKE HIM, have an aura of strength and power. In reality, his actions are weak and cowardly. That's not merely gratuitous name-calling, it's a clinical observation: his methods are objectively sneaky and dishonest—the traits of a coward. At any point during the interaction, especially early on, Luanne could have outmaneuvered him, had she only recognized his tricks and known how to respond.

Unfortunately, her good nature put Luanne at a disadvantage. The Expert Aggressor's methods are usually tried and true; it takes a lifetime of practice to reach James's level of finesse. The basic tool of his trade is a ritual attack similar to the ritual of two cats or rowdy bar patrons, but he has twisted and bastardized it to suit his purposes.

Rather than a blatant verbal assault or direct threat, James starts small. For instance, he began his interaction with Luanne by greeting her rudely and plopping down into a chair before being invited to do so. This isn't a crime, but it's outside the realm of good manners. Just as the two ruffians in the pub tested each other's reactions to small transgressions, James wanted to know how Luanne would respond to this small breach of etiquette.

Whether Luanne is a "good" target or not, she may be too polite to respond directly to James's bad manners, but that doesn't matter; James doesn't need a verbal response. Sometimes the most important part of communication is non-verbal, and predators like James have an exceptional ability to read others. He will know simply by judging the minutia of Luanne's reaction whether he can safely proceed to the next level of his attack. If he gets the green light, he will continue. Like a bird of prey designing ever-narrowing circles around its target, James will subtly raise the amplitude of his aggression until he ultimately lashes out after the true object of his desire.

This entire process takes time and requires a great deal of stealth. If Luanne knew what tricks James had up his sleeve—if she knew his ultimate goal—she would have left the room and sought help, and James wouldn't have accomplished his objective. Instead, she assumed he was sincere. Testing rituals provide the cover that the Expert Aggressor needs.

The aims of predatory testing rituals are twofold. First, they're designed to distract the target and push him or her off-balance. Like the magician's lovely assistant, testing rituals provide a lot of flash and detail that redirect the target's attention and mask the aggressor's true intent. Second, testing rituals are designed to test a target's willingness to defend themselves on issues of little consequence. If the target won't defend boundaries that seem inconsequential—as when James rudely straddled the back of his chair in Luanne's office—a pattern of compliance begins. As each undefended boundary is breached, it becomes increasingly unlikely that the target will defend larger and more important boundaries—as when James insisted that Luanne violate the rules of his contract.

Many of these techniques have the added advantage for the aggressor of creating self-doubt in the target. Tricks that play on emotions such as guilt, sympathy, or insecurity can cause the target to forfeit trust in themselves and place that trust with the aggressor—the one person they absolutely *shouldn't* trust.

Here are seven rituals that predators use to examine and soften their prey:
- overaccommodation
- getting a foot in the door
- invading personal space and violating social conventions
- exploiting sympathy and guilt
- exploiting insecurity and dispensing insults
- intimidation and exploiting fear
- distraction and information overload

Although by no means an exhaustive list, these examples offer an overview of the Expert Aggressor's methods. After exploring these rituals through the case studies below, you'll be able to recognize most testing behaviors even if they don't appear on this list. In addition, we'll discuss four basic traits shared by most testing rituals. And, of course, we'll explore how to respond as early and as safely as possible.

In each of these case studies, pay attention to the details. That's where you'll find the devil.

Overaccommodation

I was enjoying a springtime vacation in New Orleans with a close friend. One bright and sunny morning as we were walking toward the French Quarter, I was approached by a man who introduced himself as Dan the Shoeshine Man.

Dan was a happy and entertaining fellow who seemed to have appeared from nowhere. He reminded me of an elf. He smiled broadly, and with a cheerful little dance he told me in rhyme how he would shine my shoes "like no one can."

I was wearing shorts, a T-shirt, and ratty, worn-out hiking boots that couldn't take a shine if he had used a floor buffer. But that didn't matter to Dan. He knew an easy mark when he saw one; he spotted my vulnerability. I had left my sense of awareness and street savvy in the hotel room, and Dan knew it. From my clothing right down to my unguarded, unaware demeanor, I had "tourist" written all over me, and at the sight of this happy, dancing little man, I dropped my guard even further.

Before I realized what he was doing, Dan had kneeled down in front of me and sprayed a neat pile of foaming polish on each of my shoes. By the time I noticed what was happening, Dan had already stood up—always one step ahead of me—and was grinning widely and holding out his left hand. In his right hand was a well-worn rag. "Three dollars to shine your shoes, mister!" he happily exclaimed.

The reality of the situation finally dawned on me. I could either give the man three dollars to remove the white piles of foam from my shoes, or I could walk around the French Quarter with each foot looking like a banana split. Without hesitation—almost as if acting under remote control—I reached for my wallet and handed three dollars to Dan the Shoeshine Man.

Dan took the money, bent over, and with his dirty rag knocked the little mounds of cream off my shoes. Within seconds, he was gone and my ratty old shoes were still every bit as ratty and old.

My question to you is: Why did Dan introduce himself to me with a song and dance? Why not simply spray foam on my shoes and demand three dollars to remove it? For that matter, why not simply demand three dollars?

The answer is that he didn't know how I would respond. Bending over and spraying foam on the shoes of a complete stranger could be a dangerous proposition. In order to do it safely—and thereby obtain his *real* goal of three dollars—he had to distract me, assess my demeanor to make sure that I would not retaliate, and soften my defenses.

He accomplished all of this by being *too* entertaining, *too* charming, and *too* funny for the circumstances. Dan didn't know me from Adam. It simply wasn't appropriate for this complete stranger to take time from his busy day to entertain little ol' me.

Had I been more awake and aware that day, rather than walking around in a relaxed stupor, I might have stopped to ask myself why this stranger was being so nice to me. But, as I have heard from so many class participants, "It all happened so fast!" Dan had probably used the same scam hundreds, if not thousands, of times. He was an expert.

During my career of studying and experimenting with de-escalation skills, I've had a number of successes and quite a few spectacular failures. I usually keep the failures to myself, but this is a valuable one to share because it keeps me humble. It's a constant reminder that like all of us, I must learn from my mistakes.

I share it also to encourage you not to take your errors in judgment too seriously. The next time you're duped by any of the testing rituals I'm about to share, rather than expending energy on beating yourself up and feeling foolish, do this: take a moment to picture me, your intrepid and supposedly street-savvy author, standing in the hot sun with neat mounds of white foam on each shoe. All that's needed to complete the picture is a cherry on top.

Now let's look at an overaccommodation case study of a more serious nature. Make a mental note the first time you notice the aggressor being too nice, too friendly, or too accommodating for the circumstances. Watch for the point at which his helpful gestures become inappropriate.

THE HELPFUL STRANGER

Becky had been working late at the office, something she was known to do quite regularly. As she walked toward the parking lot, the sun was sinking behind the hills and only a few cars remained. She was carrying a large box of papers and an overstuffed briefcase, and wasn't looking forward to the long walk across the parking lot to her car. After she'd taken only a few steps, a stranger approached her.

"Here, let me help you with those," he said with a smile.

Becky was startled. "Oh, God! You scared me!"

"Sorry about that," he smiled. "Let me give you a hand."

The tall, muscular man seemed to have materialized out of thin air. He was nice-looking, but something about him made Becky uncomfortable. Perhaps it was his excessive familiarity, or maybe it was the fact that he had appeared so abruptly, almost as if he had been waiting for her. Maybe it was the baseball cap that he wore low on his forehead; it seemed strangely out of place in this corporate office park.

"No thanks, I've got it," she said abruptly. She wanted the man to just disappear, but something told her that he wouldn't, and she was right.

"Oh, come on now, what kind of guy would stand here and watch you struggle with all of that? Here, let me take that one." With that, he reached over and took one of the boxes.

"Really, I've got it!" she protested.

"It's nothing!" he said cheerfully. "Let's go!"

This made Becky terribly uncomfortable. Not only had he appeared out of nowhere, not only was he following her to her car, but now he had her property. She felt as if she were tethered to him, and she had no idea what to do. She didn't want to return to the building or demand the box back because she didn't want to look like a bitch. Besides, she needed that box of papers. She wished he would just vanish.

The stranger made small talk as he walked next to Becky. "So, you work here? My cousin Paul works here. Maybe you know him?"

"Umm—no," Becky answered. She desperately wanted to get away. Not knowing what else to do, she quickened her pace, hoping that would bring a speedier end to the situation. The stranger easily kept up. With each step she took away from the building, she felt more isolated.

After what seemed like a trek of forty years across the parking lot, they finally arrived at her car, a luxury sedan. "Well, this is me. I can take it from here. Thanks." She reached into her briefcase with her free hand and pulled out the car keys. She pointed a small remote control at the car and pushed a button. The car made a chirping noise and all of the doors unlocked.

Immediately the helpful stranger dropped his box of papers. He grabbed the key chain with his left hand, and with his right hand punched Becky in the face so hard that she went reeling to the ground.

When she awoke many minutes later, her head was pounding and she was nauseated from the pain. Both the stranger and her car were gone.

When Politeness Becomes Rudeness

The helpful stranger in this case study shows us that there *is* such a thing as being too nice. The stranger insisted on helping Becky in spite of her clear protest. Like Dan the Shoeshine Man, this "helpful stranger" was far too accommodating. A truly helpful stranger might have offered assistance but would have sensed Becky's discomfort and wouldn't have forced the issue. Anyone who insists on helping in spite of your protests is probably not acting in your best interest. Politeness becomes rudeness at the point when it defies your wishes.

This case study also underscores the fact that no matter how hard we try, we cannot wish an aggressor away. In fact, by losing herself in wishful thinking and fantasy (the affliction of abiding in ignorance), Becky played right into the stranger's hands. Before he could attack her, he needed to know how she would react to small transgressions such as surprising her and taking the box from her hands. When she offered no meaningful resistance, he had his answer; he knew it was safe to proceed.

Leading the criminal to the crime scene

Predators like the helpful stranger in this last case study rely on physical as well as psychological stealth to commit their crime. It's clearly to their advantage to isolate their victim. Becky made two common mistakes.

First, she failed to plan her environment. She would have been better off had she parked closer to the building or, better yet, used the buddy system and walked with a friend or coworker to her car.

Second, she allowed the predator to accompany her to an isolated area, where he could commit his crime with minimal risk to himself.

Had the helpful stranger asked her point-blank, "Will you accompany me to that distant area of the parking lot so I can assault you and steal your car?" she obviously wouldn't have done so. But by using a covert testing ritual, he was able to accomplish just that. That's what is so insidious about the methods of the Expert Aggressor.

Never accompany a stranger to an isolated location.

Getting a Foot in the Door

A telemarketer once called me during dinner. Before launching into her sales pitch, she opened the conversation by asking, "How are you doing this evening, Mr. Smith?" Come to think of it, *every* telemarketer who has called to interrupt my dinner began with a similar line.

This is no accident, of course, and they don't open the conversation in this manner because they're polite. If they were polite, they wouldn't interrupt my dinner seeking to sell me sell vinyl siding or a fabulous new credit card. They're using an age-old strategy: they're trying to figuratively get their foot in the door by forcing me to invest in the conversation through the usual pat response "I'm fine. How are you?"

Telemarketers understand that if I invest in the conversation, I'm more likely to stay on the line. If I stay on the line, I'm more likely to listen to their spiel. If I listen to their spiel, I'm more likely to buy a product. They also understand that the initial investment doesn't need to be a big one. A simple greeting is enough. Simple greetings lead to conversations, and conversations lead to sales.[42] Once the telemarketer gets a foot in the door by engaging me in conversation, it becomes much more difficult for me to defend my limits and control the course of the conversation. (The sidebar titled "The bottom-line technique" on page 181 offers an excellent way to handle telemarketers as well as others who pester you.)

Expert Aggressors understand this principle all too well. Watch for it in this case study.

THE CONVENIENCE STORE

Marty, a convenience store attendant, had closed up shop for the night and was counting out the cash in his drawer when he heard a knock. He looked between the aisles of snack food and auto supplies to the double glass doors at the front of the store.

Standing outside was a man in his mid-twenties dressed in jeans and an expensive leather coat. He had parked close to the building and left the driver's-side door open. It looked to Marty as if the engine was still running. "Excuse me!" shouted the man.

Marty acknowledged him with a quizzical look.

"Do you know where 1320 Saint Paul is?" the man shouted not quite loud enough for Marty to hear.

"What?" Marty yelled.

"1320 Saint Paul. Do you know where it is?"

"Sorry, couldn't tell you." Marty looked back at his drawer but then couldn't resist glancing up at the fellow outside. The man had turned his back to Marty and was nervously surveying the neighborhood. He seemed confused and hurried.

The man knocked on the glass door again. "Hey man, do you know this neighborhood at all?" He was shouting, but again not quite loud enough for Marty to make out what he was saying.

"Sorry, what?"

"I said, do you know the neighborhood?"

Marty began to move toward the door. "Do you know what intersection it's close to?" he asked.

"No, man. I'm from out of town and my best friend is having a baby. Is there a chance I could use your phone?"

"There's one just around the corner of the building," Marty answered. He was still walking toward the door.

"Yeah, I tried that. It's broken." The man spun around for another look at the neighborhood before continuing, "Hey man, I'm hopelessly lost and there's nothing but houses around here. Could you help a guy out? Just one phone call. I'll only take a minute of your time, I promise."

By this time Marty was standing almost face to face with the man on the other side of the glass. He hesitated for a moment and then sighed, "Yeah, I sup-pose. Come on in." He reached into the pocket of his smock, pulled out the keys, and unlocked the door.

"Hey, thanks. You saved my life," said the man. He quickly followed Marty to the counter. As Marty began to reach for the phone, the man in the leather coat took one last nervous look around, then pushed Marty face first onto the count-er. He shouted that he had a gun, and ordered Marty to empty the cash drawer into a sack. Marty, with his face smashed against the counter and a gun to the back of his head, had never felt so terrified and betrayed.

One Step at a Time

The man outside the store understood something important about Marty: the closer he got to the door, the greater the chance that he would open it. The further he moved from the safety of his counter, the more willing he was to sac-rifice his boundaries.

Had the man simply asked to be let in, Marty would not have allowed it. But by engaging Marty, by capturing his attention and his interest, the man knew he had a chance. If he could slowly move Marty away from the counter by any means at all—in this case, by not speaking loudly enough and by sustaining a protracted conversation—then he would eventually work his way inside. Gaining entry was a matter of getting his foot in the door, of gaining some small com-mitment from Marty. The size of the initial commitment rarely matters. In this case, the commitment to carry on a conversation was quite enough.

Had Marty promised himself beforehand that he would not open the door for a stranger, no matter what the situation, he wouldn't have this unpleasant story to tell.

Invading Personal Space and Violating Social Conventions

You're at a block party. You've heard about Sarah and Brent, who live on the corner, but you're just meeting them for the first time.

"So Brent, I understand you're a marketing executive?" you begin.

"Yep, twelve years now," he answers proudly.

"Have you had any interesting clients?" you ask.

"Well, I don't mean to brag, but have you ever heard of [insert name of large, multinational company]?"

You're genuinely impressed. "Are you kidding? You bet I've heard of [large multinational company, preferably the same one]. That's great. Things must be going really well for you. And how about you, Sarah, what do you do?"

Beware the puny promise

Just before Marty opened the door, the man outside uttered those famous words "I'll only take a minute of your time, I promise."

Think back to the last time someone used these words on you. They probably didn't really want just a minute of your time, but something much more substantial. The puny promise—the unnecessary guarantee that the borrower won't ask for anything else—is a dead giveaway that they have something larger on their mind than the small item they've requested.

The last time you asked someone for glass of water, you probably phrased the request in plain English: "May I have a glass of water, please?" If your request was an honest one, you probably didn't feel the need to add any promises or conditions: "All I want is a glass of water, I promise."

That type of phrasing usually belies a larger ambition. Granting their wish helps them get their foot in the door.

"I'm a schoolteacher. Fourth grade." she answers.

"That is truly impressive," you answer. "That must be incredibly rewarding."

"And difficult!" she smiles.

"And how's the sex life, Sarah? Is he, you know, doin' it for ya? In the sack, I mean?"

Jaws drop. The room falls silent. All eyes are on you.

"What?" you say to the room at large. "It's just a question!"

No, it isn't.

It can be argued that where we, as a society, draw the line on social etiquette and personal boundaries is arbitrary.

But arbitrary or not, we know what the rules are for almost any given social situation. In an elevator, for instance, we know that all eyes are to be directed up and to the front. Conversation is to be limited to "Nice weather" and "Uh-huh."

We know that at the ATM machine, you should allow an arm's length between yourself and the person in front of you conducting a transaction. Violate that space at the risk of incurring the evil eye.

We even know different rules for different lines. We know, for example, that at McDonald's, the arm's-length rule doesn't apply; the correct distance is probably between one and three feet, depending on the number of customers. In Europe, the prescribed distance is even smaller: if you can squeeze an object the width of a French fry between yourself and the person ahead of you, you're technically not in line.

How do we know all of these "arbitrary" rules? Others taught them to us by modeling ideal behavior—our parents, our siblings, our teachers, our friends, and our business relations. Over the course of a lifetime, we somehow manage to memorize and instantly recall thousands of social subtleties.

Expert Aggressors know these rules, too—perhaps better than the rest of us, because they've learned to violate them in order to test a target's willingness to defend boundaries.

THE BUSINESS TRIP

Jillian was on her first business trip to New York City. She was walking down a busy avenue on an idle Saturday afternoon when she sensed someone's eyes on her. She looked instinctively to her right and noticed a group of young men talking among themselves and looking directly at her.

This naturally made her nervous. She averted her eyes and quickened her pace as she approached the group of men. She hoped she would be able to walk past them without incident. But as she drew nearer, one of the men spoke up: "Hey baby, where you from?" The others laughed like jackals.

Jillian felt a knot in her stomach. Perhaps if she were in her own element, she would know how to respond. But she was completely alone, and she had a bad feeling about these men.

As she attempted a subtle escape, the lead man made more rude comments, and then rose from the stoop and began to follow her, calling out lewd sugges-tions. *Maybe he won't follow me very far*, she thought. She walked quickly and stared forward, as if fixing her eyes on some distant goal, but the man kept following. The faster she walked, the more aggressively he pursued her and the more insis-tent his comments became. "Hey, honey! What's the hurry?"

Jillian was truly frightened. Her pulse quickened and the world seemed to slow to half speed. She could hear the other men sitting on the stoop still laugh-ing and jeering.

She glanced back at the man following her. His stare was like ice; a thin, evil smile formed across his lips. "Why don't you stop and talk to me, bitch?" he sneered. The others cheered him on. Jillian snapped her gaze forward, hoping to escape his eyes, and strode as quickly as she could without breaking into a full run.

Suddenly she felt his cold hand grasp her elbow in a vicelike grip. She didn't know if it was the pain of his grip or the force with which he attacked her arm, but she found herself stopped dead in her tracks and spinning to face him.

His eyes were horribly cold; his intentions seemed pure evil. The other men, still laughing and jeering, rose from the stoop and began to approach. Jillian was certain she would be attacked. She began to struggle, but his grip was too strong. The other men drew nearer.

A Small Transgression

Allow me to pose this question again: If the man wanted to assault Jillian, why not simply do so? The answer, again: because he didn't know how she would respond. He needed to test her first by being rude, invading her personal space, and measuring her responses.

He began, as we have seen before, with a mild transgression. "Hey baby, where you from?" The question is rude, but not overtly so. Had he been challenged on this behavior, he could easily have backed down, claiming that he was just trying to be friendly.

When he was not challenged, he knew it was safe to raise the intensity of the assault. He moved on to more brazen comments; then he began to follow her, making lewd comments; then he insulted her; then he grabbed her. Each of his maneuvers was a slight increase in hostility, culminating in his ultimate attack. At the completion of each interval, he became more confident; with each successful increase, he improved his chances of a risk-free assault.

Good fortune was with Jillian that day. Before the struggle became life-threatening, she was rescued by a passing taxi driver. Had she not been so fortunate, her story might have had the usual unpleasant ending: robbery, assault, rape, or even murder. Like millions of people each year, she was quickly being led down a dangerous path by an experienced predator. He had probably been practicing this type of ritual since childhood, and he could learn all he needed to know about Jillian simply by watching her early responses to his tests.

Incidentally, Jillian reported that not long before the man approached her, she had watched him begin to harass another woman, but for some reason he had stopped his advance and returned to his perch on the stoop. It's possible that the first woman bore the "don't mess with me" demeanor that city dwellers sometimes cultivate, or perhaps she disarmed him with humor or a snappy comeback ("Hey baby, when are you gonna go out with me?" "We'll talk when you get a J-O-B, honey!"). During the first moments with an Expert Aggressor, humor can provide a face-saving escape for all concerned. Either way, we know that the woman didn't break her stride or show fear.

A person may break social conventions or invade your personal space because of a mere lack of social skills, or because of something more sinister. In either case, a gentle correction is in order before the situation escalates and becomes highly uncomfortable. (The next chapter discusses such responses.)

Here are a few particular social violations to watch for:

- touching in either an overly friendly or intimidating manner
- inappropriate comments that instill guilt or fear (see the next three case studies)
- invasive questions that any reasonable, objective person would find inappropriate
- aggressive questions that are meant to subordinate you, such as "Why are you so touchy?" or accusatory questions, such as "What gives you the right to judge me?"
- invading physical boundaries by standing too close, staring too long, touching when it's inappropriate, and so on
- invading psychological boundaries by raising deeply personal issues or steering the conversation toward inappropriate subjects

A Quick Inventory

Let's take a quick inventory of the testing rituals we've looked at so far.

First, there's *overaccommodation*. This ritual allows Expert Aggressors to wiggle their way into a target's safety zone (or a second environment) by being *too* nice, *too* funny, *too* charming for the circumstance. Once they've gained trust and isolated their target, they attack.

Next is the ritual of *getting a foot in the door*. Here, the predator tricks the target into investing in an interaction. The more committed to the interaction the target becomes, the weaker their defenses are.

Finally, we looked at *invading personal space and breaking social conventions*, in which the aggressor breaches the target's boundaries incessantly, one by one, until it's clearly safe to attack.

The next three testing rituals, *exploiting sympathy and guilt*, *exploiting insecurity and dispensing insults*, and *intimidation and exploiting fear*, take a slightly different approach.

The predator using these tricks is manipulating the target's emotional state rather than simply tricking them. The goal is to put the target in such a state of mind that they misplace trust or feel obligated to comply. These rituals can be particularly insidious because they're so manipulative, and they carry the added sting of making the target feel foolish for being emotionally duped—an overly harsh judgment, considering the skill of most Expert Aggressors.

Exploiting Sympathy and Guilt

This ritual is a favorite among men who seek to exploit women, although it isn't limited to that purpose.

ANNE AND CHARLIE

Anne had had a long day of waiting tables. The pancake house had been busy from the moment she walked in, and after nearly eight hours she was ready for a break.

Charlie, a lone customer, sensed her exhaustion and wasted no time in establishing a rapport. When she presented him with his bill at the end of his meal, he smiled and handed her a large payment in cash. "Thanks, hon. You keep the change."

Anne's eyes grew wide. "Wow! Thanks! Are you sure?"

Charlie smiled. "Absolutely. I just want someone to have a better day than me."

Anne sat down at his table, pulled a disheveled wad of bills from the pocket of her smock, and began to arrange her money and receipts. "Rough day, huh?" she asked.

Charlie flashed a shy smile. "Well, I probably shouldn't burden you with it—but let me tell you, this day has been one for the books." He laughed quietly.

Anne continued arranging her bills. "What happened?" she asked.

"Oh, it's really no big deal," Charlie said. "You've got enough on your hands to worry about."

"No, really," Anne protested, "it's no problem. Talk to me."

"Well," Charlie began hesitatingly, "it started when my dog woofed his cookies all over the carpet this morning. He was on the linoleum when he got the urge, but he decided he'd rather get sick on the living room carpet." He shook his head.

"Yeah," Anne laughed, "they prefer to go on the carpet!"

"Unfortunately," Charlie added. "Of course, I was already late for a sales meeting. Now I'm on my hands and knees, cleaning up dog barf and trying to think of the best way to tell my biggest client that the dog made me late. Let me tell ya—that line didn't work in grade school, and it doesn't cut it in the real world either!"

They both laughed.

"But after twenty minutes of reflecting on the nature of partially processed dog chow on the wife's new carpet, I was off to meet the client. And let me tell ya, his day wasn't going any better than mine."

"What do you mean?" Anne asked.

"Have you ever heard of Chapter 13 bankruptcy? That's when a guy like my client decides to close his doors forever. The best part is, all the bills he owes me are null and void. So not only did I lose a sale, I lost the whole flippin' account, and now I have to explain to my boss that we won't be getting paid anytime soon."

Charlie sighed and pulled his fingers through his hair wearily. "Suddenly, cleaning up after the dog seems like a ray of sunshine!" He looked up at Anne and smiled, as if trying to disguise his dismay.

"Is your job going to be OK?" Anne asked.

"As safe as ever, I guess. Anyway, the rest of the day was various degrees of embarrassment and proverbial kicks to the groin. To top it all off, I blew a tire out here on Broadway, which is why I find myself in your lovely presence. I managed to roll into the back lot, only to find out that using the jack that comes with that car is about as safe as propping up a boulder with a number two pencil." Charlie sighed, smiled, and straightened up in his chair. "But I really should stop bothering you with all of this."

Anne stuffed the now neatly ordered bills and receipts into her pocket and began to pick up Charlie's dirty plates. "It's no trouble, really," she said. "Besides, I'm sure things will pick up for you. I wish I could help."

"Well," Charlie began but then stopped himself. There was an awkward pause.

"What?" Anne asked.

"No—I really couldn't ask," Charlie said as he looked down at the table.

"Go ahead, ask me," Anne said.

"Well—if it wouldn't be too much trouble, would you mind steadying the car while I work on a stubborn lug nut? I'm worried that the jack is going to slip, and I just need someone to push on the back of the car while I try to loosen the thing."

There was a pause while Anne considered the query.

"It's not hard, and you won't even get your hands dirty. I promise."

Anne looked around at the busy restaurant and hesitated. "Well, I really shouldn't leave."

Charlie smiled out of embarrassment. "You're right, of course. I'm sorry. I shouldn't have asked. Anyway I shouldn't expect a beautiful girl like you to help an old fart like me," Charlie joked. He began to gather his belongings and steel himself for the impending tire-change battle.

Anne looked concerned. "Is it really going to fall?"

Charlie sensed her hesitation. "The way my day is going? You can count on it! I suppose the worst that can happen is that I have to start over a few times. But it really would be nice to have some help if you have a minute. Besides, you look like you could use some fresh air."

Anne took one more look around the restaurant and after a pause announced, "All right—but you owe me one!" She pointed a finger at him playfully.

He returned her playfulness and bowed deeply. "I am forever in your debt, madam."

A few minutes later, the two of them rounded a corner in back of the building. Charlie pointed to a car parked between a dumpster and a fence. "It's the far wheel there. Just let me get the jack handle out of the back seat."

Anne, following his suggestion, began to walk around the car for a better look as Charlie opened the car door and pulled out a jack handle.

She never made it to the back of the car to find out that there was in fact no flat tire. Before she had a chance to figure out what was going on, Charlie took a quick look around, then struck her from behind with the jack handle and threw her limp body into the back seat.

He started his car and merged slowly into traffic, taking care to use his turn signal.

Laying the Groundwork for an Attack

The extra-large tip, the charming smile, the down-home conversation about dogs and the trials and tribulations of holding down a 9-to-5, and of course the subtle but contemptuous comment "I shouldn't expect a beautiful girl like you to help an old fart like me": all of it was intended to instill in Anne a sense of sympathy, guilt, and obligation. Unfortunately for Anne, Charlie was just smooth enough to pull it off.

As with our previous case studies, Charlie knew that Anne would never agree to his goal—that she accompany him to the parking lot—if he simply requested it. So instead, he resorted to manipulating her emotions and taking advantage of her good nature. It may seem that Charlie went to extraordinary lengths to trap Anne, but in fact, the effort he put forth was not unusual for an Expert Aggressor as advanced as he was.

Dr. David Lisak has done a great amount of research on what he calls "undetected" rapists. In one especially startling interview, a college student named "Frank" details the plan that he and his fraternity brothers used successfully, week after week, to rape dozens, if not hundreds, of female college students:

We would all invite girls, all of us in the fraternity. We'd be on the lookout for good-looking girls, especially freshmen, the real young ones. They were the easiest, it's like we knew they wouldn't know the ropes kind of, it's like they were easy prey. They wouldn't know anything about drinking, about how much alcohol they could manage, and they wouldn't know anything about our techniques.

"What were those techniques?" Dr. Lisak asked.

We'd invite them to the party and we'd make it seem like it was a real honor, like we didn't invite just any girl, which I guess is true [laughs], and we'd get them drinking right away.[43]

Frank proudly describes in detail how he and his fraternity brothers would get the girls too drunk to defend themselves, take them to a prepared room, and forcibly rape them.

He doesn't detail the techniques he used to persuade girls to attend the party, other than to say that he painted the invitation as "a real honor." One can only assume that the fraternity had a negative reputation on campus and that the initial persuasion relied heavily on the same techniques that Charlie used in the restaurant.

Not all Expert Aggressors will go to these lengths, but some, like Frank, aren't afraid to do their homework. They can be quite skilled at laying the meticulous groundwork necessary to complete their crime in relative safety to themselves.

Know Your Boundaries

The best defense against the overtures of predators like Charlie and Frank is to know your boundaries *before* entering a situation. It is *not* okay to accompany a stranger into a secluded environment alone (e.g., the restaurant parking lot). It is *not* okay to enter a risky environment (e.g., a frat party) without using the buddy system. Knowing your limits beforehand prevents you from falling into a quandary of indecision when an unpredicted situation arises.

Exploiting Insecurity and Dispensing Insults

Some testing rituals are built on bolstering the target's self-image and playing on positive emotions such as sympathy. Other rituals function by emotionally tearing down the target, by destroying confidence and playing on negative feelings such as fear or self-doubt, as in the following case study.

PARALLEL PARKING

My friend Mary worked in Capitol Hill, a busy downtown section of Denver. At lunch she would sometimes drive to her favorite grocery store to buy her favorite lunch. Parking in this area of town was always a challenge, and particularly so during the lunch rush.

Mary's favorite grocery store happened to face a busy avenue. On the day in question she spied an open space directly in front of the store. Being unskilled at parallel parking, she was not excited at the prospect of pulling in while traffic raced around her, but being an intrepid soul, she was willing to give it a try. She turned on her blinker to indicate her intentions, pulled one car length ahead of the space, and put her car in reverse.

Her first attempt was a miserable failure. Forgetting to reverse the steering wheel in time, she hit the curb hard, nearly crushing an innocent parking meter. She pulled out and tried again. Her second attempt was no better, although she did manage to miss the curb this time—by many feet. That's when Hank[*] appeared.

Hank had been standing on the curb watching Mary struggle. He now offered help by standing within sight of her rearview mirror and offering direction. With large, flailing motions he guided her first right and then left, frantically shouting directions: "Turn hard! Turn hard! Now cut it! *Cut it!*"

But try as he might, his directions were of no help. Mary began to think that either his guidance was a disservice, or she was completely inept at parking. After a couple of failed attempts, Hank moved to the passenger side of the car and indicated with a circular hand motion that she should roll down the window so he could speak to her directly. Mary obliged.

Mary made another attempt with Hank shouting impatient verbal instructions through the open passenger-side window. Still no luck. Finally, he grew impatient. He leaned in through the window, extending his open hand, and said, "Women can't park. Give me the keys and let me do it."

A Brief Quiz

Question: What is the first of the two techniques that an Expert Aggressor uses in choosing a victim? Think back; this is important.

Answer: The first step is the search for vulnerability. Mary is by no means a weak person; in fact, she's one of the strongest, most independent people I know. Nevertheless, we all have our insecurities. To the Expert Aggressor, our insecurities are opportunities, and Mary's Achilles heel was parallel parking.

Hank, seeing her struggles, wasted no time in seizing upon that opportunity. He assumed a position of authority by directing her into the space. He added to her insecurity by giving her ham-handed instructions, thereby ensuring her failure. And he took one final blow at her self-confidence by insulting her before finally demanding the keys: "Women can't park—let me do it."

Fortunately, this case study has a happy ending. Mary didn't fall for Hank's tactics. As soon as he insulted her and extended his hand for the keys, she drove away and found a more accessible spot.

---

[*] We'll call him Hank because he wore a mechanic's jumpsuit bearing a red-and-white name patch over the left breast pocket. Having shopped at many thrift stores during my poverty-stricken college years, I can attest that these jumpsuits are easy to come by and that nearly all are emblazoned with the name "Hank."

By all appearances, Hank makes his living conning people, and Mary believes that he wanted to steal her car. When she returned to the store many minutes later, she noticed Hank loitering on the street, waiting for the next potential victim. She later reasoned that any man who ostensibly works as a mechanic probably has better things to do during his lunch hour than help people park—and do a poor job of it.

Mary's story shows us that even when an Expert Aggressor leads us far down the dangerous path, it's never too late for a Warrior to turn back.

We've seen insults at work in prior case studies. Recall the situation involving Peter and Gary, in which Peter used insults and intimidation to gain Gary's cooperation. Rarely do people insult one another for no reason. Insults are usually an attempt to change the balance of power. In this case study, Hank used an insult as part of a larger strategy to gain Mary's trust—or, more accurately, to destroy her trust in herself.

Insults are pretty standard fare for Expert Aggressors, as is another age-old tactic: plain old fear and intimidation.

Exploiting Fear

The Magnificent 13 were a volunteer graffiti cleanup crew in the Bronx more than twenty years ago. The group was started in 1978 under the leadership of a McDonald's night manager named Curtis Sliwa.

Sliwa and his group became local heroes for their cleanup and beautification projects. But it didn't take them long to realize that cleaning up the city meant more than just removing graffiti. No matter how clean the streets were, they were still dangerous—so dangerous, in fact, that Sliwa and his fellow employees would often walk elderly McDonald's patrons home to see that they arrived safely.

One evening, a retired transit worker made a desperate plea: Do something about the crime. Sliwa and his group, comprised mostly of his fellow McDonald's employees, began patrolling one of New York City's toughest subway lines, known as the Mugger's Express. Carrying no weapons other than their wits and their teamwork, they detained the gang members and muggers who preyed on innocent straphangers and held them until the police arrived.

The Magnificent 13 soon grew to hundreds of members and changed their name to the Guardian Angels. They now have thousands of members, in chapters around the world, conducting volunteer safety patrols on some of the world's most dangerous streets.

The Guardian Angels don't rely on weapons or physical force. In fact, weapons are forbidden, and patrol members are frisked before each and every patrol to ensure that everyone's "clean." This means that verbal skills and street savvy are vital, especially for patrol leaders, who must make critical decisions during heated moments.

The case study you're about to read describes one of the thousands of incidents in which violence has been prevented thanks to Guardian Angel know-how and verbal intervention.

It's fitting to look at a case study involving the Guardian Angels when discussing the testing ritual of *intimidation and exploiting fear*. The Angels have shown us in dozens of cities, through thousands of examples, that the good need not fear the evil. Since the group first began patrolling the Mugger's Express in 1978 they've enjoyed a phenomenal safety record, and not a single Angel has been killed in the line of duty.

All of this experience has its rewards. Along the way the Angels have amassed an impressive body of knowledge about dealing with irate, frightened, and desperate individuals. And of course, they've learned a thing or two about Expert Aggressors.

A NIGHT ON THE TOWN

This Guardian Angels patrol consisted of a highly experienced patrol leader, known on the streets as Rock, and three newer members still in training, some of whom had been on patrol only a few times. The trainees knew their single obligation well: let Rock do the talking, and follow his instructions.

It had been a fairly typical patrol. They had been confronted by the usual drug dealers, gang members, and one altercation over a fender-bender. It was nearly 2 A.M. and the patrol was on its way to headquarters for a much-needed break when they heard a commotion about a block away.

As they rounded the corner, they saw a large crowd gathering outside a nightclub. They approached the scene quickly, but didn't run. Rock had learned long ago not to rush headlong into a risky situation. As they neared the ruckus, the details of the scene came into focus.

A crowd had formed an arena of sorts in the middle of the street. Occasionally a car would struggle to get by, but the crowd was so focused on the event at its center that they were oblivious to anything else. In the midst of it all were two combatants, obviously patrons of the bar, as were the majority of the crowd, judging by their stylish clothes. The two weren't yet involved in an all-out fight, but they seemed to be on the verge of it.

One of the combatants was much larger than the other. He was an athletic man, with large, muscular arms that bulged through his stylish blazer. His appearance was immaculate, his presence was commanding, and his deep voice boomed at his opponent as they circled and baited each other.

The other man, although much smaller, had his strengths as well. He too was well dressed and impeccably turned out. Although he was lacking in physical stature, he compensated for it with a powerful voice, unwavering eye contact, and frenetic energy.

The two danced and circled each other, all the while hurling directives and expletives. "You best back off!" the large man would shout at his diminutive opponent.

The crowd, of course, was no help. The majority watched in glee, while shouting partisans encouraged their favorite contestant to launch a true assault: "Don't take that! Hit him!" Standing out from the crowd was a very pretty, very nervous woman who would occasionally position herself between the two men. She would try to hold back the larger man, a giant in relation to her. She was obviously pleading with him to stop, only to be repeatedly pushed aside.

The spectacle was one that Rock had seen many times before. While enjoying a night on the town, one of the combatants had found himself under the scrutiny of the other. Perhaps he had stared at a woman for too long, or inadvertently blown smoke in the other's face, or maybe one of them had simply walked into the establishment with a chip on his shoulder.

In any case, hard feelings had led to hostile eye contact (the infamous stink eye!), and eye contact had led to verbal contact. Challenges begat insults; insults begat physical contact; physical contact led them to confront each other in the street. In all likelihood, the initial physical contact hadn't been as devastating as the old Hollywood bottle-to-the-head trick, or even a solid punch in the face. If so, the two wouldn't have ended up circling each other. Instead, it had probably been a light shove or a finger to the chest, all in accordance with ritual.

And now the two men found themselves at the end of a ritual that could easily lead to genuine violence. Judging by their actions, especially the fact that the situation had probably taken several minutes to evolve without any serious damage being done, both probably wanted a way out but were too proud to back down.

Had the two men been alone, they might have walked away. But the presence of the crowd (and the woman) prohibited such a commonsense approach. Rock knew they had no way out of this ritual unless somebody provided it for them. Ideally, this is the function of friends and associates or, better yet, some authority figure. But nobody was stepping up to the plate.

The situation was quickly escalating. Voices were getting louder and pushes were getting harder. Very soon the scene would erupt into all-out violence, and somebody could get seriously hurt. Rock had to respond immediately if he was to respond at all. The only immediate response he could offer was to restrain one of the men, giving both men the opportunity to back down.

But which one? This was the tricky part. Rock had to choose the one who had initiated hostility and remained the aggressor. When only one intermediary exists, there's no room for error in this decision, and Rock knew that his patrol was too inexperienced to make informed decisions. He would have had to explain the situation to them, and there was simply no time. They would have to follow his lead.

If he chose the wrong person to restrain, the results could be devastating. That combatant would feel as if the crowd were ganging up on him, in addition to his original assailant. This could cause him to panic and transform into a truly frightened and dangerous Desperate Aggressor. Moreover, the true aggressor would now have free rein, and might very well capitalize on the distraction and deliver a serious blow. These are just a few of the reasons that intervention is tricky and dangerous, especially for a lone individual.

Rock made the least obvious choice and restrained the smaller man. He grabbed the man by both lapels, walked him backward, and stated calmly and repeatedly, "That's enough. He just wants to walk away."

He chose correctly. As soon as Rock had detained the smaller man, interrupting his ritual, the larger man uttered a few obscenities, took the woman by the hand, and strutted away. Meanwhile, the smaller man struggled to get past Rock and resume the battle—but he didn't try very hard.

As soon as the combatants were out of each other's sight, Rock and his patrol slipped away into the darkness and the disappointed crowd slowly dispersed.

The Whole Story

Unless you have the whole story, you can be dead wrong about violence.[44]

—Debra Niehoff

Debra Niehoff, an expert in aggression, is referring in the above quote to a long-standing mistake in the world of aggression research: the confusion between offensive and defensive aggression. Defensive aggression is actually not aggression at all, but merely an attempt to escape.[45]

Rock, the Guardian Angel in the preceding case study, never studied aggression in the classroom. But he did understand, as does Niehoff, the importance of "the whole story." The casual observer, watching the tussle outside the nightclub, could easily have mistaken the larger man for the aggressor. He towered over his opponent, pushed the smaller man repeatedly, and shouted protests in a booming voice.

Rock knew better, though. He looked beyond the obvious and sized up the entire situation. What he saw in the larger man was not anger and hostility, but frustration and fear. In the smaller man he saw pride, vengefulness, and lust. Like an alley cat in a dispute over territory, the smaller man's actions were expansive and loud. He was the one who'd picked his victim and started the altercation. He was the one who'd attempted to bolster his self-esteem at another's expense.

The larger man could clearly have pummeled the smaller man, but didn't. The smaller man had succeeded in intimidating someone much larger and more capable than himself. The same could be said of James Taggart in the scenario in Chapter 10, "The Expert Aggressor." This is yet more evidence that bullies and predators can go only as far as we allow them.

Distraction and Information Overload

Christina Rivera is a motivational speaker and an outspoken activist against sexual assault. Her main message: listen to your intuition.

Christina is one of those amazing people who have turned personal tragedy into an offering for others. Her desire in life is to see that what happened to her doesn't happen to those around her.

Her story began as she was leaving work one sunny afternoon. She was waiting for a ride to a company picnic when her attacker approached. Like so many of the attackers we've already read about, this man didn't resemble an attacker at all. He was a friendly-looking man dressed in a service uniform, giving the appearance of having business at Christina's building. He pulled up next to her on the street and, with an air of sweet purity, offered her a ride.

Christina reports that "he was very charming and made himself seem familiar and trustworthy. He even made out to be looking out for me: 'You don't want to be on that highway driving by yourself.'"

Christina was initially hesitant about accepting a ride from the man, but he eventually persuaded her through persistence, refusing to take no for an answer, and painting himself as someone who could be trusted. Christina is confident that her attacker had done this before. Through heavy doses of charm and information, the man was able to divert Christina from the larger truth of the situation: that he was a stranger, and one should never get into a car with a stranger.

Once the man had Christina securely in his car, of course, he didn't drive her to the picnic. Instead he took her to an isolated spot in the mountains, where he repeatedly beat and raped her.

Christina bravely offers her story as a cautionary tale to others. She tells her audiences that she "had a feeling" she shouldn't accept a ride from the man. On some level, Christina knew that the man's story was too polished and detailed. Her "little voice" was trying to tell her that this predator was using the diversionary tactic of information overload. He was highly skilled; she was good-natured and overly trusting. Now she advises others to listen to that little voice.[46]

The woman in the following case study has never met Christina, although they live only miles apart. She found herself in a similar situation and made a different choice. That's not to say that she's smarter or stronger than Christina; Christina is both strong and smart. This woman was simply more willing to listen to her intuition at the time of her incident, and because of that, her story has a much happier ending.

CAR SHOPPING

Michelle had finished her weekly shopping and was packing her many bags of groceries into the back of her car. The sun was beginning to set and the shadows in the parking lot were long on this cool summer evening.

The trunk was filling rapidly, and Michelle was momentarily distracted while she tried to find homes for the few remaining bags. That's when she sensed a presence behind her. She turned to find a middle-aged man standing only inches away.

"Howdy!" he said with a smile. Michelle said nothing. She was shocked that the man had been able to get so close without her hearing him. Unable to stand up straight without coming nose to nose with him, she remained uncomfortably bent and twisted over the open trunk of her car.

"I couldn't help noticing your car. I've been looking for one like it myself."

Michelle stared in silence as the man began to size up her vehicle.

"Is this a new model?" he asked. "It looks like it's in good shape."

"No," Michelle said hesitantly, "it's eight years old."

The man wandered to the driver's side and peered in. At last, Michelle could stand up straight. "Most of the models I've looked at have wood paneling on the dash, and yours doesn't. I think I like it better without."

He began to walk back toward Michelle, but she'd had enough. Without bothering to finish packing or close her trunk, she quickly marched back into the grocery store and asked for an escort to her car. When she returned with a store employee, the man was nowhere in sight. With the employee's help, she finished packing and was on her way, no worse for wear.

A Bland Conclusion

At first glance, this final case study seems to be a rather bland conclusion to the set. There was no struggle, no harsh words, not even a veiled threat. We don't even know for sure that the man had any ill intent toward Michelle. It appears to be a simple story about an encounter between a woman loading her groceries and a man lacking in social skills. But there's much more to this story. It illustrates the delicate interplay between testing rituals and intuition.

After Michelle drove out of the parking lot and was on her way home, she realized a couple of important facts that probably subconsciously alerted her intuition.

First, she remembered that her model of car, no matter what year it was manufactured, did not include wood paneling. Second, her car had a body style that hadn't been produced for several years. While it was in good shape, it wasn't new.

It seemed to her that if the man had truly been shopping for her model of car, he would have been aware of these basic facts. That, combined with the fact that he had approached her silently and stood so close—violating social conventions—gave her "a funny feeling." It seemed to Michelle that he wasn't shopping for a car at all.

Instead, it seemed as if he was trying to paint himself as an "insider." By showing appreciation for her taste in cars, and by feigning interest in purchasing one for himself, he was preparing Michelle to accept him as a trusted associate. Michelle knew better. She listened to her intuition.

Predators don't want their victims to listen to their intuition, nor do they want them to stop and think. We subconsciously process details that take time to be realized by our higher, conscious mind—details such as the absence of wood paneling, or the body style of the car.

Intuition doesn't speak to us directly through words or images; it communicates through emotion. Only when we have time to reflect on a situation, as Michelle did when she was driving home, do inconsistencies become obvious on a conscious level. That's why predators prefer to keep the interaction moving, and that's why some predators inundate their targets with detailed information designed to interfere with rational thought and cloud the big picture.

Am I certain that the man intended to harm Michelle? No. Am I thankful that she heeded her intuitive warning? Absolutely.

Mix-and-Match Rituals

The speed, dexterity, and relentlessness with which predators apply their testing rituals make them difficult to perceive, especially at the moment when those rituals are being used. And predators often use rituals in combination; rarely will they rely on, for instance, overaccommodation and nothing else.

Take the case study involving Marty at the convenience store, for example. The methodical way in which the stranger lured Marty to the door and patiently manipulated him into opening it offers an excellent example of the *foot-in-the-*

door ritual. But the robber didn't rely on that technique alone. He also applied heavy doses of secondary rituals, including *exploiting sympathy and guilt* (his story about the pregnant friend and being lost in a strange town) combined with *distraction and information overload* (the details he provided concerning his friend and his search for a phone).

The table below gives a brief synopsis of each case study along with the primary testing ritual used in each. Please take a few moments to think about each case study and determine which secondary rituals were used to augment the primary ritual.

You won't find an answer key for this exercise. Simply review the facts and let your intuition be your guide. Here's a list of the rituals we've discussed:

- overaccommodation
- getting a foot in the door
- invading personal space and violating social conventions
- exploiting sympathy and guilt
- exploiting insecurity and dispensing insults
- intimidation and exploiting fear
- distraction and information overload

Case Study #1: Becky, a devoted employee, leaves her office late and encounters a stranger in the parking lot who insists on helping her with her burden. This stranger accompanies Becky to her car in an isolated section of the parking lot. He assaults her and steals her car.
Primary ritual: Overaccommodation
Secondary rituals:

Case Study #2: Marty, a convenience store clerk, is drawn to the aid of a man standing outside his store. Despite the fact that Marty has closed for the evening, he allows the stranger to enter. The man robs him at gunpoint.
Primary ritual: Getting a foot in the door
Secondary rituals:

Case Study #3: Jillian is on a business trip to New York. She is walking down a busy avenue on a Saturday afternoon when she is accosted by a young tough. His friends cheer him on. Jillian is rescued by a passing taxi driver.
Primary ritual: Invading personal space and violating social conventions
Secondary rituals:

Case Study #4: Anne is waiting tables in a busy restaurant when she encounters a charming but downtrodden customer named Charlie. After a lengthy conversation she accompanies him to the back parking lot. Charlie knocks her unconscious and abducts her.
Primary ritual: Exploiting sympathy and guilt
Secondary rituals:

Case Study #5: Mary is attempting to parallel-park in a bustling downtown business district when a stranger in a mechanic's jumpsuit tries to assist her. After a couple of failed attempts, the stranger insults her and demands the keys to her car. Mary leaves the man and finds another parking space. Many minutes later she sees the same man loitering in the same spot.
Primary ritual: Exploiting insecurity and dispensing insults
Secondary rituals:

Case Study #6: A large man in a nightclub is bullied and intimidated by a much smaller man. An altercation ensues and the two men find themselves in the street, about to come to blows. A passing Guardian Angels patrol impedes the smaller man long enough for the larger man to escape.
Primary ritual: Intimidation and exploiting fear
Secondary rituals:

Case Study #7: Michelle is packing groceries into the trunk of her car when she suddenly discovers a man standing close behind her. The man expresses an interest in buying a car similar to hers, but doesn't seem to have his facts straight. Michelle returns to the store and asks for an escort. When she arrives back at her car, the man is gone.
Primary ritual: Distraction and information overload
Secondary rituals:

CHAPTER THIRTEEN

Telltale Signs

WE'VE LOOKED AT SEVEN CASE STUDIES involving seven different testing rituals. This is by no means an exhaustive list; no one book could possibly cover all the variations of these rituals. Nevertheless, this list gives you a good start toward understanding predatory communication. Think of these seven tricks as a basic bug collection of nasty predators and bullies pinned neatly to a corkboard and covered with glass. We'll never be able to add *all* the bugs in the world to our collection, but we have enough information to know a bug when we see one.

To recognize variations that aren't present in the collection, we now know what characteristics to look for. Most testing rituals, regardless of their surface appearance, share a few common traits:

- persistence
- talking too much
- contradictions between words and behavior

  and, of course, the most important warning sign of any testing ritual—

- triggering your intuition

The first three items in this list each involve some level of interaction with the target. Remember, however, that the *first* step toward finding a target is surveillance and the search for vulnerability. Intuition can provide a warning even at this early stage; we'll discuss how that works later in this section.

Now let's take a look at the basic characteristics of almost any testing ritual, beginning with persistence. If the mark of a predator is a testing ritual, then the mark of a successful predator is immunity to the word *no*.

Persistence

Predators need their targets to stand still long enough to establish a submissive posture. Trying to gain entry to the target's environment, or persuading the target to accompany them to a different environment, can take a great deal of time and interaction. The successful predator must learn to ignore the protests of the victim. The more inexperienced or unsure the target is, the more likely the aggressor is to succeed.

People between the ages of sixteen and nineteen are the most victimized group in our country. Nearly one in ten will suffer some sort of violent crime. As a person ages, the chances of becoming a victim of violent crime substantially decrease.[47]

One of the most reasonable explanations for this trend is that with age we become more knowledgeable, more street-savvy, more risk averse, and more willing to define and defend our limits. We become more willing to say no, and we know when to do so; we're less likely to enter compromising situations.

This isn't always the case when we're young, invincible, and naive. Consider this typical date-rape case study: a girl in her late teens goes out for a night on the town with a boy she has just met. Having given little thought to her boundaries, she is easily persuaded to tolerate questionable situations and finds it difficult to defend what boundaries she does have. When she knows it's time to go home, the boy says, "Let's stop by my friend's house—just for a minute."

When the girl protests, the boy persists. "It will only take a minute, I promise." He has just denied her wishes and ignored the word *no*. She acquiesces: "OK, but just for a minute." When they arrive at the friend's house, she soon asks to leave. "Let's just stay a little longer," he protests, ignoring her wishes yet again. After some discussion, she gives in.

Then the boy offers her a drink. When she declines, stating that she'd like to leave, he ignores her wishes and uses every measure of persuasion at his disposal to "sell" the drink. Having already established a solid pattern of giving in, she finally accepts the alcohol. One drink becomes two, and two become three. He then asks her to accompany him to a room upstairs where "the real party is going on."

"I don't know," she protests meekly. But by now the boy has deciphered the code necessary to obtain whatever he wants from the girl. Once again he refuses to take no for an answer, and once again she submits. Four times she has said no, and four times he has persisted, each time learning more about her defenses. Once the couple are upstairs, he has no trouble getting what he wants.

This type of sequence plays out in the lives of many young people. We're taught as youngsters that persistence is a prized quality and that, in the end, perseverance will always win out. If we stick to our guns long enough, eventually we'll wear down the competition, defeat obstacles, and slowly forge a new path to success. Predators know this all too well, and persistence is an integral strategy in most testing rituals.

We can see this strategy at work in many of the case studies we've examined.

When Becky encountered the "helpful stranger" in her office parking lot, she refused his aid. He insisted on helping her nevertheless.

When Marty, the convenience store clerk, declined entry to the man standing outside, the man persisted until Marty opened the door. The man wouldn't take no for an answer.

Anne, the waitress, clearly stated to Charlie that she should not leave her post. Charlie persisted with his strategy of manipulation and guilt. Eventually she caved.

Persistence can be difficult to recognize when we haven't flatly stated the word *no* but simply implied it, as did both Marty and Anne. But rest assured that predators and bullies know full well when they're violating your boundaries. They know when they're not taking no for an answer. And when they succeed in some small victory, they know they're on their way to their ultimate goal.

Always keep this in mind, for it's terribly easy to forget: when a person acts against your spoken or implied wishes, they're not acting in your best interest. They're not acting like a friend, no matter how friendly they may look on the outside. Ignoring the word *no* is a powerful warning signal.

Talking Too Much

Expert Aggressors usually have a story—a long and detailed story.

I'm reminded of a situation that many of us will experience at one time or another. I was walking downtown, en route to an appointment, when an unkempt young man approached me.

"Excuse me, sir," he said. I knew that he was going to ask for something, but being in no hurry, I decided to hear him out. He proceeded to give me a blow-by-blow account of the last month of his life. It went something like this:

He had lost his job in a town ninety miles away and had no luck finding a new one and since his wife was pregnant he was forced to find other sources of income and so he sold his washer and dryer to a friend here in town but when he tried to deliver it his truck broke down on the highway about five miles away and his wife was still sitting in it and if they didn't get the washer and dryer delivered today they would lose out on the deal which would mean they wouldn't have enough money for groceries this week and they would have to sell their purebred malamute which he was willing to do "but my wife—did I mention that she's pregnant—would be devastated and you can see the bind I'm in and all I need is a buck-seventy-five for the bus ride back to the truck."

This young man was by no means an Expert Aggressor. He was just a kid looking for a few dollars. There's no crime in that.

His technique, however, bears a striking resemblance to that of an Expert Aggressor. He didn't share his life story to be friendly. It was an investment of time and energy designed to garner sympathy, and he expected a return on his effort.

Many of the case studies we've examined involved just such an investment.

The man who robbed Marty had a detailed story about his reasons for needing a phone.

Anne's assailant engaged her in a lengthy but purposeful discussion about his job, his life, and his car.

The man who tried to help Mary parallel-park outside the grocery store didn't share his life story, but he did initiate a great deal of interaction—much more than is necessary when parking a car.

The man who expressed an interest in buying a car like Michelle's put forth a level of detail and effort that simply wasn't appropriate for a stranger in a store parking lot.

Even the nightclub bully engaged in entirely too much talking. Had he *truly* wanted to fight the larger man, he would have done so. His words betrayed a ritual that is much more flash than substance.

You may be rightly thinking that some people simply like to chat and will do so at the most inopportune times. True, but there's an important distinction between innocent chitchat and the ritual of an Expert Aggressor. The conversation of an Expert Aggressor usually seems directed toward some end. For instance, Charlie's conversation with Anne seemed to be orchestrated entirely to obtain her help with the imaginary flat tire. He painted the illusion that there were simply no other options; that if she didn't help him, he might end up pinned helplessly beneath his car, and it would be her fault. The Expert Aggressor doesn't chat for the sake of chatting; there's always a vague sense that the target is being led down a dark path.

The man who robbed the convenience store took a similar approach. He absolutely *had* to get into the store to make a phone call, because all other options had been exhausted—or so he would have us believe. Of course, there were plenty of other options. For instance, Marty could have offered to place a call for the man, but the criminal deftly steered the conversation toward entering the store.

Even the man who insisted on helping Becky carry her burden after work seemed absolutely bent on accompanying her to her car. It seemed much more important to him that he walk with her than it was to help her.

In each of these cases, the perpetrator had a fairly obvious, but unspoken, goal. As talkative as this group was, you would reasonably expect them to simply state their goals, if indeed they were legitimate. Instead, they hid their true agendas behind a veil of too many words.

Contradictions Between Words and Behavior

A woman once told me the story of a man who came to her workplace after hours. She was the only one left in the building, and when she spoke to him through the locked glass doors, he promised that all he wanted was a glass of water.

She told me that in spite of his small and seemingly insignificant request, he seemed nervous. He was fidgety and occasionally checked over his shoulder. She opted not to let him in.

She had noticed something that has probably appeared in most of the case studies we've looked at: a contradiction between words and behavior. Any man who wants nothing more than a glass of water has no reason to be nervous. There are two types of contradictions to be aware of:

- contradictions between words and physical behavior
- inconsistencies between stated goals and the demonstrated intent

Noticing contradictions between words and physical behavior is a matter of watching body language. Someone who speaks of simple matters, like a glass of water, but shows a heightened sense of alertness, restlessness, or any of the signs of stress or adrenaline that we discussed in Chapter 11, "Early Warning Signs of Expert Aggression," is probably not telling you the whole story.

Expert Aggressors are usually polished and practiced enough to avoid amateurish slip-ups like these. It's difficult to mask inconsistencies between stated goals and demonstrated intent, however. This person *says* he wants one thing, but behaves as if he wants something entirely different. This behavior was readily apparent in many of our case studies.

The man who insisted on helping Becky carry her load said he was interested in her welfare. If he were truly interested in her welfare, he would have respected her wishes and left her alone. His actions demonstrated that his main interest was in following her to her car.

When Mary was attempting to parallel-park her car, the man on the sidewalk implied that he wanted to guide her. His actions, however, only served to muddle the situation and ultimately lead him to asking for the keys.

And the man who told Michelle that he was shopping for a car like hers clearly didn't behave like an informed consumer, even though he obviously wanted to be perceived as one.

Incongruities like these signal a large information gap. There's something you're not being told, and that's reason enough to raise your guard and find an escape. Noticing contradictions and inconsistencies requires a large capacity for quickly processing details. Sometimes that's a tall order for the conscious mind, but it's the perfect task for intuition.

Triggering Your Intuition

The reticular system, which we discussed briefly in Chapter 5, "Listen to Your Intuition," is Information Central for your brain. It gathers information from your senses, measures it, prioritizes it, and passes some of it up to the level of conscious perception. Much of the information, however, remains behind in the subconscious, and many believe that this is the stuff of intuition.

Even when information remains at the subconscious level it's still scrutinized, perhaps even more thoroughly than we typically scrutinize on a conscious level. When the information that remains behind contains a danger sign or inconsistency, we receive a warning signal in the form of a "gut feeling." If, for instance, you're walking down a street and catch a barely perceptible shadow out of the corner of your eye—not quite enough of the shadow to reach the level of conscious perception—you'll undoubtedly get the inexplicable sense that you're not alone.

Having studied the testing rituals of Expert Aggressors on a conscious level, you'll now be much more adept at detecting these rituals on a conscious level. You'll be more skilled at noticing inconsistencies between words and behavior, between action and intention.

Of course, you (at least at a subconscious level) were already well aware of testing rituals long before you picked up this book. We simply reinforced your knowledge. By giving the phenomenon a name and discussing the finer points and inner workings of basic predatory behavior, we've created a powerful link between your conscious knowledge and your innate subconscious wisdom. From now on, when your intuition tries to talk to you about aggressors, you'll have a much better understanding of what it's saying.

That is, if you do your pushups. Most of us spend the better part of our lives being discouraged from paying attention to our intuition, so rebuilding it requires effort. Here's a brief review of the exercises and techniques we discussed in Part One.

- **Allow your curiosity to flourish.** The mind is always in search of new information. Feed it by altering routines and occasionally playing the "what if" game.

- **Alter your routines.** Habits save time, but too much reliance on habit can cause tunnel vision.

- **Play the "what if" game.** Use some of your idle moments to explore things that could happen around you (e.g., the person in front of you in the checkout lane could have a heart attack) and how you might respond.

- **Build awareness of surroundings, others, and self.** Review the exercises on page 56 and do your pushups every day.

- **Don't dismiss your emotions.** Don't act against your own self-interest simply to be polite or to appear rational. Feelings of trepidation arise for a reason.

- **Balance goals with awareness.** Narrow-minded pursuit of a goal, such as escape, can lead you to be blindsided. When you choose a goal, be flexible in the path so that you don't sacrifice your intuition.

- **Read.** Explore the wealth of literature on developing intuition.

- **Stop.** When you get that funny feeling and you don't know why, *stop*. Take a moment to ask yourself why you feel the way you do.

In the heat of the moment, when you are truly being tested by a predator, you probably won't have time to sort it all out as it's happening. The types of situations that we've been discussing move very fast. Fortunately, you don't need time; your intuition has already done the work for you, if you're willing to listen.

CHAPTER FOURTEEN

Early Response: The Bottom Line

PREDATORS DON'T WANT YOU TO STOP and think, to listen to your intuition. They want to execute their ritual the same way they did last time, and the time before that. They *don't* want to be interrupted in the middle of their routine.

Responding to an Expert Aggressor means not playing by their rules. Sun Tsu, the famous Chinese strategist, advises us to attack the plan, not the person. Interrupting their routine—their plan—is the topic of this chapter.

Much of what I know about aggression and hostility has its roots in my father's bar, that institution of higher learning where I spent my formative years. In Chapter 5, "Listen to Your Intuition," I recounted a case involving intuition, in which my father avoided disaster by taking a soft approach to a serious danger. Like the samurai's third son at the beginning of this book, he sensed trouble early enough to avoid it completely. Unfortunately, it isn't always that easy; some Expert Aggressors force themselves upon you, and they require a more active, assertive approach.

When my father first bought the bar and took over the business, the clientele was rough. It wasn't unheard of for an unruly customer to test the limits of the proprietor, especially a new owner like my father. One such episode stands out to this day.

It was late on a Saturday night, and a group of pool players, mostly bikers, were becoming loud and destructive. My father approached the leader of the group and calmly asked them to finish their drinks and leave. One man, several years younger than my father and several inches taller, laughed out loud. He stood face to face with my father and said, "You know, I could turn you into hamburger."

My father moved so close to the man that their noses were practically touching, and calmly said, without batting an eye, "You'll never have a better chance to try."

Let me assure you that my father *wasn't* spoiling for a fight. That was the last thing he wanted, and he later admitted to being nervous (okay, scared). His strategy was simply to call an end to the type of ritual that we've been studying—in this case, playing on fear and intimidation. He effectively told the man that he refused to be a willing victim, that he would not go down without a fight.

The biker might have been able to physically hurt my father, but it wouldn't have been worth the risk. We might refer to this as *bluffus interruptus* or, better yet, "getting to the bottom line," for reasons that will become obvious.[*]

When the biker heard my father's response, he laughed derisively. For a moment it looked as if my father had made the wrong move. But soon the man joined his friends, all of them laughing with him, and said, "Let's go." The men jeered and called my father names all the way out the door, but they left, and that's all that matters.

If used against a Desperate Aggressor (discussed in Part Two), this could be a dangerous strategy indeed. Challenging someone who already feels cornered could push them beyond their limit. However, defending boundaries *early* in the interaction can have a desirable effect on an Expert Aggressor.

The key to responding to an Expert Aggressor is to interrupt their ritual as early as possible. The sooner you can make it known that your boundaries are nonnegotiable, the less effort it will generally require.

This is easier said than done. Responding to Expert Aggression can be a frightening experience. But remember our definition of a victim: one who knowingly allows a problem to progress too far. We must be willing to recognize the true nature of a dangerous situation in spite of wishful thinking or the desire to appear polite or reasonable.

The instant you detect a testing ritual, you're charged with two responsibilities in order to remain as safe as possible:

- Take control of your physical surroundings.
- Take control of the interaction.

The most basic function of predators' testing rituals is to keep them safe. If they deem you to be a poor choice of victim, they'll probably move on before they've invested too much time and energy. Even if they don't move on, you'll be in a position of much greater power should you need to force an escape.

---

[*] I didn't select this example because it showcases good technique, but because it demonstrates the principle that boundaries must be defended. There is a vital distinction between maintaining your boundaries and challenging an aggressor. My father did not merely maintain boundaries by saying, for instance, "I can't let you do that" or "Don't come any closer." Instead, his response was a clear and blatant challenge. While there may be times when this approach seems appropriate, rarely is that so. Expert Aggressors can become Desperate Aggressors if they're not provided with an exit, and one should never block an exit for any type of aggressor. (By challenging the biker in front of his friends, my father ran the risk that the man would see no alternative but to attack.) This chapter will provide other alternatives.

Take Control of the Environment

Notice that this section isn't titled simply "Run away." Taking control of your environment doesn't necessarily mean running to a different location. When dealing with Desperate Aggressors, escape means creating as much distance as possible, as quickly as possible. It means moving yourself to a secure location where they cannot get to you.

Expert Aggressors, however, must sometimes be dealt with differently. Of course, we still want to get to a safe location and create distance as quickly as possible, but we must redefine "safe location."

When dealing with a Desperate Aggressor, a safe location is essentially any place far away. With an Expert Aggressor, a safe environment is one in which the predator is unlikely to carry out their act of aggression. Far away will do, of course, but it's not the only option.

In several of the case studies and scenarios we've looked at, aggressors attempted to isolate their target; to get "up close and personal" in a private location, or at least a location filled with their friends and associates.[*] The likelihood of an unpleasant consequence increases exponentially when strangers are around, and that's why isolation is generally so important to an Expert Aggressor. (The Desperate Aggressor has no such sensibility, having an impaired regard for consequences.)

The moment an Expert Aggressor approaches, you are engaged in a battle over your surroundings. The aggressor wants to lure you into their web, while you want to keep total control over your environment. You have four ways to achieve your goal:

- **Move yourself to a safe place.** This means a place where you are surrounded by people—preferably authority figures, or your friends and associates (as opposed to your aggressor's friends and associates). Anyone who can provide aid and discourage an attack is acceptable. This is precisely what Michelle did when the man approached her in the grocery store parking lot to discuss her car. Without speaking a word, or even bothering to close her trunk, she marched back into the supermarket.

---

[*] Expert Aggressors generally prefer isolation, but we've seen a few notable exceptions to this rule. The small bully outside the nightclub acted in front of a crowd; the young man who assaulted Jillian on the busy New York avenue was surrounded by friends; the man who threatened my father was also not alone. Friends and associates are a dangerous aggravating factor when dealing with some aggressors.

- **Bring the safe environment to you.** Call the authority figures, or friends and associates, to your aid. This is a slightly more difficult proposition, as it involves contacting the outside world.

- **Drive the aggressor away by taking control of the interaction.** Taking control of the interaction means not playing by the aggressor's script; it means stopping the ritual as early as possible. This can be a daunting task, so the next section is entirely devoted to it.

- **The last resort.** The final option is to fight your way past an aggressor. That discussion is beyond the scope of this book, except to say that the only time to fight is when you sense imminent danger, and the only purpose is to find an escape.

You want to spend as little time as possible with an Expert Aggressor. If you can get to a safe environment without exchanging words, like Michelle, then you've done an outstanding job. But it may not be that easy. You may already be isolated with the aggressor, or they may be blocking your exit and you're not ready for a physical altercation. When that happens, it's time to take control of the interaction with strength and confidence.

Often, most of the messages conveyed in interactions between people come from the nonverbal cues. This is especially true when you are communicating with Expert Aggressors, who are usually quite adept at reading the subtleties of human expression. That's why we're not simply going to *ask* the Expert Aggressor to back off; we're going to *demonstrate*, through words and body language, why they should.

Take Control of the Interaction

Most bugs want to remain hidden from the world, given that the world is full of critters that would like to eat them. The moths, caterpillars, and flying insects that I chased as a child (but never harmed) were usually difficult to find among leaves, bark, and branches. I felt especially lucky when I was able to find a praying mantis or walking stick. These creatures are so well camouflaged that they seem to become one with a tree, and their shape and coloring protect them from becoming lunch for birds. Who knows how many walking sticks I had looked at before I actually *saw* one?

Some creatures, on the other hand, *want* to be seen by predators. They have bright, contrasting colors that seem to beg for attention. Yellow and black, for instance, is a common combination for these creatures; they're literally as bright as road signs. They want to be seen because their colors actually serve as a warning: I *taste bad, I'm poisonous, and if you eat me I just might be your last meal.* This safety mechanism is called *aposematic coloration*—warning colors. Predators have to eat only one of these tainted critters to learn that they'd better not eat another, hence the easy-to-remember color scheme.

We learned in Part One that those of us who are successful at avoiding conflict—particularly those who repel Expert Aggressors—have a coloration of sorts that warns predators: *If you're looking for a victim, I'm not the one you want.* Predators are engaged in a constant cycle of sizing up potential victims: looking for vulnerabilities and measuring reactions, over and over again. If they see warning colors, they move on.

Understand this about Expert Aggressors: they're *deeply* self-centered. They'll back off only when it's in their own best interest to do so. Our job is to convince them that, like the brightly colored animal, we aren't worth their trouble, that they would be better off picking on someone else. Let's examine a few specific "warning colors" that predators don't like to see when sizing up a potential victim:

- plain English
- confident body language
- confident eye contact
- unwavering commitment to boundaries
- self-assuredness (a.k.a. respect for intuition)

It's never too late to show your warning colors, although as we've mentioned, the earlier you can do so, the better. The task here is to interrupt the testing ritual as early as possible.

We'll begin with a defense strategy that is like fingernails on a chalkboard to an Expert Aggressor: plain English that cuts through innuendo, deception, and pretense.

PLAIN ENGLISH

Predators rely on cover to mask their true intentions. A barrage of words can provide that cover, if we allow it, by creating a distraction (like the magician's lovely assistant) or by planting a seed of doubt within us.

Many politicians have taken a page from the strategy book of the Expert Aggressor, especially those who wish to conceal their true agenda during interviews and speeches. They're geniuses at being coy and evasive. The next time you listen to an elected official being interviewed on a tough subject, count the number of times they evade a question, answer a question with another question, or simply ignore the question altogether and launch into a prepared speech:

JOURNALIST: "Mayor Jones, you've been accused of accepting money from land developers in exchange for condemning private property. How do you answer these charges?"

POLITICIAN: "That's a fair question. I'd like to take a moment to discuss the state of land development in our great city. If we are to become truly visionary in the way we develop our land . . ."

And so on.

Politicians who avoid plain English have no intention of answering any question that reveals their hidden agenda, misdeeds, or lack of knowledge. They get away with it because too many of us have become far too tolerant in allowing our elected officials to distract us with meaningless jabber.

And it's not just politicians who baffle us with B.S. We're surrounded by meaningless language in advertisements, marketing campaigns, and business communications. For example, sometime in the 1980s tall, thin halogen lamps became a popular household item. They were well designed in that they provided bright, indirect light, they didn't take up much space, and a person could adjust the level of brightness for that just-right ambiance.

They've enjoyed spectacular success, but they haven't had a smooth ride. In the early years, some of these lamps were deemed to be fire hazards. In 1985 one manufacturer sent out an "Important Message to Users of [brand name] Multi-Vapor and Mercury Lamps" to notify users of the potential hazards of these lamps. The page-and-a-half-long notice overflowed with language like this:

There exists the possibility with any of these lamp types, regardless of wattage, that the arc tunnel may unexpectedly rupture due to internal causes or external factors, such as a systems failure or misapplication. When this occurs, the glass outer jacket surrounding the arc tube could break and particles of extremely hot quartz from the arc tubes and glass fragments from the outer jacket will be discharged into the fixture enclosure and/or the surrounding environment thereby creating a risk of personal injury or fire. Users must recognize that metal halide lamps and mercury lamps are not risk-free. Few products found in industry today could claim to be totally risk free. This does not mean, however, that such products should be considered "unsafe."[48]

This mishmash of words is meant to distract consumers from the fact that "fire" and "hot flying pieces of metal and glass" are indeed "unsafe."

Distractions like this are all around us. Countless companies on the Internet claim to offer "solutions," a meaningless term that is often modified by meaningless adjectives such as robust, seamless, end-to-end, turnkey, or, my favorite, mission-critical. Consider this sample, pulled at random from a website:

> [Our company's] platform provides a business, financial and technology framework enabling deployment, management, distribution and utilization of both business-critical information and other intellectual property.

> **Power phrase: The bottom-line technique**
>
> This technique will help you short-circuit testing rituals and bring the aggressor's intentions out into the open. If you don't get a straightforward answer to the question "Bottom line, what do you want from me?" then assume you're being tested.

[Our company] enables companies to deploy data-centric, Web-centric and user-centric solutions that address issues of Corporate Web-Strategy—solutions involving strategy definition, application development and multiple-platform implementations. [Our company] elegantly transforms Web sites into winning business solutions.

What service does this company provide? Your guess is as good as mine, but you can be sure that the price has been inflated as much as the description.

Why is this discussion of political and corporate babble important to the study of aggression? Because if we're not vigilant, we can become desensitized by the constant barrage of doubletalk and jibber-jabber present in our daily lives. If we're not ever-critical and aware of intentional distractions like these, we can become susceptible to the overtures of any silver-tongued devil who wants to disguise their true agenda.

It takes effort for Expert Aggressors to devise their doubletalk. Consider the amount of time, effort, and expense that Frank and his fraternity brothers invested in persuading young women to attend their parties. We, the good guys, have it easy. We can refuse to become players in their script simply by insisting on plain, direct English and settling for nothing less:

- **State your limits in plain English.** "That's far enough. Don't come any closer" or "I said no and I *meant* it."

Using deception

Deception is a perfectly legitimate strategy for driving off a predator (although it's not the same as bluffing, discussed on page 116). Don't hesitate to use lies such as "My ride will be along any minute" or "I think I feel a seizure coming on." You can shout to an imaginary friend, rant and rave, or act insane. Do or say whatever you think will drive a predator away.

• Demand to know, in plain English, their motives. "Bottom line—what do you want from me?"

We can learn a great deal about aggressors' motives by their response to these statements, particularly the bottom-line technique. If they meet you with a barrage of words—or with *anything* other than a direct answer and a solid respect for boundaries—then they are probably testing you for a larger assault. Don't be drawn into a discussion, and don't be derailed from the larger picture. You decide what to talk about; *you* control the interaction in spite of all their efforts to distract you.

Predators and bullies detest plain English as much as cockroaches detest the light. More often than not, it's enough to send them scurrying. If not, then at least we know where they stand. Most importantly, they'll realize that you see their true agenda; they'll know you're not to be trifled with.

CONFIDENT BODY LANGUAGE

You probably know what an assertive, confident person looks like. What you may not be aware of, like most of us, is what *you* actually look like when you communicate. Most of us have habits and tendencies that we're not aware of.

The Guardian Angels have a training exercise, called the Draw-the-Line exercise, that's designed to build confident and assertive body language. In it, Person A assumes a preparatory stance (see page 40).

Person B attempts to enter A's personal space three separate times. On the first attempt, A raises her hands as if to say *stop* and says, "That's close enough." A is not to move forward or backward, but simply maintains her position. B takes a step back and regroups for the next attempt.

On B's second attempt, A is more forceful about defending her boundaries: "I *said* that's close enough." Again, she is simply to maintain her position and keep B at a safe distance.

On the third attempt, A shouts, *"Back off!"* Again, she is not to move forward or backward. Her only job is to keep B at a safe distance, at least an arm's length away.

When the exercise is complete, B gives A feedback on her body language, verbal expression, and eye contact. With practice, even the most timid and slight of stature can become extremely convincing, and the key lies almost entirely in body language. Words, in this case, are secondary.

This exercise also underscores the fact that predators want to reduce distance and get close to their intended targets. The exercise provides excellent skills for overcoming the tenacity of Expert Aggressors.

We don't have room here to discuss all of the physical nuances of appearing confident. There are countless books on the subject of body language, but you probably don't need them; you know what confidence does and doesn't look like. The biggest challenge in managing your body language during stressful situations is being aware of your unconscious and involuntary gestures. Scenario training can help you overcome this challenge.

Here are some general guidelines for sending the proper nonverbal message to an Expert Aggressor:

- **Posture.** As your mother said, stand up straight. Don't cross your arms and legs or put your hands in your pockets; keep your head and eyes up. Don't break your stride. You have someplace to go, so act like it. If you're cornered and your personal boundaries have been invaded (the person is closer than two arms' lengths), then don't just stand there. Assume the preparatory stance discussed on page 40.

- **Facial expression.** If you have a snarl, get rid of it; it's a sign of weakness. Your facial expression should be at least neutral, preferably confident. You want to be nonthreatening and nonthreatened. Beware the nervous smile. It can sneak up on you.

- **Gesticulations.** Hands can send powerful messages. When you speak (e.g., "I said that's close enough!"), punctuate your message with a *stop* hand signal. Don't go for weak gestures such as crossing your arms or nervously putting your hands in front of your face.

- **Intonation.** Speak clearly and forcefully. Be aware of nervous tendencies such as mumbling or giggling. If you choose to scream or shout, do it with all your might, using powerful words. Compare the phrase "Somebody please help me" to "I said, '*Back off!*'" The second phrase commands respect and is more likely to draw a crowd.

- **Eye contact.** This one's so important it gets its own section.

CONFIDENT EYE CONTACT

In the chapter on the early warning signs of Expert Aggression, we covered both verbal and physical indicators of an impending attack. But we left out one crucial indicator of a testing ritual: extended eye contact and gazing. Predators tend to look longer and more directly at their intended prey than does someone engaged in a normal conversation.

Researchers have shown that people tend to lengthen the intervals and increase the frequency with which they look at others when they're trying to be convincing or to be accepted, and, of course, when they're attempting to intimidate or frighten other people.[49] Research has also confirmed that avoiding eye contact communicates submissiveness and appeasement.[50]

The topic of eye contact always generates debate and discussion during training sessions. What's the best way to use eye contact prior to and during an interaction? Some people believe that eye contact conveys strength. Others see it as an unintended challenge.

People are often advised not to look others in the eye when walking down the street: *If you go to New York, whatever you do, don't—for the love of all that's holy—don't make eye contact!*

Nonsense. There's absolutely no evidence to suggest that calm, confident, neutral eye contact increases one's chances of being involved in a crime. On the contrary, research demonstrates that strong eye contact is interpreted by most people as a direct reflection of self-confidence[51] and dominance.[52] In the interest of gathering my own anecdotal evidence, I spent many, many hours making eye contact with the population of Manhattan, and am happy to report that I'm still alive.

The advice to avoid eye contact, I believe, is based on fear and a couple of valid concerns. The first (particularly for women) is that establishing eye contact with a stranger will be interpreted as flirtation. The second (particularly for men) is that eye contact will be interpreted as a challenge. Both of these fears are valid, up to a point.

Yes, gazing directly into a person's eyes can be interpreted as an invitation or as a challenge,[53] particularly if that look is a stare, and that stare is accompanied by facial expressions and body language that seem to say, "Let's go outside and settle this like men" or, alternately, "Let's go outside and settle this like a pair of amorous rabbits." That's why we don't stare in a challenging or flirtatious manner.

The key to establishing eye contact with strangers is to make it fleeting, polite, and firm: acknowledge the people around you, and nothing more. This is where self-awareness is crucial. Just as with unintentional body language, your eyes and facial expression may be saying things that you're not aware of. If you just suffered a rotten commute, then you might have a rotten expression on your face without knowing it. Combine that rotten expression with an extended stare, and you have a recipe for an unintended challenge.

Fleeting, firm eye contact doesn't last long—a fraction of a second most of the time. In addition to giving you a calm and confident appearance, it allows you to truly look at the other person—not simply to recognize that someone is taking up space in front of you, but to actually *see* them. This is enough to inspire many predators to look for a new target.

If you find yourself engaged in an interaction with an Expert Aggressor and leaving isn't an option, then direct, consistent eye contact is a must. Eye contact is one of the most important nonverbal cues to your state of being. If your eyes are darting, looking down, or involuntarily looking away as if trying to escape, you can be sure that an Expert Aggressor will take notice.*

Making eye contact, both prior to and during the early stages of an interaction, may be difficult and uncomfortable. But consider the only alternative: avoiding eye contact, and possibly conveying fear or weakness.

Unwavering Commitment to Boundaries

I cannot emphasize enough the importance of maintaining boundaries, *especially* those boundaries that don't seem very important. Expert Aggressors don't profit by violating small boundaries; their interest lies in violating large, important ones. But predators scan for vulnerability. They look for any indication, no matter how small, that you are willing to let your boundaries slide. That's why defending small boundaries is important. Failing to defend them can ultimately provide Expert Aggressors with exactly what they want.

Consider this common case study. Erin works in a small company. She's on a coffee break in the company kitchen when John approaches. She has dealt with John on many previous occasions, and while he seems like a happy-go-lucky, generally harmless guy, she knows that he is tenacious in seeking what he wants.

John spots Erin in the break room. He goes to talk to her, placing himself between her and the door. He greets her with a large smile.

JOHN: "Hey, Erin!"

---

* There are most certainly some very important exceptions. During a hostage or other situation in which you are at another's mercy, demonstrating submissiveness by averting eye contact can help you avoid inadvertently challenging the aggressor. The discussion here refers to the early stages of a typical one-on-one interaction.

ERIN: (not pleased to see him) "Hi, John."

JOHN: "Hey, do you know when the budget meeting is?"

ERIN: "I think it's at 2 o'clock in the east conference room."

JOHN: "Great! Thanks. . . . Speaking of meetings, when are you going to go out with me?"

ERIN: "John, I've told you that I don't want to go out with you."

JOHN: (laughing) "All right! Fine! But will you at least have lunch with me today? I have some questions before we go into the meeting. Just lunch. Strictly business—I promise!"

ERIN: (sighing) "Fine. But just lunch. And strictly business."

JOHN: (beaming) "Great! I'll be by your office around noon!"

Erin's concession to have lunch is more important than it might seem. John wasn't interested in discussing business over lunch—he brought it up only after his first advance was rejected. John's true interest was in isolating Erin. Make no mistake, he succeeded against her will.

Most likely, Erin will have a "dammit moment" when she returns to her desk. (*Dammit! Why did I do that?*) Of course, she's not out of options. She can always cancel the date, take the issue to her supervisor, or bring a third party along for security.

However, she would've sent a much clearer message to John if she'd had an unwavering commitment to her boundaries from the beginning. Consider this alternative:

JOHN: "Hey, Erin!"

ERIN: "Hi, John."

JOHN: "Hey, do you know when the budget meeting is?"

ERIN: "I think it's at 2 o'clock in the east conference room."

JOHN: "Great! Thanks. . . . Speaking of meetings, when are you going to go out with me?"

ERIN: "John, I've told you that I don't want to go out with you."

JOHN: (laughing) "All right! Fine! But will you at least have lunch with me today? I have some questions before we go into the–"

ERIN: (interrupting) "John, I'm sure you're a nice guy, but if you don't stop asking me out, I'll have to take this to HR."

JOHN: (incredulous) "What? I just wanted to talk business!"

ERIN: "If you have questions, we can go over them here at work. Do you want to sit down and discuss them before the meeting?"

JOHN: "Never mind. It's no big deal."

This time Erin defended her limits immediately and consistently. She had decided long before this interaction began that it was inappropriate to isolate herself with John, or any other person with whom she's uncomfortable, no matter what the pretense or circumstance. Had she not defined that boundary clearly to herself, she might have left herself open to any number of manipulations. Instead, she was able to draw the line before the situation had a chance to escalate—in other words, before she was alone with him.

Maybe John is a predator; maybe he isn't. It doesn't matter. What matters is that Erin held her ground. While she did negotiate with him in order to answer his questions about the upcoming meeting, never did she sacrifice her boundaries; never was she in a compromising position.

SELF-ASSUREDNESS (A.K.A. RESPECT FOR INTUITION)

Criminals, and sometimes even your friends, don't want you to listen to your own intuition. They'll argue that you're being silly and illogical. They'll tell you to look at the bigger picture. They'll reassure you that nothing shady is going on and that you should trust them.

The truth is that anyone who would talk you out of listening to your own intuition isn't behaving as a friend. Anyone who in essence says, "Don't trust your own perception or judgment; trust mine instead" is not to be trusted.

Defending physical boundaries: about martial arts training

Verbal and mental skills are much more important than physical defense skills. Martial arts should never be relied upon to extricate yourself from a dangerous situation. The hard, cold truth about martial arts training is that it rarely works in real life the way it did in the classroom. More importantly, martial arts training doesn't prevent conflict in daily life. And like weapons, it can lead to a false sense of security.

That said, martial arts training is fun and useful. It can improve your physical fitness, awareness, and confidence. Martial arts styles range from soft (meeting force with deflection) to hard (meeting force with force). Some styles require a great deal of finesse and take years to master, while others are more crude but provide more immediate results.

On the soft end of the spectrum are arts such as aikido and tai chi. These styles consist of brilliant deflections, control holds, and escapes. Many of these techniques require years of practice in order to become proficient.

On the hard end of the spectrum are ballistic arts such as karate and tae kwon do. They provide excellent exercise, and while you can spend a lifetime polishing these techniques as well, they provide more immediate results than the flowing soft styles. The techniques consist mainly of punching, kicking, and blocking. The practical street application of these styles can be limited, since "street fighters" often rely on grabs, chokes, throws, and cheap shots rather than the kicks and punches typically found in most karate and tae kwon do training halls.

Also on the hard end of the scale are more street-oriented styles such as jujitsu, which combine the effectiveness of soft styles with the quicker results of hard styles. They provide realistic escapes, deflections, and other responses to the cheap shots taken by Expert Aggressors. They also include all-important lessons in defending yourself at close range and on the ground.

Before you pick a school, it's best to shop around and find one you'll enjoy. Any reputable school will allow you to observe a class before signing up; just ask. Avoid schools that ask you to sign a contract in which you promise to pay for several months or years of classes.

People are often aware of a dangerous situation on a subconscious level long before they consciously understand what's going on. The phrase "I knew something bad was going to happen" is unfortunately all too common.

Your intuition is already well aware of the predatory tricks and testing rituals that we've been discussing. Now that you've weighed this information on a conscious level, your intuition will have a much easier time communicating messages of danger.

All that's left for you to do is to give yourself permission to listen. Make it a daily exercise at home, at work, and in your personal life. When you get that funny feeling that something isn't right, *stop*. Take a breath and reflect on the situation. Whenever your intuition is right on some small matter, reward yourself.

Not in It for the Challenge

Now that we've looked at some of the defenses against Expert Aggression, let's reexamine the scenario at the beginning of this section involving Luanne, the benefits administrator. James Taggart, the consummate Expert Aggressor, strutted into her office and manipulated her with a shamefully high degree of skill. But like most Expert Aggressors, James isn't in it for the challenge.

Let's revisit the scenario, this time arming Luanne with a solid knowledge of predators like James.

SCENARIO: The Bullying Client—Version Two

Luanne was new at her job. She had just graduated from college and had eagerly accepted a position in her hometown welfare office as a benefits administrator. As she sat busily ordering papers on the new desk of her new office, she was startled by the terse ring of the intercom. "Luanne, James Taggart is here to see you."

"Thanks, Mike. Send him in, please."

After several minutes James appeared. He had clearly taken his time, giving Luanne an uneasy feeling she couldn't quite explain. She stood to greet him as he ambled into the room.

"Good morning, James!" she said with a smile. "At last we meet!" After reviewing James's lengthy case file, which she'd inherited from her predecessor, she'd called him in to discuss the fact that his benefits would be ending if he continued to neglect the terms of the contract he had signed earlier in the year.

James looked at her with a smile that bordered on a sneer. "Mornin'," he answered, then plopped down into a chair before being invited. Luanne's vaguely uneasy feeling increased.

> *Those vaguely uneasy feelings are her intuition's first warnings of trouble. James is beginning to ever so subtly test her boundaries. Luanne should have her guard up, and she should start thinking about escape routes.*

Luanne seated herself. "Well, James, how are things going for you?"

> *Politeness: the preemptive strike! Displaying good manners in the face of adversity shows strength.*

James huffed disdainfully as he reached for a folded letter in his shirt pocket. "You oughta know. You're the one who set me this damn letter." He held up the letter as if displaying the physical manifestation of a profound injustice.

"Go on," Luanne said.

"It says my benefits are ending. What the hell is that about?"

Luanne was flustered by James's directness, but only for a moment. "Um, yes, Jim. When I took over your case file from Sandy, she and I went over the requirements that you need to fulfill in order to receive your benefits. And we found that you've come up short in a few areas. For instance, you were supposed to complete course work at our career center. You haven't been there once since I took over your case last month."

James stood up and shouted, "This is *crap*! Sandy knew I didn't need to take those classes!"

Luanne kept her composure. She thought about leaving but decided that she wasn't in any immediate danger. She decided to give James a chance, but she knew she'd better be firm. "Mr. Taggart, I'm only willing to continue this conversation if you take a seat."

> *Stating boundaries right from the start. Let's assume she spoke the words with the appropriate body language. Will she stick to her boundaries, or will she give in if James pushes on?*

James grudgingly obliged. He spun his chair around so that the back was facing Luanne, and straddled it. He crossed his arms over the back of the chair and stared at Luanne defiantly.

Luanne had had enough. Her intuition told her that this conversation was going nowhere fast. She needed backup. She stood up and, in her most professional tone, asked, "Will you please excuse me for a moment, Mr. Taggart?"

She didn't wait for a reply. Before he could respond, she was out the door. Several minutes later she returned with Pam, her supervisor. Not wanting to take on James alone, she had invoked the buddy system. James stood up. The defiant look had vanished.

She did it! She maintained her boundaries. James did sit down at her request but, in typical fashion, did so in a testing, prodding manner. It would have been terribly easy for Luanne to convince herself that James had complied, when in fact he had only pretended to do so. She didn't fall for his tricks.

Also note that while she didn't escape from James in the strictest sense of the word, she did create an environment in which James was not likely to attack by bringing a buddy to the scene.

"Mr. Taggart, I'd like you to meet my supervisor, Pam. Pam, I asked you in here because Mr. Taggart has some questions. There seems to be some confusion over the training listed in his benefits contract. Since you worked with Sandy, you might be able to clear things up."

Luanne was not derailed from the topic of discussion, which was James's lack of effort.

Pam had barely begun to speak when James interrupted. "Look, I'm a busy guy. All I'm saying is, I don't see why I have to take these classes."

Pam examined the contract. "Well, Mr. Taggart, you did sign the contract. Didn't your previous caseworker explain the terms?"

James gave a disdainful huff. "I know what it says."

Luanne spoke up, looking James squarely in the eyes. "I'll get right to the bottom line, James: no class, no benefits. You know how it works. I'd like to think we can work this out."

First she took control of her environment; now she's taking control of the interaction, setting up crystal-clear boundaries for James.

"Fine!" James said, avoiding eye contact by glancing out the window. "I'll take the stupid class. I still think it's a waste of time." He started toward the door and the two women stepped aside, giving him a wide berth. "Thanks for your time," he huffed sarcastically.

Never block an exit.

When James was gone, Luanne let out a sigh of relief, walked behind her desk, and plopped down in her chair.

"What was that all about?" Pam asked.

"He came in here, obviously testing me to see if he could push me around. I tried to get him to be civil, but when he kept giving me attitude, I knew I wasn't going to get anywhere alone."

Pam started toward the door. "I'm glad you called. Don't ever hesitate to get help. I'm going to have security make sure he gets out of the building. I'll let the other folks know what happened, in case he comes back. We'll make sure you have an escort to your car from now on."

> Debriefing, and preparing for a repeat attack. More on
> that in Part Four.

Nip It in the Bud!

Let's visit Mayberry one last time. Deputy Barney Fife had a favorite saying, issued in a high, squeaky voice whenever he became nervous about an impending problem: "Nip it! Nip it in the bud!" Wise counsel. Solve the problem the instant you detect it; solve it before it gets out of hand.

Responding to an Expert Aggressor is comparable to stopping a train. If the train has just started and isn't moving fast, then it will take a relatively small effort to put on the brakes. But if the train is careening along at full speed, then all of that mass and momentum will be difficult to stop in an emergency. There may be a train wreck coming. At the least, it will be a noisy, frightening affair.

The same holds true for situations involving Expert Aggressors. The sooner you put on the brakes, the easier it will be to stop their advances. You cannot wish a predator away; if you ignore them, they'll only become more bold.

The best response is one that attacks the plan. If they want to get you alone, then stay with people no matter what. If they want entry to your safe haven, bar the door and call for backup, no matter what the situation appears to be on the surface. If they try to bully and intimidate you into compliance, use the buddy system and call the law no matter what vague threat they imply.

And do it all as quickly as possible. You can be polite to the *person* if you wish. Good manners show strength. But the *plan* must be given absolutely no chance of success. None.

Some people understandably worry that standing up to aggressors will only enrage them. There may be a grain of truth to this concern; there's no guarantee that every aggressor will back down as James Taggart did. And even when aggressors do back down, there's no guarantee that they won't return to exact their vengeance—hence the protective measures that Luanne's supervisor suggested, such as notifying security and escorting Luanne to her car for the foreseeable future.

It's true that standing up to an Expert Aggressor is frightening and sometimes dangerous. I offer no illusions about the possible ramifications. But my personal philosophy—and I bear no ill will against those who disagree—is that the only alternative to resistance (barring escape) is submission. Imposing boundaries on someone like James Taggart may be frightening and dangerous, but giving in can be ultimately devastating.

A victim is one who knowingly allows a situation to progress too far. Whether one is dealing with a Desperate Aggressor or an Expert Aggressor, taking control of a situation before it gets out of hand is the key to a successful outcome. Barney Fife may have looked like a buffoon at times, but he knew enough to *nip it in the bud*!

Practice, Practice, Practice

A teacher once asked me how I thought Muhammad Ali became such a great boxer.

"Practice," I said.

"Right," he answered. "And then what?"

I thought for a moment. "Practice?" I asked meekly.

"Right. And then what?"

"Practice," I said. I'd gotten the point.

It's time once again for scenario training. Just as we ended Part Two by referring you to Appendix C for two scenarios of the type of aggression discussed in that section, so we end Part Three by referring you to scenarios 3 and 4 in Appendix C, which relate specifically to the information discussed in this section. As before, you don't need to stick to the scenarios provided; they're just a starting point.

Again, if scenario training is impossible for you, then at least run through the exercises mentally.

A word about weapons and gimmicks

Imagine that you're defending yourself from a surprise attack. Would you take the time to notice which way the wind is blowing, how drunk or drugged your attacker is, or what kind of clothing they have on? These are a few of the factors that can affect the performance of pepper spray, Mace, and other chemical sprays. Sprays, stun guns (usually useless, and illegal in some states), personal alarms—the list of "self-defense" products seems endless. Some can be helpful; for instance, O.C. spray (derived from a potent pepper plant) may actually distract an assailant long enough for you to escape. But weapons like these can also backfire or be turned against you, and they can pose a threat to younger members of your family, who may be tempted to experiment with them.

The reality is that no self-defense tool is foolproof, and none will prevent an attack from happening in the first place. The only tool that can be counted on to extricate you from a nasty situation is the one between your ears.

I don't mean to imply that weapons are a bad thing. Countless times they've helped save lives and avert attacks. The key to using them effectively is knowledge and training.

If you feel the need for the extra punch provided by chemicals, guns, or other weapons, take the time to train with them under a competent instructor. Buying a weapon, placing it in your pocket, and pulling it out only when you need it is like washing red clothes with your whites. You just never know how things will turn out.

Before you carry a weapon, you'll also want to check the laws in your area. And by all means, don't let the weapon give you a false sense of security. Weapons may make you more dangerous, but they won't necessarily make you safer.

PART IV
THE PATH TO PEACE

THE ABILITY TO MANAGE PROBLEMS AND potential violence is like a little fire that burns inside you for all the world to see. To those who use violence for profit, it's a warning to choose other prey. To those who are desperate for help, it's a beacon of hope.

That little fire is a signal of skill and ability, and it's apparent through the most subtle of signals—the manner of your walk, the position of your eyes, and the directness of your speech.

A friend of mine was walking through a nearly deserted train station in France, loaded down with luggage and looking painfully out of place. As he entered an empty corridor he sensed a pair of eyes scanning him. My friend turned his head toward a dark corner, where he saw a man in a large coat staring at him. The man had no luggage and appeared to be merely loitering in the train station. My friend stopped, looked the man squarely in the eyes, and smiled. Nothing more. Almost instantly, the stranger broke eye contact and disappeared around a corner, never to be seen again. My friend had dispatched an apparent threat with nothing more than a confident expression.

This small episode doesn't look like much on the surface, but it showcases that which we've been studying: early detection and early response.

The truth is, we cannot expect a peaceful existence in this world without the ability to respond to violence. When we make reasonable preparations for war—when we develop the skills, strength, and ability to allay a hostile encounter—we're rewarded with peace. That paradox lies at the heart of this book.

There are essentially three steps to preventing, or at least surviving, a potentially violent encounter:

- early recognition of hostile intent
- early response
- cleaning up after the incident

Recognizing Hostile Intent

When an opponent is brandishing his sword behind him or to his side, when he is suddenly about to strike, he shows his intent in his sword. . . . If you are inattentive, you will miss the rhythm.[54]

—MIYAMOTO MUSASHI

We've spent much of this book discussing early recognition of the aggressor. Most aggressors fall into one of two camps: those who resort to hostility for lack of other options, and those who turn to hostility for profit.

Desperate Aggression	Expert Aggression
• Likely to occur when the aggressor has run out of options.	• Likely to occur when the aggressor finds a suitable "victim."
• Generally an attempt to regain control.	• Generally an attempt to profit.
• Characterized by signs of stress.	• Characterized by testing rituals.

These two categories aren't the be-all and end-all to understanding aggression. Plenty of aggressors in the world don't seem to resemble either one of our categories, at least on the surface. Your intuition will be your guide with these aggressors. It's also important to know that Expert Aggressors don't always remain Expert Aggressors. They can quickly transform into Desperate Aggressors, or vice versa.

Picture a pair of burglars in the midst of a crime. They strike when they can be reasonably sure that the owners aren't home. This is a good example of simple Expert Aggression.

Now let's suppose that the owners come home and catch the burglars in the act. They turn on the light in the living room, and there stand the burglars with the family's most prized heirlooms in a knapsack—even Uncle Herb's coveted Silver Salesman award. Suddenly visions of prison guards and a large cellmate named Bubba begin to flash through the burglars' minds. Their pulse increases. Their blood pressure rises. They begin to sweat and panic. They want nothing more than to escape, and they will stop at nothing in pursuit of that goal. They have just transformed into Desperate Aggressors, and I wouldn't want to be the one standing between them and the door.

You may well discover, when dealing with what you reasonably judge to be a Desperate Aggressor, that they suddenly begin to test your boundaries in the manner of an Expert Aggressor. You may also find, when dealing with an Expert

Aggressor, that they begin to panic and show the signs of stress and adrenaline that indicate desperation.

When this happens, you must be willing and able to adjust your response. You may not expect your boundaries to be tested by a Desperate Aggressor, but you must be willing to maintain boundaries anyway while *at the same time* remembering that you must not push the aggressor into a corner. You may not expect to see signs of panic in someone who is behaving like an Expert Aggressor, but when it happens you must be willing to soften your approach and begin to use the LEO formula if it seems appropriate. With practice and scenario training, you'll learn to adjust to almost any situation.

There's one more type of threatening behavior that we haven't fully discussed yet: direct verbal threats.

A Word about Threats

We've spent a lot of time discussing nonverbal warning signs, and not much time discussing verbal threats, because aggressors' actions are more important than their words. In addition, not all verbal threats result in a crime, and few crimes are preceded by direct verbal threats.

When threats do exist, however, they become extremely important and should be taken seriously. They provide a window to the aggressor's intent, and they usually give a target time to respond. If an aggressor issues a threat, then they're *thinking* about causing harm and *talking* about causing harm, but they're not actually *doing* it—at least not at the moment. Threats can, in a sense, be a blessing; you should take full advantage of the advance warning they provide.

So what is a threat, exactly? See if you can determine which of the following six statements are actual threats, and which are attempts to manipulate:

> "I'll kill you if you don't sleep with me."
> "Get out of the way or I'll flatten you!"
> "If you fire me, so help me, you'll live to regret it."
> "There's a bomb in the office. It will go off at 3:00."
> "You'll pay for that! I swear, you'll pay!"
> "I'm going to cut you!"

A true threat is never conditional. It doesn't contain words such as *unless* or *if* or even *could* ("I *could* turn you into hamburger"). A true threat is a simple statement of intent with no stipulations attached.

198 ■ SURVIVING AGGRESSIVE PEOPLE

The first three statements in this series are difficult to classify as threats. They're the manipulations of Expert Aggressors; they're ploys, devices, strategies designed to force compliance. That isn't to say that the aggressors aren't willing to follow through—they might be perfectly willing to carry out their evil plans. But the true intent of these statements is to gain compliance, not to warn the target of impending danger.

The last three statements in the series are very different. They're unconditional statements of intent to do harm. They're genuine threats with no conditions attached.

The Federal Bureau of Investigation places most threats into one of four categories:[55]

- **A direct threat** describes a specific act against a specific target, in plain English: "I'm going to run him down with my car after work." (This type of threat is often a sign of Desperate Aggression.)

- **An indirect threat** is vague and ambiguous. The threat may be missing a clearly defined target or action: "I'm going to hurt someone before the day is out." "Somebody is going to pay for what this company has done." (Again, possibly a sign of Desperate Aggression.)

- **A veiled threat** is one that strongly implies a harmful act toward a specific person: "We'd all be better off if you vanished from the face of the Earth." "This company won't function without me—and I mean it." (This one could also be the sign of a desperate person.)

- **A conditional threat** is a statement meant to intimidate a target into compliance. (I don't consider this a true threat, but rather a sign of Expert Aggression.)

In deciphering how realistic a threat is (i.e., how likely the aggressor is to complete the act), the FBI tends to look at the level of specific, plausible details, the emotional content, and the precipitating stressors. In general, a threat that is detailed and specific, has a high emotional content, and was preceded by a great deal of stress on the aggressor is deemed a highly realistic and dangerous threat.

Genuine threats (direct, indirect, or veiled) may be a sign of Desperate Aggression. If you receive a genuine threat, follow the steps presented in Part One: find the first available exit or, if no exit is available, begin the LEO formula.

Conditional threats are typically a sign of Expert Aggression, and should be treated as such. Immediately take control of your surroundings and the interaction.

Responding

Half of this book has been devoted to detecting potential violence. The other half has been devoted to response.

Escape is usually the first and best option, provided that you're not "escaping" into an isolated area with an Expert Aggressor. When that isn't possible, then words are necessary. You should now have several verbal options at your disposal, and scenario training will ingrain these new skills.

Responding to Desperate Aggression	*Responding to Expert Aggression*
• Escape • Listen, Empathize, provide Options • Repeat if necessary • Set alternatives	• Escape or create a safe environment • Take control of the interaction

One particular challenge you may face, even in scenario training, is maintaining control over your own emotions. Fear, anger, and even rage can turn a bad situation into a terrible one. Managing your emotions while under threat is easier said than done, but it is possible.

Managing Your Emotions

Fear and anger are the most powerful and destructive emotions you may encounter during a violent or potentially violent situation. Two primary tools can help you manage these emotions.

To counter the effects of anger, frustration, rage, or fear, stay goal-oriented from start to finish. If you keep yourself busy and moving in a positive direction, as we discussed in Part One, you simply won't have much time to dwell on your fears. Recognize your emotions—they're important indicators—but keep moving toward the next step. Here are some other tips.

- **During the beginning stages** of an interaction, track your own emotions and manage anger by switching perspectives, even if just for a moment. If you have the time, look at yourself and the situation from the other person's point of view. Like a true Warrior, take a broad perspective.

    At this stage, start thinking about how you want the situation to end. Pick a goal and a means of arriving safely. You can always adjust your plans later. Having a goal in mind will give you much peace of mind if the situation degrades.

- **During the interaction,** manage your anger by being aware of any sudden surge of emotion. If what you are about to say *feels good* but serves no other purpose, then don't say it.

  Manage fear by following through on the goals that you set during the beginning stages of the interaction. Keep things moving. Even if your plan involves listening, don't allow yourself to become passive and mentally drift away. Actively pay attention.

- **After the interaction,** manage anger by avoiding the temptation to do or say something that will reignite the situation. If it *feels good*, then think twice before speaking.

  Manage fear by setting a new goal: to get to a safe location. Even if the situation appears to be over, don't stop moving until you know you're safe. If you've been injured, keep moving toward safety if at all possible. Know that your body was designed to have exceptional strength, even when damaged.

Regrouping and Recovering after an Attack

You've successfully dealt with a potentially violent aggressor. Everyone is speaking rationally; you've moved to (or created) a safe location, and the crisis seems to have been averted. Congratulations. But don't start the celebration just yet; there's still plenty of work to be done.

Once the initial crisis is over, it's time to regroup for a possible repeat attack. Following that, you have a responsibility to care for yourself, those around you, and perhaps even the attacker. Even when others may be sounding the "all clear" signal, there's work to be done.

REGROUPING IMMEDIATELY AFTER AN ATTACK

After an attack, attend to these tasks in roughly this order (obviously, different situations may call for different responses):

- Get to a safe location by escaping. Or establish a safe environment around you by barricading yourself and bringing other people to your aid.
- Apply first aid, if necessary, to yourself or others.
- Notify the authorities even if you don't want to prosecute. They may be able to use your information to prevent future problems.
- Seek medical attention for yourself, others, or the aggressor.
- Communicate the threat to others, as Luanne's supervisor did after James Taggart left the office.

In the event of a rape, don't bathe, change clothes, or clean up in any manner until you've received medical attention. Doing so may destroy evidence that could lead to an arrest. Immediately contact a rape crisis center, friend, relative, or doctor.

Of course, you can complete these tasks only to the best of your ability. Delegating them will help ensure that they get done if you're not physically or mentally able to do them yourself, and it also helps prevent those around you from panicking.

When delegating, you must be specific. Avoid vague or general statements such as "Somebody call 911!" It may not get done if everyone expects someone else to do it. Be specific: "Mary—There's a first aid kit and some bandages in the kitchen. Bring them here, please. Mike—please call 911. Use the phone at the reception desk. Stay on the line with them." And so forth.

LONG-TERM RECOVERY

Sometimes it seems that when a violent incident is long over and the physical damage has ended, that's when the real work begins. The one who suffered the assault must come to terms with what has happened.

People sometimes have trouble returning to normal life after a serious assault. Physical and psychological symptoms can linger for weeks or months. It can be a life-changing experience for the victims, and for their friends and loved ones.

The most important thing to keep in mind is that the target of an assault was in no way responsible for the harmful actions of another. Victims often question themselves and even feel guilty about their actions prior to, or during, a crime. This is flat-out wrong thinking. The decision to harm another person is entirely the perpetrator's, and that is where the responsibility for the incident begins and ends.

Friends and loved ones can also fall prey to a damaging line of thinking. Out of concern, they may question the victim's actions. However, even if the target of the assault could benefit from changing some habits, these types of questions soon after the event rarely help. There will be time later to take an objective look at the event and the precipitating factors.

Physical and psychological effects of an assault can last for days, weeks, or longer. They can include headaches and body aches, anxiety, lethargy, changes in eating or sleeping habits, nightmares, mood swings, and depression.

The feelings of fear that follow an attack can be profound. The target of the assault may feel that no one can be trusted, and may even believe that their own loved ones won't believe or support them. They may also be fearful that the assailant will return, or that another perpetrator will strike. These fears may make it difficult to return to normal life.

The emotional impact of a serious assault is not limited to fear but also includes guilt and anger. The target of an assault may not want to speak about the incident to important people in their lives because of the shame they feel. Patience, along with a message of kindness and understanding, will help them a great deal.

Simple messages such as "I'm glad you're OK" or "You did nothing wrong" are powerful sentiments of support. Friends and loved ones should avoid phrases such as "I'd like to hunt that creep down." While the intentions are good, such statements serve only to underscore feelings of helplessness.

A healthy diet and exercise, along with a regular schedule, will help the target of an assault avoid becoming obsessed with the incident, and counseling will help them regain a sense of control and power. You might encourage them to seek counseling when the time is right.

Friends and loved ones may also discover feelings of guilt, anger, or frustration after the incident. Just as the assault wasn't the target's fault, neither was it the fault of friends or family. It's unrealistic to think that you can protect your friends, family, or coworkers from all the dangers of the world.

Eventually the target of an assault or violent incident can come to thrive in spite of the experience, and even become stronger for it. Part of this process, for organizations as well as individuals, involves a frank examination of the incident—a debriefing—after emotions have quieted and control has been reestablished.

THE DEBRIEFING

A general of great merit should meet with at least one defeat.[56]

—ASAKURA NORIKAGE

Debriefing is a fancy, military-sounding term meaning only this: "Let's talk about the incident, what we did right, what we could have done better, how we're going to recover, and how we can prevent it from happening again."

Debriefing is one of the most important and overlooked steps in managing a violent incident, whether from the standpoint of an individual or an organization. We've all heard the rather clichéd advice that crisis always presents an opportunity for growth, but that holds true only for those willing to take an objective look at the event.

Here are a few guidelines to help organizations, as well as individuals, ensure that debriefing is an objective and positive experience.

- **Take care of each individual.** Each person involved in the incident will experience their own unique emotional reaction. Some will be angry, some will feel guilty, others will have reactions that may seem inexplicable. In the wake of a crisis, adrenaline rules the day. The atmosphere in your organization may be an emotional powder keg for days to come. A professional counselor's assistance may be necessary to sort out the emotional aftermath.

- **Solicit all points of view.** Each person involved needs the opportunity to describe the event, as well as their thoughts and feelings, in a safe and unbiased atmosphere. Let those who are willing to talk do so. Others won't want to discuss their feelings or perceptions; don't force the issue. Encourage them to simply provide an account of the facts.

- **Identify precipitating factors.** Look for patterns among descriptions that may point to weaknesses in security or policy. Nobody is more aware of your organization's vulnerable spots than those who work on the front lines. Be prepared to act on the advice they offer.

- **Follow up with the aggressor.** In a therapeutic or professional environment, it may be necessary for the aggressor to come to terms with the incident. Ignoring the situation only encourages a repeat performance rather than uncovering why it happened in the first place and enabling you to take preventive measures for the future.

For the individual recovering from an assault, the same guidelines apply. Rarely is it helpful to approach such situations alone. Your friends will probably be all too happy to listen to you, but make sure they understand your needs (you might have them read this chapter). If you just want a sympathetic ear, let them know you're not interested in hearing suggestions about what you could have done differently. It may be more appropriate to use the services of a counselor.

The Peace Paradox

What is called cherishing the Way of the Warrior is not a matter of extolling the martial arts above all things and becoming a scaremonger. It is rather in being well-informed in military strategy, in forever pondering one's sources of pacifying disturbances, in training one's soldiers without remiss . . . in being correct in one's evaluation of bravery and cowardice, and in not forgetting this matter of "the battle" even when the world is at peace.[57]

—KURODA NAGAMASA

In 1998 approximately 31.3 million crimes were committed in America, including 8.1 million crimes of violence. Violent acts occur in vast numbers and at times of day when most of us are out and about, attending to our daily business and expecting to arrive home safely.

The question of how we, as individuals and as a society, respond to violence isn't a question of weaponry, punishment, or self-defense tactics. It's a question of philosophy. If we are forgiving and tolerant of violent ways, then violence is what we shall have. Such a policy doesn't equip us to prevent violence. On the contrary, it encourages us to sit and watch as the world and all we cherish is torn down around us. Eventually we may become enraged at the injustice that we have allowed. But having been forgiving of evil ways—having developed no responses to the slings and arrows of evil people—we will be loath to do anything about it. In a sad irony, a philosophy of tolerance will soon enough bring misery.

One of the great paradoxes is that peace can come only through strength. Not the brute physical strength to club a malefactor into submission, but the mental strength to recognize and respond to an attack while the stakes are still low, and the strength and ability to respond peacefully even when the stakes are high.

Some argue that preparedness leads to paranoia. Worse yet, they say, preparing for a battle only enrages the enemy. Nothing could be further from the truth. The person who makes reasonable preparations against a likely threat (and violence in America is a very likely threat) will earn both peace, and peace of mind.

You should know this as well as anybody. Having read this book, do you fear that your new skills will enrage criminals across the land, causing them to seek you out and force you into submission? Or instead, do you feel reasonably confident that you could detect and respond to the early stages of Desperate and Expert Aggression?

This peace of mind, however, comes with a price. You must be vigilant of complacency, you must maintain awareness, and you must practice. You may as well start now.

Escape Cues

Desperate Aggression

- Adrenal effects
  - Changes in breathing
  - Shaking and tremors
  - Fidgeting and restlessness
  - Vocal changes
  - Offensive or defensive physical posture
  - Protective facial gestures (such as furrowed brow)
  - Flushed or reddened face
- Agitation
- Uncharacteristic or poor judgment
- Paranoia and defensiveness
- Extreme pessimism
- Nervous confusion
- Withdrawal
- Hurtful language or attempt to draw you into a fight
- Direct threats

Expert Aggression

- Testing rituals
- Overaccommodation
- Foot in the door
- Invading personal space
- Exploiting sympathy and guilt
- Intimidation and exploiting fear
- Distraction and information overload
- Persistence and ignoring "no"
- Talking too much
- Contradictions between words and behavior

And of course, don't forget the most important escape cue: your intuition.

Power Phrases

HELPFUL PHRASES

Desperate Aggression

"I want to help you, but I'll only do so if . . ."

"Tell me if I understand you correctly . . ."

"I see some options here. Would you like to hear them?"

"I'd like to think we can find an answer. Is there *anything* I can do to help?"

Expert Aggression

"Bottom line, what do you want?"

PHRASES TO AVOID

"Calm down. Relax. Take it easy."

"I understand."

Bluffing, except as a last resort.

If you don't know what to say, don't say it. Keep the other person talking.

Scenario Training Exercises

We called it the Summer of 10,000 Kicks. I was in my late teens, and my karate instructor had posted a graph on the wall of our training studio. At the bottom of the graph were several categories of blocks and strikes: front snap kick, upper rising block, side thrust kick, and so on. Ten basic techniques in all. At the left side of the graph was a gradation of numbers: 100, 200, 300 . . . all the way up to 1,000.

The plan was to execute each technique 1,000 times before the end of the summer. For those of you keeping track, that's a total of 10,000 kicks, punches, and blocks, all done in a tiny studio without air conditioning.

My teacher didn't devise this assignment because he was sadistic—he *was* a bit ornery, but that's not why he proposed it. He offered this assignment because he knew that mastery comes from repetition and practice.

Managing a hostile or potentially violent individual is no different: it takes practice. There are no easy answers to this complex problem, and anyone who tells you otherwise is selling you a bill of goods. Practice is like an insurance policy: if there ever comes a time when you must protect yourself or someone you hold dear, the small amount of effort that you put forth now will pay huge dividends.

Need evidence? Imagine any of the frightening case studies or scenarios that we've examined in this book. Think back to Charlie luring Anne, the waitress, from the restaurant. Or consider the armed stranger talking his way into the closed convenience store, where he robbed Marty at gunpoint. What do you suppose Anne or Marty would have given not to have been in that situation?

A little bit of practice isn't too much to ask in light of that question. The good news is, it doesn't have to be nearly as arduous as the Summer of 10,000 Kicks. In fact, it can be fun.

Part Three discussed a number of forms of practice that can be done on a daily basis—playing the "what-if" game, altering your routines, being aware of your surroundings, others, and yourself, and refusing to accept everyday doubletalk. All are excellent exercises for keeping the mind sharp, relaxed, and ready to respond. Scenario training exercises are a bit more involved, but the benefits are immeasurable.

All you need are a few friends or coworkers, a room with some privacy, and some prearranged scenarios in which one person is the aggressor and the other is the target. The goal of this game is simple: use the skills you've learned to talk your way out of an (imaginary) potentially violent situation.

Of course, the first and best option in any dangerous situation is to move yourself to a safe location. For the sake of these exercises, we pretend that escape isn't an immediate option—you must earn your escape.

The rules of the game are simple:

- One (or more) person(s) will act as an aggressor. Their job is to study the role of the aggressor thoroughly, and to consider alternatives beforehand. This person should know how to respond if the target draws the line, gives in, yells for help, and so on.

- The second person will act as the target. This person doesn't know what to expect from the aggressor, other than that the aggressor won't actually hurt the target, because this is a safe atmosphere. The target is informed of only the location and the general situation.

- A third person acts as a mediator. This person will set the scene, provide instructions for both participants, start the scenario, and end it. This person is also responsible for intervening if the scenario gets out of hand (e.g., the participants are stricken by an overwhelming attack of the giggles, or the scenario is emotionally overwhelming for one of the participants). The mediator should call for a break any time emotional or physical well-being is in question.

- All others present should observe quietly, watch out for the safety of the participants, and make mental notes as the scenario progresses. They'll be asked for their opinions later.

- There is to be no physical contact—no grabbing, pushing, punching, wrestling, or other touching. When the aggressor gets to the point in the situation where they would commit a physical assault, they should simply say *attack* or some similar phrase to signal the end of the scenario.

- Decide on a stop phrase that any participant can use at any time, such as "stop the scenario." This phrase must be respected completely and immediately, no matter who says it. Of course, once a scenario is stopped, it can be resumed at any time.

- Each scenario training should end with a debriefing. Start with the person who played the target. What did they think of the situation and the way they handled it? Next, the aggressor should state their goals in the scenario, as well as appraise the target's performance. Finally, the observers and the mediator should share their thoughts. Just as in a real debriefing, all points of view should be considered.

Remember that mistakes *will* be made during the course of a scenario training, and that's the entire point of this exercise. By making mistakes in training, we increase our chances of success in the real world, and we greatly improve our chances of recovering from a mistake in the real world. "Do-overs" are not only permitted but encouraged. It's important to feel the sensation of success, and it's even more important to ingrain good habits.

When sharing observations, please be mindful that the person who played the target may feel agitated and defensive due to the stress of the experience. Be honest, but also empathetic and encouraging.

Four scenarios are included to get you started, but the best scenarios are the ones you devise yourself based on your experiences, your concerns, or the particulars of your workplace or neighborhood.

There are no right or wrong endings to these scenarios. As in life, any time you escape a situation without harm should be counted as a success.

SCENARIO 1: Dismissal

This scenario is based on the information presented in Part Two: Desperate Aggression.

Instructions for target: This scenario is similar to Kim's story at the beginning and end of Part Two. You are a supervisor who has been charged with the task of dismissing your employee, the aggressor. You've called a meeting between yourself and the employee to break the news. The employee is being let go for chronic tardiness and for being absent for work several times without calling. They've been formally warned on several occasions. In an uncharacteristic lapse of judgment, you've inadvertently blocked your easy escape route by placing your employee between yourself and the door. By the way, the termination is nonnegotiable; you have your orders from on high. And, as in real life, you may want to have an observer or human resources specialist present.

Instructions for aggressor: Although on some level you are aware that you're going to be fired, you're not prepared to accept the news. You're having several problems in your personal life, which is why you've been late and absent from work on so many occasions. Although you've been warned on several occasions, you just didn't remember to call. You feel like the victim. In your mind, you've done nothing wrong. You believe your supervisor is "out to get you." You stand up and pace, shouting and cursing. You are panicked because you don't know how you're going to find a new job, cover the bills in the interim, and deal with your personal problems. It's all just too overwhelming. The only thing that will calm you down is a concrete approach to solving at least some of your problems.

SCENARIO 2: No Receipt, No Return

This scenario is based on the information presented in Part Two: Desperate Aggression.

Instructions for the target: You work at the customer service counter of your local department store. A worried-looking customer approaches your counter and asks to get a refund for a large grill purchased recently with cash. The grill looks unused and does appear to have come from your store. However, the patron has no receipt and your store has a strict policy: no receipt, no return.

Instructions for the aggressor: You recently purchased a top-of-the-line grill at this department store. But before you had a chance to use it, you came upon a bit of hard luck. First, you lost your job last week. There was no notice, and no severance package. Your company simply folded.

Following that bit of news, part of your roof collapsed. Insurance won't cover the damage, and you have a spouse and two kids to support. In the week since you were laid off, money just seems to have evaporated. Your job prospects aren't coming through, and the first of the month is fast approaching. Many bills are coming due, and the pantry is bare.

In an effort to lighten your load, you've decided to sell some of your possessions. This grill represents more than $500 to you. That money would go a long way toward groceries, and frankly, you've become desperate. If the clerk stands between you and your money (read "you and your family's safety"), you're likely to become violent. You feel that you've run out of options.

You present your story to the clerk with restraint at first. When they explain the "no receipt, no return" policy, you begin to show signs of desperation, and you attempt to bargain. As the argument continues, you become increasingly desperate—that is, of course, unless they are able to give you a good reason to calm down.

You're feeling cornered. Ideally, the clerk should employ the LEO strategy and quickly become aware of the gravity of the situation. From that point, they must be willing to exercise a bit of creativity in devising options. The store policy is hardly worth dying for.

If the clerk fails to attempt any type of assistance, you will take this very personally and eventually commit an assault. When you get to this point, simply say *attack* or some similar phrase to signify an assault. (It's assumed that a genuine attacker would commit a physical assault at this point.)

SCENARIO 3: Parking Lot Helper

This scenario is based on the information presented in Part Three: Expert Aggression.

Instructions for the target: You've just finished shopping and are loading groceries into the trunk of your car. It's late in the day, few cars are in the lot, and no people are around.

Instructions for the aggressor: You see a person loading groceries into the trunk of their car. You offer to help. If the person refuses, you press on. You won't take no for an answer. You'll even take bags from the target's hand if possible. Of course, your goal isn't to help the person, but to get at their car keys and steal the car. Your strategy is to get the groceries loaded and then accompany them to the driver's-side door, where you'll pretend to open the door, but will in fact steal their keys at the first opportunity. Use a word such as *attack* to signal the end of the scenario if you are able to get this far.

Throughout the scenario, be as jovial and charming as possible. You want to gain your target's trust.

SCENARIO 4: Elevator Man

This scenario is based on the information presented in Part Three: Expert Aggression.

Instructions for the target (female): You are riding an elevator alone in a nearly deserted building when the elevator stops and a solitary man enters. You think of exiting, but he positions himself so that you cannot escape while the doors are open without rudely pushing past him. In an uncharacteristic lapse of judgment, you decide to stay on the elevator car alone with this man.

Instructions for the aggressor (male): You've been waiting for the opportunity to catch this woman alone. Your ultimate goal will be to take her to a second environment, such as the rooftop or utility basement, where you plan to assault her. However, you don't want to have a scene on your hands. Ultimately, you'll give her an ultimatum: *Come with me or you'll be sorry.* But since you don't know how she'll respond, you have to proceed in small increments. First you'll stand too close. Then you'll move closer and make suggestive comments. All the while you're making direct and inappropriate eye contact, leering at her. If at any point she puts up a fight or pushes past you to get at the controls, you'll back down. But if you feel it's safe to proceed, you'll eventually deliver your ultimatum. At that point, say the word *attack* to end the scenario. Move quickly through the stages of your testing ritual.

Notes

Part I

1. U.S. Department of Justice, *Bureau of Justice Statistics: At a Glance* (Publication No. NCJ 183014, August, 2000), 3.

2. U.S. Department of Justice, *Criminal Victimization in United States, 1998 Statistical Tables* (Publication No. NCJ 181585), 62.

3. U.S. Department of Justice, *Criminal Victimization in United States, 1998 Statistical Tables*, 69.

4. U.S. Department of Justice, *Criminal Victimization in United States, 1998 Statistical Tables*, 64.

5. Fifty-four percent of all violent crime victims knew their attackers prior to the crime. Where sexual assault was concerned, 7 in 10 victims knew their attackers. U.S. Department of Justice, *Criminal Victimization in United States, 1999: Changes 1998–99 with Trends 1993–99* (Publication No. NCJ 182734), 1.

6. At the core of our brains, we humans have a great deal in common with reptiles. Imagine the human brain as an archaeological dig site, with older structures buried underneath structures that evolved later. On the surface of the brain is our most modern structure, the cerebral cortex. Of all the structures of the brain, these have been around for the least amount of evolutionary time, and they give us our highest and most human reasoning abilities. They allow us to invent Salad Shooters, to build cathedrals, and to solve differential equations.

    Go beneath this thick surface (and backward in evolutionary time) and you find a middle layer consisting of older structures, differing in chemistry and much more primitive in function (including the limbic system, which is central to aggressive behavior).

Go even deeper, to the center of the brain (or the top of the spinal column, depending on which way you're looking), and you discover structures common to most creatures, right down to and including cold-blooded reptiles. This "reptilian brain" provides the templates for such basic behaviors as hunting for food, establishing territories, mating, and self-defense. See Paul D. MacLean, A *Triune Concept of the Brain and Behavior* (Toronto: University of Toronto Press, 1973).

7. Aaron T. Beck, *Prisoners of Hate: The Cognitive Basis of Anger, Hostility, and Violence* (New York: HarperCollins, 1999), 8.

8. John Monahan, *The Clinical Prediction of Violent Behavior* (London: Jason Aronson, 1995), 27.

9. For those of you unfamiliar with the intricacies of a rat's social life, they tend to dwell in groups. (Eibl-Eibesfeldt was interested in wild brown rats and house rats, not the cute, pink-eyed albino variety you can find at the pet store.) They don't seem to recognize each other on a personal basis, unlike other animals such as monkeys and some birds. Nevertheless, they're social creatures, and family is very important to them. Konrad Lorenz, an expert on animal aggression, gives us some sense of a day in the life of a big, brown, smelly, stiff-haired rat:

    > Within the pack, there is no real fighting, at the most there is slight friction, boxing with the forepaws or kicking with the hind paws, but never biting; and within the pack there is no individual distance, on the contrary, rats are contact animals . . . and they like touching each other. The ceremony of friendly contact is the so-called "creeping under," which is performed particularly by young animals while larger animals show their sympathy for smaller ones by creeping over them.
    > —KONRAD LORENZ, *On Aggression* (New York: Harcourt, Brace and Company, 1963), 160.

10. Lorenz, *On Aggression*, 160. Lorenz was commenting on Eibl-Eibesfeldt's experiment.

11. D. Stroble, "Dehumanization among soldiers and the effect of sociopolitical transformations on aggression," *Aggressive Behavior*, 23(3):163–164, 2001.

12. There may be sound reasons for our natural reticence toward apologizing. Almost by definition, apologizing puts you in a "one-down" position relative to the apologizee. It's an admission of guilt, which for all intents and purposes is an admission of subservience: "I stepped on your toe, you graciously forgave me, and now I'm in your debt, oh purple-toed one." Many would argue the opposite, that apologizing in fact makes one the bigger person; that may be true in the philosophical sense, but we're not always in a philosophical mood, especially when our toe is throbbing. The theory of evolutionary psychology suggests that early in our evolution, too much apologizing among the tribe quickly put a person in a submissive position, which in turn could lower that individual's chances of procreation. Robert Wright, speaking of typical acts of reconciliation after a fight among chimps, points out that

> a peace overture can carry intimations of submission; and submission during a leadership struggle carries real Darwinian costs, as it may bring secondary or still lower status. So a genetically based aversion to such submissions (up to a point, at least) makes evolutionary sense. In our species [as opposed to chimps], we call this aversion a sense of honor, or pride.
> —ROBERT WRIGHT, *The Moral Animal: The New Science of Evolutionary Psychology* (New York: Vintage Books, 1994), 255.

13. Takeda Nobushige, "Opinions in ninety-nine articles," *Ideals of the Samurai*, William Scott Wilson, trans. (Burbank: Ohara Publications, 1982), 102. Original work composed circa 1500 A.D.

14. Rollo May, *Power and Innocence: A Search for the Sources of Violence* (New York: W. W. Norton and Company, 1972), 23.

15. James Gilligan, *Violence: Reflections on a National Epidemic* (New York: Vintage Books, 1996), 66.

16. Gilligan, *Violence*, 112.

17. David Lisak and Susan Roth, "Motivational factors in nonincarcerated sexually aggressive men," *Journal of Personality and Social Psychology*, 55(5):795–802, 1988.

18. George Orwell, 1984 (New York: Penguin Books, 1950).

19. Takuan Soho, *The Unfettered Mind*, William Scott Wilson, trans. (New York: Kodansha International, 1986), 19. Original work composed circa 1600 A.D.

20. Takuan, *The Unfettered Mind*, 19.

21. Takuan, *The Unfettered Mind*, 20.

22. Milton Fisher, *Intuition: How to Use It in Your Life* (New York: Wildcat Publishing Company, 1995), 3-4.

23. Matthew Lieberman, "Intuition: A social cognitive neuroscience approach," *Psychological Bulletin*, 126(1): 109–137, 2000. Lieberman, a Harvard psychology professor, believes there is a link between the subjective sensation of intuition and implicit learning (learning without conscious effort and without the knowledge that we're learning). He believes that the study of intuition has a place in information-processing theory:

> It may seem strange to think of intuition in terms of information processing because phenomenologically, intuition seems to lack the logical structure of information processing. When one relies on intuition, one has no sense of alternatives being weighted algebraically or a cost-benefit analysis being undertaken. Oddly, it is just this lack of subjectively experienced reasoning that suggests intuition may have a home in the world of information-processing theory. In recent years, research on implicit learning has suggested that our behavior can be rule-like and adaptive without a concomitant conscious insight into the nature of the rules being used.

He goes on to demonstrate, in great detail, that intuition probably has a biological beginning, and that implicit learning and implicit logic may provide the basis for intuitive insights.

24. W. R. Wilson, "Feeling more than we can know: Exposure effects without learning," *Journal of Personality and Social Psychology*, 37, 811–821, 1979. In this study on selective attention, participants were asked to repeat what was said through one earpiece of a headset while novel tunes were played through the other earpiece. After the experiment, the participants couldn't identify the tunes they'd heard when those tunes were interspersed with others. However, when they were asked to rate the tunes by order of preference, they expressed preference for the tunes they had heard during the listen-and-repeat task. Although the participants were not consciously aware of it, it appears that they did become familiar with those tunes.

25. Miyamoto Musashi, *The Book of Five Rings*, Thomas Cleary, trans. (New York: Barnes & Noble Books, 1997), 16. Original work composed 1643 A.D.

26. Robert L. Spencer, *The Craft of the Warrior* (Berkeley: North Atlantic Books, 1993), 49.

27. Spencer, *The Craft of the Warrior*, 56.

Part II

28. Terry Dobson and Victor Miller, *Aikido in Everyday Life* (Berkeley: North Atlantic Books, 1993), 40.

29. Lorenz, *On Aggression*, 28. The importance of perception in aggression isn't unique to humans. While studying the "fight or flight" patterns of threatened animals, ethologist Heini Hediger coined the term "critical reaction." A physical attack, he said, is triggered by at least one of four criteria: the animal is trapped, the danger is too close to turn away, the animal is surprised, or its "critical distance" is invaded (meaning the animal was in hiding, but someone got too close). In other words, the critter lashes out because it feels threatened.

Nowhere does Hediger state that the threat has to be a real one. He simply says that the animal has to *feel* threatened. The animal may be cornered by a group of benevolent people who are attempting to move it from harm's way. That doesn't matter to the animal; all it knows is that it's trapped and something is trying to capture it.

30.   Leslie W. Kennedy and David R. Forde, *When Push Comes to Shove: A Routine Conflict Approach to Violence* (New York: State University of New York Press, 1999), 10. Kennedy and Forde point out that even the threat of severe consequences for violence isn't a deterrent when an aggressor feels that other options don't exist.

      Still, we have examples of people who act in violent ways whom we would not expect to do this. The bank executive who assaulted an airline stewardess on a plane may be as incapable of explaining why he did this (not likely the normal way in which he gets service) as the young tough who complained that he was bored prior to popping an unsuspecting victim. Both individuals appeared to run out of options of how to manage others and to get something they wanted (more booze and more excitement, respectively). Violence becomes an option under these circumstances, surprisingly, even in the face of the not unpredictable consequences of severe sanctions for these actions.

      The conditions that Kennedy and Forde speak of in their examples are much less severe than the threat Molly faces in the preceding scenario (losing her livelihood and her only source of support for her children), but the notion is the same. Lack of options may be as much a trigger for human violence as Hediger's critical reaction is to animals. It can cause us to abandon common sense and to disregard consequences.

31.   MacLean, A *Triune Concept of the Brain and Behavior,* 9.

32.   Debra Niehoff, *The Biology of Violence: How Understanding the Brain, Behavior, and Environment Can Break the Vicious Circle of Aggression* (New York: The Free Press, 1998), 74. Many laboratory researchers and animal behaviorists once considered any and all aggression to be a simple reaction to stimuli. For example, predatory aggression in animals was once considered a knee-jerk reaction to the presence of prey; territorial aggression was considered a reaction to the presence of an intruder; fear-induced aggression was a reaction to attack when escape was impossible. Stimulus-reaction, stimulus-reaction—that's what some psychologists thought we were made of.

      Like most theories this one contains a grain of truth, but it makes for a very mechanistic interpretation of aggression. Rarely does aggression have a solitary trigger, particularly in humans. That's evidenced by the fact that a person will react differently to identical stimuli depending on innumerable conditions. For example, if you poke Joe with a sharp stick as he's leaving an IRS audit, you might be met with a punch in the nose. Poke him with the same stick after he receives a big job promotion, and he might smile and say, "You'll need a bigger stick than that to ruin my day!"

While a simple stimulus-reaction model is useful in some cases, it simply doesn't hold up against the complexity of real-world experience.

33.   Niehoff, The Biology of Violence, 62. She observes,

> Aggressive activity [in rats] tends to occur in bursts, followed by quiescent intervals with little social contact. . . . Aggression in mice and other rodents follows a similar burst-gap pattern, although the duration of both bursts and gaps differs for each species. Even human aggressors—the abusive spouse who rages at the end of the work week, the boss who terrorizes his staff before a critical deadline, or the serial killer who strikes, then vanishes—tend to act out intermittently rather than continuously.

34.   William Manchester, The Last Lion: Winston Spencer Churchill, Visions of Glory, 1874–1932 (Boston: Little, Brown, and Company, 1983), 7.

Part III

35.   Stanton E. Samenow, Inside the Criminal Mind (New York: Times Books, 1984), 95.

36.   D. G. Perry, S. J. Kusel, and L. C. Perry, "Victims of peer aggression," Developmental Psychology, 24: 807–814, 1988.

37.   Samenow, Inside the Criminal Mind. Samenow, an expert in human aggression, has seen this type of behavior all too many times:

> Intimidation is the criminal's other great weapon. [The first is stealth.] His domineering manner may be so menacing that he need never utter a threat, raise his voice, or clench his fist. People cower in fear of the criminal's tearing into them, revealing their inadequacies, and making fools of them. . .
>
> There are times when a display of anger accomplishes his purpose. This may occur in a carefully orchestrated, dramatic manner to

make a point, or he may simply fly off the handle. In either case,
the result is the same. (page 99)

The result, of course, is that those around criminals tend to quickly
give in to their demands.

38. Lorenz's beliefs fell out of favor, along with the beliefs of many other
behaviorists, when psychology took a hard turn toward social theories,
which generally posit that a person's problems can almost always be
traced to childhood experiences. This new school of thought found it
repugnant to suggest that a person's actions were due solely to biology.
For many years during the 1970s and '80s (an interval that archaeologists
have dubbed "the Phil and Oprah period"), the pendulum swung to the
opposite extreme. Behaviorists couldn't get a word in edgewise.

As is usually the case, however, both theories contain a grain of truth.
Biological sources of aggression are wired into our brains, and our life
experiences profoundly shape our personalities. We can see this in animals as well as in people. Follow an ill-tempered pet home, and an ill-
tempered owner is likely to answer the door. That pet has been molded
by its environment, which has aggravated its natural aggressive potential.

39. Lorenz observes:

This territorial aggression, really a very simple mechanism of
behavior-physiology, gives an ideal solution to the problem of
the distribution of animals of any one species over the available area in such a way that it is favorable to the species as a
whole. Even the weaker specimens can exist and reproduce, if
only in a very small space.

In other words, thanks to a bit of controlled aggression, everyone gets a
place to live along with some company to keep them warm at night (modern evolutionary psychologists might quibble that last point, but I believe
the general principle stands). The property lines are divvied up by way of
natural, healthy aggression and competition, which oftentimes doesn't
even involve physical contact. Ducks, for instance, are known to "incite"
one another by paddling to the outskirts of their territory, quacking loudly
at their neighbor, then quickly returning to the safety of their home turf—
more ritual than substance. (Lorenz, On Aggression, 38.)

40. Lorenz, *On Aggression*, 39.

41. U.S. Department of Justice, *Criminal Victimization in United States*, 1999, 3.

42. J. L. Freedman and S. C. Fraser, "Compliance without pressure: The foot-in-the-door technique," *Journal of Personality and Social Psychology*, 4:195–202, 1966. In this experiment on voluntary compliance, researchers traveled door to door, asking people to sign a petition for a "safe driving campaign" (a small request). Weeks later, they returned and asked the petition signers, as well as a control group who were never presented with the petition, for permission to post a large, ugly "Drive Carefully" sign in their front yard (a much larger request). Within the control group, only seventeen allowed the sign to be placed. But within the group that had signed the petition, three times as many granted permission. Granting a small favor makes a person much more likely to grant a larger one in the future.

43. David Lisak, *The "Undetected" Rapist* (videotape) (New York: National Judicial Education Program, 1990). Lisak is associate professor of psychology and director of the Men's Sexual Trauma Research Center at the University of Massachusetts–Boston. He seeks to discover why far more rapes are reported than men are indicted for the crime, hence his interest in the "undetected" rapist. This video is a reenactment of an interview with an undetected rapist who describes in shocking detail the lengths to which he and his accomplices have gone in order to prey on unsuspecting college-aged women. The video can be obtained from the National Judicial Education Program, 395 Hudson Street, Fifth Floor, New York, NY 10014.

44. Niehoff, *The Biology of Violence*, 65.

45. Niehoff, *The Biology of Violence*, 65. Beginning in the 1930s, researchers began publishing dozens of papers highlighting the correlations they had found between "aversive stimuli" (pain) and aggression in laboratory animals. For instance, by electrifying the floor of a rat's cage and frying its tender feet, they could cause the rat to rear up, box, and even attack other animals. By all appearances, these researchers had established a positive correlation between pain and aggressive behavior: they concluded that tormented animals can become hostile. This less than astonishing discovery evoked yawns.

Nearly fifty years later, researchers began to scrutinize these experiments. They noted that placing a solitary rat in a cage and tormenting it with forces beyond its control completely factored out the social forces at play in a rat's normal day-to-day life.

[The researchers] suspected that while electric shock certainly produced a consistent [aggressive] response, it was far from clear whether this was the response an angry rat might make under less stressful circumstances. The researchers questioned whether the rearing, boxing animals were really "fighting" at all. To uncover the true nature of pain-induced aggression, they compared the behavioral response elicited by foot shock with "aggressive behaviors occurring in the real world." (page 65)

By studying rat aggression in the context of a real-world colony, these researchers discovered that the rearing and boxing behavior of the caged rat was in rat parlance not *aggressive* but *defensive*. A rat attacked by another rat will at first try to run away. If an exit isn't available, he'll turn and box in an effort to protect his back from being bitten. The solitary rats who were suffering foot shock in the original experiments, finding no escape from the attack to their feet, displayed the same defensive behavior.

46. Christina Rivera offers talks on intuition and safety. She can be reached via email at christina_rivera@usa.net.

47. U.S. Department of Justice, *Criminal Victimization in United States, 1998 Statistical Tables* [Special issue]. Retrieved May 2000 from www.ojp.usdoj.gov/bjs/.

48. As quoted in William Lutz, *Doublespeak* (New York: Harper & Row, 1989), 135–136.

49. Chris L. Kleinke, "Gaze and eye contact: A research review," *Psychological Bulletin*, 100(1):78–100, 1986.

50. Kleinke, "Gaze and eye contact."

51. Joyli M. Droney and Charles I. Brooks, "Attributions of self-esteem as a function of duration of eye contact," *Journal of Social Psychology*, 133(5):715–722, 1993.

52. Stephen Thayer, "The effects of interpersonal looking duration on dominance judgments," *Journal of Social Psychology*, 79:285–286, 1969.

53. Kleinke, "Gaze and eye contact."

54. Musashi, *The Book of Five Rings*, 41.

55. U.S. Federal Bureau of Investigation, *The School Shooter: A Threat Assessment Perspective*, 2000. Downloaded October 15, 2001, from www.fbi.gov/publications/school/school2.pdf.

56. Asakura Norikage, "The recorded words of Asakura Soteki," *Ideals of the Samurai*, William Scott Wilson, trans. (Burbank: Ohara Publications, 1982), 81. Original work composed circa 1550 A.D.

57. Kuroda Nagamasa, "Notes on regulations," *Ideals of the Samurai*, William Scott Wilson, trans. (Burbank: Ohara Publications, 1982), 137. Original work composed 1622 A.D.

Index

W

warning colors, 179
warning signs. *See* aggression; Desperate
    Aggressors; Expert Aggressors
Warriors, 11, 24, 45, 59, 72
    and broad perspective, 199
    characteristics of, 1–2, 29, 35
    and focus on problem solving, 25
    intuition of, 59
    principles of, 2

flexibility, 42–44
force vs. finesse, xvii
intolerance of violence, 204
power of intuition, 47, 53, 187-89
reacting vs. responding, xiii, 3
soft approach, xvi–xviii
training, 45–46, 193, 204
weapons, 194
what if game, 58
words. *See* language
Worf (*Star Trek* character), 17

About the Author

SHAWN T. SMITH is the founder of Peaceful Paths, a company that has provided violence prevention training and security consulting since 1997. He developed and teaches two violence prevention programs: *Managing a Hostile Public*, designed mainly for the workplace, and *Defense Skills for Women*, which includes both verbal and physical defense skills. Smith's company has presented these courses to students, government entities, private corporations, and the general public. He's received coverage for his work in numerous newspapers, on radio talk shows, and on television.

In addition to degrees in Communication and Psychology from the University of Colorado at Denver, Smith has had years of first-hand experience with violence prevention. He has patrolled the streets with the Guardian Angels and served for four years as a trainer and senior patrol leader for the internationally renowned organization. His background also includes work in a group home for troubled and violent teens, and in a drug and alcohol detoxification facility. Shawn has studied the techniques and philosophies of the martial arts for seventeen years. He is currently working toward his Doctorate in Clinical Psychology at the University of Denver.

SENTIENT PUBLICATIONS, LLC publishes books on cultural creativity, experimental education, transformative spirituality, holistic health, new science, ecology, and other topics, approached from an integral viewpoint. Our authors are intensely interested in exploring the nature of life from fresh perspectives, addressing life's great questions, and fostering the full expression of the human potential. Sentient Publications' books arise from the spirit of inquiry and the richness of the inherent dialogue between writer and reader.

Our Culture Tools series is designed to give social catalyzers and cultural entrepreneurs the essential information, technology, and inspiration to forge a sustainable, creative, and compassionate world.

We are very interested in hearing from our readers. To direct suggestions or comments to us, or to be added to our mailing list, please contact:

SENTIENT PUBLICATIONS, LLC

1113 Spruce Street
Boulder, CO 80302
303-443-2188
contact@sentientpublications.com
www.sentientpublications.com